REACHING
the
RESISTANT

OTHER TITLES IN EMS SERIES

#1 SCRIPTURE AND STRATEGY: The Use of the Bible in Postmodern Church and Mission, by David J. Hesselgrave

#2 CHRISTIANITY AND THE RELIGIONS: A Biblical Theology of World Religions, Edward Rommen and Harold Netland, Editors

#3 SPIRITUAL POWER AND MISSIONS: Raising the Issues, Edward Rommen, Editor (now Out of Print)

#4 MISSIOLOGY AND THE SOCIAL SCIENCES: Contributions, Cautions and Conclusions, Edward Rommen and Gary Corwin, Editors

#5 THE HOLY SPIRIT AND MISSION DYNAMICS, C. Douglas McConnell, Editor

REACHING the RESISTANT

Barriers and Bridges for Mission

J. Dudley Woodberry
Editor

Evangelical Missiological Society Series #6

P.O. BOX 40129
PASADENA, CALIFORNIA 91114

EMS Series #6

Published by
William Carey Library
P. O. Box 40129
Pasadena, California 91114
(626) 798-0819

ISBN 0-87808-380-4

Library of Congress Cataloging-in-Publication Data

Reaching the resistant: barriers and bridges for mission / J. Dudley Woodberry, editor.

p. cm. — (Evangelical Missiological Society series ; no. 6)

Includes bibliographical references.

ISBN 0-87808-380-4 (alk. paper)

1. Missions—Theory. 2. Missions—Theory. I. Woodberry, John Dudley, 1934- . II. Series: Evangelical Missiological Society series; no. 6.

BV2063.R38 1998

266—dc21 98-43987

CIP

4 3 2 1
00 99 98

PRINTED IN THE UNITED STATES OF AMERICA

Contents

Part III
Means of Overcoming: Finding and Building Bridges

Part IV
Preparing for the Future: Planning Bridges

Preface

Barriers and Bridges

The lands where Muslims and Christians have encountered each other are littered with the ruins of fortresses—from the Muslim Alhambra in Spain to the Crusader Krak des Chevaliers in Syria and even the small fortress tower of the Monastery of Saint Makar in Egypt. Each faith community built barriers—walls, gates, or moats—to keep out the enemies of the other faith. Each sought to control from inside any access, by gates or bridges.

The present studies look at the barriers erected by peoples considered resistant to the gospel, and the bridges God is using to carry the gospel to them.

The first part reflects on the barriers: What do we mean by resistant? Why are some people groups resistant to the gospel? What is God's role in resistance? Is "resistance" a result of the failure of God's people or of it not being the "fullness of time"? Should missionaries focus on the least reached or the most receptive? What degree of contextualization is legitimate? How did the concepts of resistance and receptivity develop in missiology? And, above all, how should we understand these terms biblically and theologically?

The second part analyzes representative case studies that exhibit many of the barriers. Judaism and Islam, Christianity's monotheistic cousins, have enough biblical content to inoculate them against the rest. Japanese resistance, to the extent that it is real, raises issues of social, cultural, and national bonds.

Finally, post-Christendom Europe raises issues of a culture that has tasted a form of Christianity and rejected it.

Part three focuses on finding and building bridges over the barriers. Writers throughout the volume mention the use of contextualization and the value of the behavioral sciences in bridging cultural barriers. In this section tentmaking with integrity is evaluated by one's intentional use of time. The majority of the chapters in this section, however, deal with aspects of spiritual power—the vulnerability of the power of the cross expressed through suffering and martyrdom and power through prayer and the paranormal.

The final part turns to preparing for the bridges of the future—in the equipping of missionaries and planning for the evangelistic task ahead beyond the year 2000.

Christians did overcome the barriers and cross the bridge into the Muslim Alhambra, for Ferdinand and Isabel did conquer it after commissioning Columbus to set sail for what became known as the New World. Yet as the Catholic monarchs entered the royal palaces they were greeted by the motto of the Nasrid kings on the wall, "There is no conqueror but God."

These are words we would do well to remember as we seek to cross bridges to the resistant, not by force of arms, but by "love and prayers, and the pouring out of tears and blood" as called for by the missionary Raymon Lull (cited below, p. 157).

My thanks go to all who helped overcome the obstacles in the publication of these studies, which grew out of the National Meeting of the Evangelical Missiological Society joined by the International Society for Frontier Missiology in Santa Clara, California, November 20–22, 1997. Kenneth Mulholland did a superb job coordinating the selection of presenters along with Gailyn Van Rheenan as publications chair and Michael Pocock as president. Thanks also go to Anne White for the typesetting and my staff of Denise Schubert, Betty Ann Klebe, and Craig Beckett for their cheerful attention to collecting and proofreading the manuscripts on their way to the printers. Finally I want to thank my wife Roberta for doing with less of my help than could be expected during some busy days of packing for work among the resistant. Each has helped to carry this manuscript across the bridge to us all.

J. Dudley Woodberry, Dean
School of World Mission
Fuller Theological Seminary
Pasadena

AUTHOR PROFILES

David Bjork has served in France. He has done doctoral studies at the School of World Mission at Fuller Theological Seminary and is completing them at the University of Paris.

David Brickner is the president of Jews for Jesus.

Luis Bush is the general director of AD2000 and Beyond.

Stan Conrad is Associate Pastor of Missions and Evangelism at the Susquehanna Valley Evangelical Free Church in Harrisburg, PA. He has served in Japan and as a district missions consultant for the Evangelical Free Church of America.

Gary Corwin is editor of the *Evangelical Missions Quarterly* and an executive vice-president of EMS. He has served with SIM in Ghana and as International Research and Education Coordinator, and most recently on loan to *EMQ*.

Gary Ginter has served as a board member of several Christian organizations including InterVarsity, Norwegian Missionary Alliance (USA), Intent, and the Midwest Center for World Mission.

Sobhi Malek has served in Spain, Morocco, and France under the Assemblies of God.

Michael Pocock is Professor and Chair of World Missions and Intercultural Studies at Dallas Theological Seminary. He served in Venezuela and has been the president of the EMS.

John D. Robb serves with MARC/World Vision and as chair of the Unreached Peoples Track of AD2000.

Timothy C. Tennent is Assistant Professor of World Missions and director of TESOL at Toccoa Falls College

Charles Van Engen is the Arthur Glasser Professor of the Biblical Theology of Mission at the School of World Mission at Fuller Theological Seminary. He has served in Mexico and has been the president of the Reformed Church of America.

Karen L. White is the Pastoral Ministries Coordinator of the First Baptist Church in Dallas, Texas. She has served in the Philippines and as adjunct professor of missions at the Criswell College in Dallas, Texas.

J. Dudley Woodberry is Dean and Professor of Islamic Studies at the School of World Mission at Fuller Theological Seminary. He has served in Pakistan, Afghanistan, and Saudi Arabia.

Part I

Foundational Issues: Reflecting on the Barriers

Chapter 1

RAISING QUESTIONS ABOUT THE RESISTANT

Michael Pocock

The theme of this volume goes to the heart of world evangelization, "Reaching the Resistant." On this theme I am reminded of a wonderful film that probably launched a new generation of fly fisherman in their pursuit of that wonderful, yet resistant species—the trout. *A River Runs Through It* told the story of a clergyman and his wife raising two sons with equal doses of love, fishing, and the Westminster Catechism along the banks of the Blackfoot River in Montana. In spite of the parents' efforts, prayers, and dreams, one son became "Mr. Responsible" and the other "Mr. Hell Raiser." One followed, in large measure, his father's aspiration, and the other went his own way, destructively as it turned out. In his later years, the old clergyman, saddened by the death of his son who rejected all counsel to mend his ways, plaintively asks his congregation these questions, "What is it about those we love? Don't we have what they need? Or is it just that they won't take what we offer?"

The reasons why some peoples resist the gospel in our day and why others are more responsive are just about as elusive as the answer to the clergyman's questions. "Lord," we may say, "we know you so loved the whole world that you gave your only son for their redemption; we have accepted your challenge to make disciples of all the nations; we believe we have been given the presence and power of your Spirit to reach them; and we've tried to get to as many as we possibly can. So how is it that two thousand years after you laid out this task so many are yet unreached? And why are so many resistant to the gospel? They have not responded even when the opportunity was given them!"

These are the tasks of this volume—to reflect on why some peoples are resistant and to formulate an idea or a "theology" of resistance as well as of overcoming resistance. We hope to be encouraged by models that bear a possibility for reaching the resistant and that describe cases that show where and how it is happening.

I will not here address the question of why many peoples are resistant. That is done in the subsequent chapters, but I would like to pose some questions and suggest some directions to frame our thinking.

Should We Be Surprised That Many of the Unreached Today Are Also Resistant?

After almost two thousand years of expansion, there is hardly a nation where the gospel has not been proclaimed, although there are many people groups in these nations that have no churches and have not really heard the gospel. One characteristic of all cultures is that, similar to the people of which they are constituted, they are wonderfully originated by God (Gen. 11:1–9 and Ac. 17:24–27) but fatally flawed by sin. These infirm cultures may be more or less resistant to the cure for their illness, but we can be sure that the easier "diseases" have been mitigated, leaving the more resistant in our day, and that some that have been repeatedly exposed to the cure have become all the more resistant.

In 1972, David Liao, writing about the Hakka of Taiwan, showed that although most missionaries considered the Hakka resistant, there had in fact been periods of great response—especially among those on the mainland of China—but he demonstrated statistically that there was proportionately less targeting of outreach, resources, and personnel toward the Hakka than toward other groups in Taiwan especially after 1950. He concluded that the Hakka were not more resistant than others but simply neglected (Liao 1972). We may be using the idea of "resistant" to comfort ourselves or excuse ourselves from engaging and living among the unreached when in reality we simply do not know what the disposition of these people may be to the presentation of the gospel.

What Do We Mean by "Resistant"?

The resistant are those who have or are receiving an adequate opportunity to hear the gospel but over some time have not responded positively. They are not simply "unreached people." Of the latter's receptivity or resistance, we may know little. On the other hand, "unreached" in modern missiological parlance does not mean "unengaged by mission efforts," but rather "there is no indigenous community of believing Christians with adequate numbers and resources to evangelize the group to its margins" (Dayton and Fraser 1990:29). So some groups that already have a mission outreach among them may nevertheless be both resistant and unreached.

Why Are Some People Groups Resistant to the Gospel?

Martin Luther seriously felt that resistance to the gospel was akin to "spiritual madness." He argued that those who resist are "demented, mad, irrational" and like sick people being offered a cure by a competent doctor only to speak abusively to him, they reject the treatment. Such a response he felt could be only accounted for by madness (Luther 1959:695).

Others speaking more temperately have suggested that the communication has been flawed, or that the culture has not been respected or adaptation has not been made. The church has failed in some cases by locking the Bible into a single language as the Roman Catholics did in keeping to Latin instead of the vernacular and the [Greek] Orthodox did in keeping to Greek (Winter 1996:6).

Donald McGavran observed in what is the now famous homogeneous principle that "people everywhere like to become Christians without crossing barriers of race, language, and class" (1970:223). He maintained that much resistance was due to forcing one culture to drop its identity and join another in coming to Christ. Instead, it should be possible for each culture to respond to the gospel and form a church movement while remaining fully a part of the same culture.

Peter Lundell, writing about resistance to the gospel in Japan, argues that the concept of *Nihonkyo* (Japanism) held even by Japanese pastors themselves is an inhibitor to church growth among that people. His argument is that churches and leaders in Japan should drop *Nihonkyo* and go for New Testament principles which are at variance with the concept. *Nihonkyo* is "a pervasive glue permeating every sector of life" (1995:401–412). It is not simply national pride or ethnocentrism but a pervasive integration of core worldview assumptions (1995:401–412). What is interesting is that this concept can be shown to develop from the 1600s onward in marked contrast to the openness found originally in Japan when Christian (Catholic) missions first began work. Like the Hakka of Taiwan, the Japanese did indeed have a receptive moment after which responsiveness was greatly reduced.

The reasons for both resistance and even failure to target a people are many. Repkin adds to those already mentioned:

- A harvest mentality that fails to see that the mandate is to share the gospel broadly whether there is a harvest or not. When harvest is the bottom line, proclaimers quit proclaiming—often prematurely.
- A monocultural view of what churches should be like.
- The need for security in publicizing efforts among limited access peoples.
- Persecution: believers are often badly treated even more so than those who go to share.
- Prejudice and ignorance of Christianity on the part of nonbelievers.
- Expense and weak support systems for those in dangerous or trying circumstances (Repkin 1996:284–288).

Samuel Zwemer, who had a lifetime of experience, argues that, while Muslims were definitely winnable, the chief deterrent to conversion was the law of apostasy. He wrote an entire book on the subject (Zwemer 1924).

More recently, a great deal has been made of Satanic opposition (Wagner 1996), and surely this needs no refutation.[1] We are told clearly that Satan blinds the eyes of unbelievers so they will not believe the glorious gospel of the Lord Jesus Christ (2 Cor. 4:4). The Evangelical Missiological Society (EMS) has considered the matter of Satanic opposition and of territorial spirits at the 1995 and 1996 conferences, and still more can, will, and should be said. I believe, though, we have ourselves resisted studying the evidence that God himself can be the author of both resistance and response. This leads us to the next question.

What Is the Role of God in Resistance?

The development of resistance due to the multiplicity of dynamics affecting it is a complex and interactive phenomenon. Both Scripture and experience show this to be true. All of the human agents in the evangelistic encounter are fallen, sinful, and limited human beings. The evangelists as both human and sinners saved by grace will do their work imperfectly. Their motivations and practical dependence on the Spirit of God whom they possess as agents of God (Ac. 1:8) may ebb and flow. The failures of the evangelists are one set of dynamics that may contribute to the development of resistance. But the unbelievers can also initiate resistance out of their own stubborn desire to live on their own terms which is a characteristic of all men and women since Adam and Eve. God as sovereign Lord may both cause resistance in the first place for his own purposes or cause continuing and growing hardness in response to human rejection.

---

1 However, this emphasis *has* been criticized, and a dialogue of sorts on the extent to which Satanic and demonic influences enter into resistance and demonstrations of power in overcoming resistance may be found in Rommen 1995.

The passages relating to the interaction between Moses, God, and Pharaoh in Exodus 7–14 show the two sides of resistance or hardening of the heart of an unregenerate Gentile. "I will harden Pharaoh's heart, and though I multiply my miraculous signs and wonders in Egypt, he will not listen to you" (7:3, 4). The confrontational chapters show that Pharaoh hardened his own heart seven times (7:13, 22; 8:15, 19, 32; 9:7, 34), and seven times the Lord is said to have hardened Pharaoh's heart (9:12; 10:1, 20, 27; 11:10; 14:4, 8). All the hardening passages are preceded by the promise of God to harden Pharaoh's heart, yet the self-hardening passages tend to precede the majority of those indicating God was doing the hardening. Several times the purpose of hardening is mentioned (9:16; 10:1; 11:9; 14:4, 17). It is to show the glory and power of God in a display of miraculous signs that identify Yahweh as the true God.

The great displays of overcoming resistance are not lost on later Scripture writers. Time and again they refer to them. Through the Exodus and other narratives, the sovereign power and discretion of the Lord in the process of resistance, which is equivalent to hardening, is shown. The Gentiles (in the case of Pharaoh) and the Lord's people can both harden their own hearts and be hardened by God. Paul in Romans 1:21, 26, and 28 shows the principle that God reveals himself to men and women in general revelation, and men and women deliberately resist this truth, leading in turn to greater hardness initiated by God.

Paul expounds at some length on God's sovereign discretion and power in Romans 9–11. He refers to the raising up of Pharaoh to display God's own power (9:17) and concludes in verse 18, "Therefore God has mercy on whom he wants to have mercy, and he hardens whom he wants to harden." The elect obtain the promises of God; others are hardened (Rom. 11:7). The method of hardening is that "God gave them a spirit of stupor, eyes so that they could not see and ears so that they could not hear" (Rom. 11:8, citing Isa. 29:10). God is the agent of hardening, but hardening is also in response to humanity's resistant spirit.

We will see David Brickner on the issue of Jewish resistance to the gospel, and he will show that, while there is a temporal, general resistance of the Jewish people, they are not as a matter-of-fact all resistant, and many do respond to the gospel. This squares with Paul's assessment that they are hardened "in part until the full number of the Gentiles has come in" (Rom. 11:25) after which all Israel will be saved.

We must be careful in our own strategic planning to recognize the hand of God in the matter of resistance. In some peoples we may see what we consider resistance and may be able to trace it to broad-scale acts of rejection of previously known truth, but there will always be a portion of those peoples who are prepared by God to respond. It is to them, by addressing the whole culture broadly, that we are to announce the gospel.

I like the confidence of earlier evangelists to Muslims who espoused the possibility of response among this generally resistant people. Zwemer cites W. H. T. Gairdner, who said,

> Those who care for Christ's Kingdom of God now know for certain that the evangelization of Moslems is possible ... the talk (about the impossibility of Moslem conversion to Christianity) is utterly baseless and has been confuted by contrary fact in almost all countries again and again (Gairdner cited in Zwemer 1924:14).

The waxing and waning of resistance is a mysterious matter. Our error would be to search solely for human, environmental, Satanic, or demonic causes while neglecting the sovereign purpose, plan, and timing of God. We are brought back time and again to the role of God in ordering history for his greater glory as the Lord of the Harvest who both sends out the workers and delays or develops the harvest according to his wisdom. While it is true that only "the Spirit gives life, the flesh counts for nothing" (Jn. 6:63), we nevertheless have been graced to be the channels of Holy Spirit power (Ac. 1:8). The treasure is in earthen vessels that the glory may be of the Lord (2 Cor. 4:7).

The following chapters will more clearly and adequately help us to understand the dynamics of resistance and the path to overcome it. To answer the questions of the clergyman in *A River Runs Through It*, I say, "Yes, we do have what our loved ones and the world need, and we must offer it to them, but we cannot make them take it. That lies in God's power, timing, and grace."

REFERENCES

Dayton, Edward R. and David A. Fraser. 1990. *Planning Strategies for World Evangelization*. Revised edition. Grand Rapids: Eerdmans.

Eenigenburg, Don. 1997. "The Pros and Cons of Islamicized Contextualization." *Evangelical Missions Quarterly* 33:3(July).

Jaffarian, E. Michael. 1994. "World Evangelization by AD2000: Will We Make it?" *Evangelical Missions Quarterly* 30:1(January).

Kobata, Daryn K. 1997. "Finishing Kick," *World Pulse* 32:20(October 17).

Liao, David C. E. 1972. *The Unresponsive: Resistant or Neglected?* Pasadena, CA: William Carey Library.

Lundell, Peter N. 1995. "Behind Japan's Resistant Web: Understanding the Problem of Nihonkyo." *Missiology* 13:4(October).

Luther, Martin. Ewald M. Plas, compiler. 1959. "The Damned Are Self-Condemned." *What Luther Says: An Anthology*. 3 Vols. St. Louis: Concordia.

McGavran, Donald. 1970. *Understanding Church Growth*. Revised edition. Grand Rapids: Eerdmans.

Repkin, Nik. 1996. "Why Are the Unreached Unreached?" *Evangelical Missions Quarterly* 32:3(July):284–288.

Rommen, Edward, ed. 1995. *Spiritual Power and Missions: Raising the Issues*, EMS Series Vol. 3. Pasadena, CA: William Carey Library.

Wagner, C. Peter. 1996. *Confronting the Powers*. Ventura, CA: Regal Books.

Winter, Ralph. 1996. "Do We Need Heresies on the Mission Field? Can Heresies Be Silver Linings?" *Mission Frontiers* 18:9–10(September–October).

Zwemer, Samuel M. 1924. *The Law of Apostasy in Islam: Answering the Question Why There Are So Few Moslem Converts and Giving Examples of Their Moral Courage and Freedom*. New York: Marshall Brothers.

Chapter 2

REVISING ASSUMPTIONS ABOUT THE RESISTANT

Gary Corwin

Having passed through many political seasons, we are all well aware of the importance placed upon poll watching. Politicians and pundits alike would hardly know what to do without these regular readings of public sentiment. Without them there would be little left for candidates but to say what they actually believe and plan to do. Wouldn't that be radical?

There is another kind of "pole watching," however, that may be quite important for those who think deeply about the world missions enterprise. This one, spelled differently, refers to the outer limits of a continuum of thought on a subject as in "They were poles apart on the issue."

Some wag has said of modern evangelicalism that the only time we seem to be in balance is at that point on the pendulum where we are swinging from one extreme to the other. There is poignant truth in that observation and much more than can even be alluded to here. But one place where we can appropriately explore its truth is in an examination of the assumptions that both underlie and guide mission outreach to what we are calling "the resistant." And even our use of that term must be held lightly as it reflects assumptions that need to be explored. While the concept of "the resistant" can be looked at from several different angles, the unifying definition that guides our discussion here is "those peoples who for whatever reason have not responded significantly to the gospel" having heard it.

I believe Hegel had a thought process that may be useful to us in this endeavor. He asserted that for every thesis there is an antithesis and that out of the interaction of the two will come a synthesis. Our approach, therefore, will follow the broad strokes of his model as we do our "pole watching," exploring the possibility of synthesis for some of the seemingly conflicting assumptions that guide our outreach to "the resistant." Obviously, we will not in this short chapter be able to treat any of these issues exhaustively, but perhaps highlighting them with at least some level of reflection will help to carry the discussion forward.

Theological and Faith Assumptions

The Failures of God's People versus the "Fullness of Time"

Some will undoubtedly consider it folly, but it is nearly impossible to consider fruitfully the need of "resistant" peoples for the gospel without getting profoundly theological. Missiology in these circumstances is driven back to its biblical roots, and the missiologist cannot escape his calling as theologian. Though some might argue otherwise, the social science aspects of missiology are profoundly under-equipped to determine ultimate reasons why the resistant remain that way.

Interestingly, there are influential voices among both the optimists and the pessimists on this subject of reaching the resistant who argue that the least reached or resistant remain that way because we simply have not done enough, or because our missiological approaches have been inadequate. God's people simply have not yet invested the time and energy necessary to reach the "resistant," or they have not gone about it in the right way.

The alternative view is that the least reached or resistant remain that way because it is not God's time for them yet. Their *kairos* moment has not yet arrived. In this view, just as the Holy Spirit guided Paul away from Asia and toward Europe, he is guiding God's people and the gospel message toward those whom he has prepared to receive it. Those who do not receive it have not yet been prepared to do so.

If you think this debate sounds a little like the centuries old debate over the relationship between God's sovereignty and human responsibility, you are correct. And the answer to it dwells in the same realm of paradoxical understanding. The apparent contradiction is just that—apparent, but not real.

Frontiers, an agency I admire very much, has used as its mobilization motto, "Muslims—It's their turn!" It is a short but catchy phrase, and while the extent to which it can be seen as causative remains unclear, this young mission has certainly grown rapidly over the last decade and a half. I have often wondered, though, how the author of that slogan came to know "It's their turn!" Did he or she have an inside track on God's plan for the ages and know for a fact that God plans to convert large numbers of Muslims from scores of people groups in our own day? Perhaps in a sense he or she did, if in reading Scripture the individual was juxtaposing God's promises in Revelation 5:9 and 7:9 (that there would one day be some from every tribe, language, people, and nation gathered at the throne of God to worship the Lamb) with his or her own understanding of scriptural teaching on eschatology, believing that the Lord's return is indeed near. If both of those things were true, it is possible to think that the author of that phrase was simply deducing an implication from the teachings of Scripture since there certainly have not been many from Muslim backgrounds who have found the savior up to this time.

A more likely explanation for the phrase, however, is that from a human effort point of view this mission is determined to put the kind of resources, energy, and effort into reaching Muslims that others have enjoyed. In other words, "It's their turn" to receive the kind of attention that has led to the major faith movements that other more "receptive" peoples have experienced. Clearly, the underlying assumption is that there would be equally large numbers of Muslim-background believers if only they had received the same kind of missiological attention that other groups have received. The history of my own mission, SIM, which has had an enormous investment in reaching Muslims for at least seventy years, might argue otherwise.

John Hall, for example, was an early SIM pioneer who for seventeen years spearheaded a highly effective outreach to the Tangale people of the middle belt of Nigeria. He later wrote a book entitled *From Cannibalism to Christ* about that work. Subsequently, he also worked among the Muslim Hausa in northern Nigeria for an additional seventeen years. This was the same man and the same country but a different people who were Muslims. Unlike his first seventeen year tenure, there was no people movement to Christ this time.

The truth, I would suggest, lies somewhere between a *kairos* moment explanation and a human effort one. Clearly God has said that he is the one who provides the necessary faith to believe as a work of his own grace (Eph. 2:8–9), but he also does it through the foolishness of preaching and that by those who are sent (Rom. 10:14–15). The human instrumentality of preaching to the resistant made receptive by the work of the Holy Spirit is the master plan of evangelism as pertains to Muslims and other resistant peoples. "It's their turn" only as divine preparation and human instrumentality combine in effective outreach. At its core, however, it is the work of the one of whom it was said, "What he opens no one can shut, and what he shuts no one can open" (Rev. 3:7). And increasingly there are signs that many hearts long resistant are being opened in many parts of the world.

"Resistant": Character Trait or Historical Description?

A legitimate question arises in discussions concerning "resistant" peoples as to whether they are resistant by nature or character (i.e., as a personality trait) or whether "resistant" is simply a historical assessment of how they have responded to the gospel to date. This is no small distinction from a theological point of view. If their resistance is simply a product of the historic or contextual circumstances that they have experienced, then their receptivity would seem to be contingent upon changing those circumstances or at least overcoming the effects of their occurrence. If, on the other hand, their resistance stems from a more deep-seated personality characteristic, whether defined corporately, idiosyncratically, or even as a part of the human condition then other kinds of remedies are required.

Clearly, there is a great deal of evidence on both sides of this issue. Much of missiology today is dedicated to discerning and finding solutions to the obstacles presented by history, culture, and communication style which hinder the spread of the gospel among a particular people group. Many profound and helpful insights have been garnered from the work of anthropologists, linguists, sociologists, historians, and others. Principles such as the high receptivity period, which characterizes the first couple of years when rural immigrants enter into urban situations, are most helpful to strategic planning in missions.

At the same time, there is a good deal of both biblical and experiential evidence to establish the fact that a far more deep-seated problem must be overcome—the universal human condition of being "dead in trespasses and sins" (Eph. 2:1, KJV). Unless God makes people alive again through regeneration, there is no hope for change. In this sense, then, the problem is one of character. All men have not only sinned and come short of the glory of God (Rom. 3:23), but they are universally in a state of open rebellion against him. In other words, all men are resistant: "There is no one ... who seeks God" (see Rom. 3:10–18).

That is not to say that all groupings of people are equally resistant to the gospel. Some are clearly more resistant than others. It is possible, for example, to resist not only the gospel itself but, through the use of social and governmental control, to resist for ideological reasons even access to the gospel of Christ. This has certainly been true in many Muslim lands and in lands where Marxist ideology has been predominate.

So, what are the implications of this for understanding resistant peoples? Simply this (and again ancient theological issues raise their heads): resistance is not the exception among the human family but the norm. Any movement of receptivity, whether in an individual or among a people group, is the product of the Father's work by the Spirit of drawing men to himself (Jn. 6:37, 44). Sometimes this requires only a work in individual lives while at other times God first changes the macro-landscape as he did with the breakup of the former Soviet Union.

Does all this then mean that good missiological principles do not matter? Not at all. As with evangelism in general, God has chosen to use human beings as the primary messengers of his gospel. As his ambassadors, we can use effective or ineffective means just as we can go forth prayerfully in the power of the Holy Spirit or not. The lessons of the Scriptures and of history are that God uses the instrumentality of human efforts to achieve his purposes, and he honors those who strive for excellence in serving him effectively. Doing less is to dishonor him and is not a condition in which the true child of God can comfortably rest. In other words, within the parameters of God's sovereign work of drawing men to himself, the harder, the more prayerfully, and the more intelligently we work, the less resistant people will be.

Strategic and Tactical Assumptions

Emphasize the Least Reached or the Most Receptive?

On the surface at least, this seems like one of those places where the obvious and time-worn answer sort of jumps up and bites you: "It's not a question of either/or but of both/and." We need to emphasize both the least reached and the most receptive. Things are not quite that simple, however.

For starters, there are those on each end of that choice spectrum who would argue forcefully that for biblical, historic, or pragmatic reasons their emphasis is the correct one. The most strident advocates on the receptivity side have been found among the church growth school. Their counterparts on the least reached side have been found among the Frontier Missions school. In between are multiple shades of accommodation and/or blending such as those who emphasize various saturation church planting or mission mobilization strategies.

The issues between the poles, of course, are not trivial, particularly as they tend to focus on the allocation of scarce resources. On the one hand is a mountain of statistical evidence that the overwhelming preponderance of resources are being (mis)directed to those who need them the least (i.e., the already Christianized world, or at least the already evangelized world). Frontier Missions school's case is both graphic and telling. "Why should anyone hear the gospel twice," they would argue, "when there are those who have never heard it once." As with Paul, their ambition is to preach Christ where he is not yet known (Rom. 15:20).

On the other hand lies the sane and pragmatic argument that scarce resources ought to be directed first of all to those places where the harvest is greatest. It makes no sense, this school would argue, to miss those seasons of special harvest when and where God's Spirit has prepared them. Harvest times do not last forever, and they ought to be maximized when they occur. "Why spend most of your energy plowing rocky soil," they would say, "when a ripe harvest is in danger of rotting in the fields for lack of attention?" Like Christ in Matthew 9:37–38, their focus is on the plentiful harvest and the scarcity of laborers.

But things get more complicated than that. The receptivity of various peoples to the gospel can change dramatically over time for a whole host of circumstantial and Spirit-inspired reasons. That is why even Donald McGavran, the father of the church growth movement, argued in favor of maintaining at least a beachhead of presence among all peoples. You never know what might occur to make a largely unresponsive people receptive in whole new ways, and you want to be ready when that happens.

It is also true, however, that huge quantities of resources can be squandered in already churched areas, where good teaching on biblical stewardship and missions responsibility might have produced a fountainhead to extend ministry rather than a catch basin to collect it.

So, what is the answer? It is the same one we began with. Both emphases are not only permissible but also essential. We must somehow provide to one another the latitude to make both cases well. We do not have to have tunnel vision to prove that we are single-minded. Both the least reached and the incredibly ready are emphases that God would have us pursue with every fiber of our being.

Extraction, Contextualization, or Super-Contextualization?

It is not altogether fair to use the critic's term "extraction" to describe what is often an unintended consequence of gospel ministry in hostile environments. It does communicate well, however, the state of affairs in which a recent convert concludes that it is necessary to leave his or her family and social relationships usually for purposes of self-preservation or at least to avoid persecution and gain freedom of religious practice. Advocates of contextualization, however, see this result as a failure of methodology.

The goal of contextualization is to remove as many foreign accouterments to the gospel as possible, thus making it far easier for the resistant Muslim, Buddhist, Hindu, *et cetera*, to receive the gift of life through Christ. By so doing, the gospel also has the opportunity to pass effectively along normal social and familial channels of communication. If there is going to be an offense in the gospel, they argue, let it be the offense of the cross and not the presence of offensive foreign practices.

The concept is relatively simple, and there are few who would argue against it in principle. There is a minefield of debate, however, present in the details of determining what is essential to the gospel and Christian integrity, and what may be scrubbed so as not to cause unnecessary offense. As they say in Washington politics, "The devil is in the details." Is Sunday worship essential, or could it take place on Friday? Is praying daily at the mosque permissible? What about keeping the fast of Ramadan? Is public baptism essential or could it be done privately? And the list could go on with a variety as rich as the religions and cultures involved.

The issue is even more complicated than that, however, with the recent advocacy of what I will call "super-contextualization" which I can only describe as a new willingness to push the envelope of cultural and religious accommodation way beyond current practice. While thankfully the parameters of genuine discussion and debate are still fluid on this, there are some guiding principles and precedents being cited which cause concern.

One of these is the general principle that we should simply win some converts among a people, provide them with the Bible in their own language, and then set them free to develop in whatever culturally relevant ways they will. Syncretism and unorthodoxy in many areas are to be expected, it is argued, but this will work itself out over time. In the end, they suggest, the Holy Spirit will guide them into all truth through his word.

While there is a large element of truth in all this, as in the commitment to historic indigenization and contextualization principles which it implies, it seems to ignore the scriptural mandates to "make disciples" by "teaching them to obey everything I have commanded" (Mt. 28:19–20). It also ignores the Pauline model for leadership development and the missionary role he exhibited of ongoing care of the churches. Sending Timothy to revitalize the relatively young Ephesian church, for example, would have had no place in this approach.

Now it is true, as in the case of most of the over six thousand African Independent Churches (denominations, not congregations), that churches can emerge with a large degree of spontaneity from outside existing church structures. That is no reason, however, for not doing responsible discipleship training (even as a Westerner) where one can. In the example cited, many AIC churches have benefited from such discipling efforts as well.

Another troubling aspect of the "super-contextualization" approach is the appeal to the precedent of Christian participation in the worship at the Jewish Temple and synagogues, arguing that this could also work in Islamic and other contexts. The case is made that there must be much greater tolerance of elements in the host religious culture just as there was with Judaism during the earliest Christian century. The difference, of course, is in the shared heritage of revealed truth communicated through common Scriptures. The same cannot be said even of Islam, Christianity's next closest religious cousin, which though it shares a high regard for portions of the Bible, considers the Qur'an its most definitive scripture. Doing so in Hindu or Buddhist contexts is an even larger stretch.

While we can and must champion efforts to de-Westernize or "de-Whateverize" all foreignly imposed additions to the gospel, we must be extremely careful not to de-gospelize the gospel. Does that mean, for example, we must insist that converts call themselves "Christians" when that is equivalent in their culture to saying "I have become a Westerner"? I do not think so, but neither does it diminish the applicability of Christ's words, "But he who disowns me before men will be disowned before the angels of God" (Lk. 12:9). Though the terminology may need to change, the principle cannot.

Rather than moving the contextualization pole further out on one end of the spectrum, it seems that our energies would be far better expended in striving to find the scripturally warranted boundaries of appropriate contextualization, which preserves the commitment to biblical holiness (indeed, even "separation" as necessary) while minimizing unnecessary and culturally bound obstacles to faith among the least reached. While we never want to acknowledge "Caesar (or culture) is lord," we should not hesitate to render unto either that which is theirs.

CONCLUSION

As with so many areas of Christian life and work, the common thread that ties these assumption issues together is the need for balance. It is such a common refrain that one almost tires of it. It lacks inspirational value, and it seldom engenders excitement even among its advocates. But it encompasses the essence of what it means to be Christian. It is modeled in God himself, who dwells in perfect and harmonious balance as the three persons of the Trinity, or who, in the second person of that Trinity, balanced perfectly the incarnational life of the God-man. It is no less essential for carrying out God's missiological task of redeeming some from every tribe, language, people, and nation.

If God has given us "the ministry of reconciliation" and has "committed to us the message of reconciliation" (2 Cor. 5:18–20), we must find ways to reconcile our different emphases and our individual passions in staying true to our high and holy calling as "ambassadors of Christ." Life out at the poles may be exciting, but fruitfulness is found by abiding together in the Vine, who said, "Apart from me you can do nothing," and "I will build my church."

Chapter 3

Reflecting Theologically about the Resistant

Charles Van Engen

Introduction

I was asked to prepare a chapter on "A Theology of the Resistant." I have changed the title for several reasons, not the least being the following. I am the father of three children, the oldest of whom, a daughter, is now twenty-three and a doctoral student in physics at the University of Colorado at Boulder. The second, also a daughter, will graduate this coming May with a BS with a major in computers and minors in business and Spanish. And the third, my son Andrew, is sixteen years old, six foot two and about two hundred ten pounds, and a junior in high school.

Now when my daughters were eight and ten, my wife, Jean, and I moved from Mexico to the U.S. At that time, I sat them both down (and I did this later with my son as well) and very seriously I informed the girls,

"Look, I want you to know that for the next ten years or so your Dad is going to get more and more stupid. Each year you will be surprised at how much dumber your Dad will be getting."

The girls, with big, wide eyes responded, "Really, Dad, what's wrong?"

"Well, I don't have time to explain it all to you now. I just want you to know that this is going to happen—and don't worry too much about it. Because you will discover that from the time you are about twenty-three or so until you are thirty-five years old, each year I will begin to get smarter! So in about twenty-five years I will be as smart as I am now—so don't worry too much about it."

Now you may wonder what this has to do with my changing of the title of this chapter. Well, anyone who has had teen-aged children will be able to explain it to you. Once each of my three children hit twelve or thirteen, they became *resistant*! Although I have played basketball for over a quarter of a century, suddenly I could not coach them, I could not teach them—I seemed to know nothing about basketball. And although I played varsity soccer in high school and college and had coached my son for a number of years, once my son was thirteen, why Dad did not seem to know anything about soccer—actually, Dad did not seem to know anything about anything, including girls! So I have found that, although I have served as a consultant to churches, presbyteries, and mission agencies, I clearly know nothing about relationships, organizations, how my children's friends are coping, or anything having to do with human relations. My children have become a *resistant people group*!

So, having learned from them, I have come to realize that I cannot do a "Theology of the Resistant"—because I do not know anything about it! You have to ask the "resistant"!

THESIS

The thesis of this chapter is the following:

> A missiological and theological understanding of "resistance" or "resistant people" must be grounded biblically in a recognition of human sinfulness that reflects the way humanity spiritually and relationally rejects God's loving self-disclosure to humankind. This would imply that a missiological discussion of "receptivity/resistance" should deal primarily with issues of spirituality, theology, and reconciliation with God, self, others, and the world—and secondarily with matters of worldview, sociology, contextualization, or strategy.

THE NEED FOR THEOLOGICAL REFLECTION WITH REGARD TO THE RESISTANT

This chapter is divided into two major sections. In the first section, I review the development of the concepts of resistance and receptivity in church growth theory. This is important if we are to understand the missiological framework of the concept about which we are doing theological reflection. This clarification must include the fact that one cannot consider the concept of "resistant peoples" apart from its association with the idea of "receptive" peoples. In the second section I will offer an outline of the theological reflections that would seem to be appropriate with regard to these concepts.

The origin of the concepts "responsive" and "resistant" are to be found in church growth theory that was predominantly based on sociology and strategy. The concept of "resistant peoples" was first popularized by Donald McGavran. In the late 1930s and 1940s, together with J. Waskom Pickett, McGavran began to ask questions about why churches in India seemed to grow among some people groups and not among others.

The Concept of Group

First, although it is beyond the scope of this chapter to deal with McGavran's concepts of "peoples," "people group," "group conversion," and "multi-individual conversion," it is important to note that the concept "resistant" was used very early by McGavran as a term describing "peoples." There is development in McGavran's writings in the way he defined the term, yet throughout, the concept of groupness, corporateness, and social cohesion remained constant. One must remember that for McGavran this issue was absolutely basic, influencing even his hermeneutic of Matthew 28:19, where he read *matheteusate panta ta ethne* as "disciple the peoples" of the world. Here are some samples of the way McGavran defined a "people."

> In the West Christianization is an extremely individualistic process.... Peoples were thought of as aggregates of individuals whose conversion was achieved one by one. The social factor in the

conversion of peoples passed unnoticed because peoples were not identified as separate entities.

However, a people is not an aggregate of individuals. In a true people intermarriage and the intimate details of social intercourse take place within the society. In a true people individuals are bound together not merely by common social practices and religious beliefs but by common blood. A true people is a social organism which, by virtue of the fact that its members intermarry largely within its own confines, becomes a separate race in their minds. Since the human family, except in the individualistic West, is largely made up of such castes, clans and peoples, the Christianization of each nation involves the prior Christianization of its various peoples as peoples ... (McGavran 1955:8–10).

A nation is usually a conglomerate of peoples, sometimes bound together by language, religion and culture and sometimes divided by just these factors (1959:41).

[People] meet the Church not only as isolated individuals but as multitudinous societies, each made up of interrelated individuals who are often of one blood, language, dialect, or section of the country.... Among the many aspects of human society none is more important to church growth than these homogeneous units of [hu]mankind.... The general population may be compared to a mosaic. Each piece of the mosaic is a society, a homogeneous unit. It has its own way of life, its own standards, degree of education, self-image, and places of residence....

This sociological viewpoint is factual and reasonable. [Humans] do live in societies.... What is commonly called group conversion is really *multi-individual conversion*. It is many individuals believing on the Lord at the same time in shared knowledge of the joint action and mutual dependence on each other. Such multi-individual action has very different marginal meanings and results from lone individual action taken in the teeth of group disapproval.

Recognizing homogeneous units and claiming them for Christ emphasizes the biblical goal of discipling the tribes (1965:69, 71–73).

Thus, essentially, the starting point for reflection on "resistant peoples" must be the concept of "peoples," from which we can then move on to make the observation that a particular people group may be "resistant." The concept of "resistant" was one that sought to describe something about a corporate group, namely, the way that group responded to mission actions carried out in and with the group (*see* McGavran 1974:2–5, 38–40; 1977:74–76).

The Concept of "Responsive" Groups

Second, we should be aware of the fact that originally McGavran's and Alan Tippett's emphasis did not fall on "resistant," but rather on "responsive" peoples. In *Bridges of God*, McGavran said,

> As we search for light as to how *peoples* become Christian, the story of the early Church has a great contribution to make. . . . Perhaps most important of all, we see how the intentional missionary labors of the early Church, headed by Paul, were devoted in large measure deliberately to following responsive peoples and to expanding existing impulses to Christ in the hearts of people (1955:36; *see* also McGavran 1959:52).

Fifteen years later, in his *magnum opus*, McGavran developed this concept further.

> The receptivity or responsiveness of individuals waxes and wanes. No person is equally ready at all times to follow "the Way". . . . This variability of persons is so well known that it needs no further exposition.
>
> Peoples and societies also vary in responsiveness. Whole segments of [hu]mankind resist the Gospel for periods—often very long periods—and then ripen to the Good News. In resistant populations, single congregations only, and those small, can be created and kept alive, whereas in responsive ones many congregations which freely reproduce others can be established (1970:216; *see* also McGavran and Hunter 1980:30–31, 112).

Earlier, in 1972, Alan Tippett had written a chapter entitled, "The Holy Spirit and Responsive Populations," emphasizing that the concept of a "people" is helpful as it allows the missiologist to take the next step and ask about responsiveness.

> When we speak of "responsive populations" we are thinking of large homogeneous units of people who, once they have made their decision, act in unison. . . . Not all populations are responsive. Fields *come* ripe unto harvest. The harvest time has to be recognized, and harvesters have to be sent in at the correct season. . . . Responsive populations should mean many people movements and great

> numerical church growth. Identifiable groups are waiting to be won for Christ. When the group responds, a congregation has to be created, preferably with the same structure as the group itself.... Those responsible, as the stewards of the ingathering, need common sense, humility, anthropological understanding, and a strong personal faith to be good stewards; but, above all, they need obedient submission to the Holy Spirit, without whose power and blessing there could be no mission at all (Tippett 1972:77–78, 97–98).

So the early emphasis of McGavran and his associates was positive, seeking to identify those people groups that were more responsive—and having identified them, to respond appropriately in terms of mission strategy and action. That brings us to the third major step in the process of theoretical construction (*see* McGavran and Arn 1973:47–48).

Selective Targeting of Responsive Groups

Third, McGavran proceeded to affirm a rule-of-thumb of mission strategy—that missions should invest much among groups that have been deemed responsive, and "inhabit lightly" the areas where peoples were not responsive (McGavran even used the term "irresponsive" [1955:120]—did he mean "unresponsive?"). Peter Wagner and others followed that thinking to the next seemingly logical step, stressing that once the responsive populations have been identified, missions should learn the art of selectively targeting those people groups that were identified as receptive.

Eddie Gibbs warns us about this which he calls an "axiom" of church growth theory.

> It is an axiom of church growth thinking that highest priority must be given to presenting the gospel to the receptive rather than wasting effort in futile attempts to convince the resistant. To help the evangelist and church planter identify receptive soil there are a number of indicators, most of which point to people in transition or trauma. But unless due regard is given to the work of the Spirit, this church growth principle is liable to be unscrupulously exploited rather than conscientiously applied.... What is clear is that there needs to be a caring, articulate Christian presence at such times (of transition or trauma) to be available to the Spirit in presenting the riches and claims of Christ (1986:192).

Recognizing the Mosaic of Varying Receptivity

Fourth, we are indebted to McGavran, Tippett, Wagner, and others in helping us see that in any given nation, and especially in any specific city or area, there may in fact be a rather complex *mosaic* of various people groups, and that the "receptivity" or "resistance" may vary from group to group—and the factors that contribute to their "receptivity" or "resistance" also may differ markedly. Thus, McGavran affirmed,

> Unless churchmen [*sic*] are on the lookout for changes in receptivity of homogeneous units within the general population, and are prepared to seek and bring persons and groups *belonging to these units* into the fold, they will not even discern what needs to be done in mission. They will continue generalized "church and mission work" which, shrouded in fog as to the chief end of mission, cannot fit mission to increasing receptivity. An essential task is to discern receptivity and—when this is seen—to adjust methods, institutions, and personnel until the receptive are becoming Christians and reaching out to win [others] to eternal life (1970:232).

Later, McGavran wrote,

> In almost every land some pieces of the mosaic are receptive to the Gospel. Church growth [folks] keep pointing out that we live in a responsive world (1984a:252–253).

The inevitable conclusion drawn from this observation was selective targeting. Mission strategists should direct most of their efforts to the receptive mosaics and "occupy lightly" the people groups or parts of the mosaic that are yet resistant (McGavran 1970:229–230).[1] As Delos Miles said in *Church Growth: A Mighty River*,

> Priority in church growth should be given to those who are most receptive to the gospel. We should put our greatest resources where they will provide the largest harvest now. McGavran calls this

---

1 It is beyond the scope of this paper to evaluate the swarming of mission agencies into certain parts of the world and specific contexts that this concept produced—with, in some cases, rather disastrous results.

"Winning the winnable while they are winnable." George Hunter is convinced that the "Church Growth movement's greatest contribution to this generation's world evangelization will be its stress upon receptivity."

Hence, church growth presents us with a priority of priorities! Top priority is to be given to evangelism. Within that priority foremost attention is to be given to winning the winnable. Gospel acceptors are to have priority over gospel rejectors (McGavran 1970:256 and Hunter 1979:104 cited in Miles 1981:90–91).

C. Peter Wagner explained it this way:

> As I mentioned previously, virtually every discussion about the principle of the harvest or resistance and receptivity raises the concern about the resistant. Missionaries have been working among specific people groups for years with little or no harvest. Nor do they anticipate a harvest in the near future. Are these missionaries out of the will of God? Should we abandon people such as Muslims? Do we bypass the unresponsive? These excellent questions need to be brought out into the open. It is at this very point that some have rejected not only the harvest principle, but the entire Church Growth Movement as well.
>
> No church growth advocate I know has ever suggested that we bypass the resistant. The Great Commission says that we are to preach the gospel to all creatures. Donald McGavran from the beginning has taught that we should "occupy fields of low receptivity lightly" [McGavran 1980:176–178]. In many cases Christian workers can do nothing more than establish a friendly presence and quietly sow the seed. God continues to call many of his servants to do just that, and I am one who supports and encourages them (Wagner 1987:88–89).

Here Wagner is echoing McGavran's strong stance on this issue. McGavran categorically stated, "No one should conclude that if receptivity is low, the Church should withdraw mission" (1970:229).

Biblical Support for Selective Targeting Drawn from the Parable of the Sower

Selective targeting was supported by appealing to the parable of the sower (Mt. 13:1–23). As far as I have been able to find, this parable was first mentioned in a contemporary missiological context by Ralph Winter, followed by Peter Wagner and others.

Subsequently, the parable of the sower became known in church growth literature as the parable of the soils, with a hermeneutical approach that concluded that the parable provided a biblical support for selectively targeting the people groups and contexts in which one chose to do mission activity.

As early as 1971, Ralph Winter affirmed,

> The ultimate missionary significance of [the parable of the soils] emerges with crystal clarity: this parable is the stoutest biblical basis for seeking receptive peoples and investing our time with those who will reproduce (1971:146).

This was echoed in that same year by Peter Wagner:

> Sowing the seed is necessary, but the parable [of the soils] refines the concept and teaches that *intelligent* sowing is necessary if the proper harvest is to come as a result. The obvious principle for missionary strategy is that, before sowing the seed of the Word, we will do well to test the soil.... As much as possible, responsible missionary strategists should strive to eliminate careless and broadcast sowing (1971:42).

In 1987, C. Peter Wagner affirmed that,

> The parable says that the seed which fell on good ground produced fruit thirty-, sixty- and one hundredfold. The fertility of the soil, then, is the most important independent variable. This "soil," according to the interpretation, is people who have been so prepared that they hear the word and understand it (see Matt. 13:23).
>
> So one way to increase the effectiveness of evangelistic strategy planning is to determine ahead of time which individuals or groups of individuals have hearts prepared by the Holy Spirit to receive the Word.... Careless sowing of the gospel message is not usually the most effective evangelistic procedure. To the degree possible, and later on I will share some of the technology available for doing this, we should test the evangelistic soil. Once we test the soil, we can use the energy and time and other resources available for our evangelistic task in a much more productive way (1987:61–62).

In Evangelical missiology, this parable has been a standard proof-text for selective targeting (*see*, e.g., McQuilkin 1973:24–32; Peters 1981:68–71; McGavran 1970:215ff; 1980:245ff; 1990:179ff; Wagner 1987:61–62; and Rainer 1993:250).

I will return to a further consideration of the parable of the sower in Part II.

Defining "Receptivity"

At this point we need to backtrack and ask how "receptivity" was first determined. On what basis was one to judge that a particular group was "receptive"? The answer appears obvious and harmless: In church growth literature, the predominant basis for judging a people to be "receptive" seemed to have been based on the fact that in the midst of a particular group *some churches were growing rapidly*. For McGavran, this meant that someone had been able to see the beginning of a "people movement." For McGavran and Wagner, it meant that when one did a comparative statistical church growth analysis of the various denominations, congregations or missions laboring among a particular people, one found that the churches (or at least some of them) were growing rapidly. As Wagner said it,

> Years of research has shown that, among many others, three major indicators of resistance-receptivity stand out and ought to be considered whenever determining where to plot a given people group on the axis. They are (1) where churches are already growing, (2) where people are changing, and (3) among the masses.... It sounds almost too elementary to say that receptivity can be expected where churches are already growing. But it needs to be highlighted because many evangelistic planners develop their strategy on the opposite consideration. They determine, on principle, to evangelize in places where churches have not been growing. For those who have a view to the harvest, such may not be the most efficient approach (1987:78).[2]

The Resistance-Receptivity Axis

This foundational definition ("receptive" peoples are those among whom many churches are growing rapidly) proceeded to give rise to the development by McGavran, Dayton, Wagner, and others of the "Resistance-Receptivity Axis" as shown below. In *Evangelism and Church Growth: A Practical Encyclopedia*, Elmer Towns defines this axis as, "A measurement scale by

---

2 In this volume Wagner then went on to elaborate, on his understanding of these three major indicators, on where a particular people group would fall on the resistance-receptivity axis. *See* Wagner 1987:78–88.

which people are designated according to their openness to the gospel" (Towns 1995:340).

The Resistance-Receptivity Axis

Highly Resistant to the Gospel										*Highly Receptive to the Gospel*
-5	-4	-3	-2	-1	0	+1	+2	+3	+4	+5
Strongly Opposed		Somewhat Opposed			Indifferent		Somewhat Favorable		Strongly Favorable	

Dayton 1980:47; reproduced in Wagner 1987:78. *See* also McGavran 1970:228; Wagner 1971:150–151; Reeves and Jenson 1984:69; Zunkel 1987:158; Dayton and Fraser 1990:129–130.

As we will see later, the "resistance-receptivity axis" fuels the question as *to what* the group may be receptive or resistant? In answer, various persons in the church growth movement developed a rather sophisticated analysis of various factors which might contribute to resistance or to receptivity. Working especially with matters of local contextual, local institutional, national contextual, and national institutional factors, one can quite helpfully sort out various issues that may be contributing to a group's place on the scale at a particular time and in a particular context. In my opinion, this analysis of factors that enhance or inhibit growth has been one of the most creative, constructive, and helpful elements of church growth theory.

"Resistance/Receptivity" as Second-Level Terms

Exactly what are we saying if the basis of our calling a group of people "receptive" is due to the fact that we can find churches growing rapidly among them? I would suggest that in using such terms, the church growth movement was actually not saying anything specific about the group itself. I do not believe the terms told us anything about a group's worldview, its cultural or religious systems, its faith-issues, its spiritual openness, or its psycho-emotional willingness to receive new ideas. Rather, the terms are, in my opinion, second-level derivative observations. The logic would go something like this:

a. Based on the fact that some churches are growing rapidly, and
b. based on the assumption that churches grow most rapidly among people whom we have termed "receptive,"
c. therefore we conclude that these people are receptive.

An associated concept that serves to demonstrate the above has to do with recent efforts in the church growth movement directed toward spiritual issues. Since 1980 or so, some folks like Peter Wagner and others have been working in areas of "strategic level spiritual warfare" and seem to be saying that "receptive" or "resistant" may be terms that should be understood to speak about the unseen cosmic-level spiritual forces operating on and in a people. In this case, again, the terms would tell us little about the people themselves. Instead, they could be understood to refer to the spiritual forces or spiritual environment operative among, and on, that people group at that particular time.

Thus, I would suggest that, viewed theologically, the early use of "responsive" or "receptive" as used by McGavran, was predominantly descriptive of the churches and their growth—not about anything inherent or intrinsic to the group itself. I am beginning to see that "receptive" and "resistant" have been essentially sociological terms, descriptive of an observable phenomenon (the numerical growth of congregations), and not theological terms speaking about the spiritual state of a people group.

Missiological Developments

Three major powerful and influential developments in Evangelical missiology flowed from the theoretical framework of resistant/receptive people groups.

Hidden/Unreached Peoples

The first major missiological implication that flowed from the theoretical framework I have outlined above has to do with the concept of "hidden peoples" and then "unreached peoples" which Ralph Winter has served the church so well in highlighting. These became very important in Evangelical missiology, first at Lausanne, 1974 (Douglas 1975), then at Pattaya, 1980 (Douglas 1980:43–44; Scott 1981:57–75; Coggins 1980:225–232; Winter 1980:79–85), then at the World Consultation on Frontier Missions held in Edinburgh, 1980 (Starling 1981), and most recently in the "Adopt-a-People" movement and the AD2000 Movement's stress on the 10/40 window. All of these have derived in some way from the theoretical framework outlined above. One could also include here the MARC research (Dayton, et al.) on unreached peoples, and specific assumptions behind some of David Barrett's research which also drew from this theoretical complex. No matter that one such as myself may strongly support the missionally activist initiatives represented by these movements in Evangelical missiology. That is not my point here. Rather, I wish for us to see that we have left unanswered one of the most significant and foundational theological and missiological questions: what are we saying when we say "receptive" or "resistant?"

Contextualization

A second missiological development that flowed from this theoretical complex was the desire for careful contextualization of the gospel in such a way that resistance could be avoided or at least lessened. As Donald McGavran suggested,

> Each population, therefore, must have its own formula.... The essentials of the Gospel, the authoritative Bible, and the unchanging Christ remain the same for all populations. But the accompaniments can and must be changed freely to suit each particular case (1970:231).
>
> Hard, bold plans for proclaiming Christ and persuading [people] to become His disciples and responsible members of His Church are a *sine qua non* of Christian mission. Their boldness will be enhanced by their sympathetic approach to the bewildering multitudes of every nation. They are essential to right strategy.
>
> Right strategy will divide the world into cultural units—those where Christian mission is correctly seed-sowing and those where it is correctly harvesting. Both kinds of culture are found, and there is no clear line between them. Wrong strategy fails to note the difference between responsive and resistant segments of society. Right strategy

not only notes the difference, but constantly explores to discover ways of identifying each variety of population and of fitting the missionary effort of each church correctly to each variety (1972a:105–106).

So in creating the School of World Mission/Institute of Church Growth at Fuller Theological Seminary, Donald McGavran brought in Alan Tippett, then Charles Kraft, to be joined later by Dean Gilliland and Dan Shaw—all experts in cultural anthropology and contextualization theory (*see*, e.g., Gilliland 1989).

Homogeneous Unit Church Planting

Although this is beyond the scope of this chapter, it is important to note here that a third missiological development was the very strong emphasis in the American church growth movement on planting homogeneous unit principle (HUP) churches. I have space only to mention some of the sample publications produced by Donald McGavran, Win Arn, Peter Wagner, and others that explained, strongly supported, and contextualized for North America the concept of planting HUP churches in North America, a stream of missiological thought flowing from the conceptual spring of measuring and responding to the resistance/receptivity of a particular people group. Here are some samples:

1971 C. Peter Wagner, *Frontiers of Mission Strategy*;
1973 Donald McGavran and Win Arn, *How to Grow a Church;*
1976 C. Peter Wagner, *Your Church Can Grow: Seven Vital Signs of a Healthy Church*;
1977 Donald McGavran and Win Arn, *Ten Steps for Church Growth*;
1979 C. Peter Wagner, *Our Kind of People*;
1980 Donald McGavran and George Hunter, *Church Growth Strategies that Work*;
1981 Donald McGavran, "Why Some American Churches are Growing and Some are Not," (in *The Complete Book of Church Growth*);
1981 Donald McGavran, *Back To Basics in Church Growth*;
1981 C. Peter Wagner, *Church Growth and the Whole Gospel*;
1984 Donald McGavran, *Momentous Decisions in Mission Today;*
1984 C. Peter Wagner, *Leading Your Church To Growth;*

1986 C. Peter Wagner, "A Vision for Evangelizing the Real America" (in *International Bulletin of Missionary Research*);
1987 C. Peter Wagner, *Strategies for Church Growth*;
1990 C. Peter Wagner, *Church Planting for a Greater Harvest;*
1996 C. Peter Wagner, *The Healthy Church;* and
1996 Thom Rainer, *The Book of Church Growth*.

We might draw two observations from surveying the above titles. First, the matter of "resistance/receptivity" has been very influential in Evangelical missiology during the last thirty years and cries for careful thought, examination, and critique. Second, the concepts themselves are quite unclear in terms of that to which they refer—especially with reference to spiritual and theological understanding. The terms have referred mostly to the fact that among a particular people group churches may be observed to be growing, and therefore the group should be targeted, and therefore specific cultural issues should be considered in missiological strategies directed towards it. But the lack of theological clarity is especially glaring when one focuses on the "resistant" part of the formula. Because, qualifiers and explanations notwithstanding, we might assume that for the "resistant" we would conclude the opposite of all the assertions previously made about the "responsive." Namely, that among the resistant we should carry out very little mission endeavor, that we should be especially careful about the contextualization of the gospel, and that we should not be too concerned about targeting resistant groups until such time as they become "receptive."

Yet, significantly—and in contradiction to the earlier perspective, in recent emphases in the AD2000 Movement, in Peter Wagner's and others' ministries, and in many mission initiatives dealing with the "10/40 window," one finds mission leaders calling for intentional and aggressive mission to be carried out precisely among some of the most resistant peoples of the world.

All of this is to say that we are in need of a thorough-going rethinking of the theological meaning of the term, "resistant." This, then, is the substance of the second section of this chapter.

An Outline of Theological Reflection about the Resistant

In what follows I would like to develop in a kind of outline form a progression of theological and biblical affirmations that may help us clarify the issue at hand. And the starting point, as I see it, must be positive (following early McGavran), not negative. So the progression of ideas is as follows:

All Humans Are Loved Always by God

God recognizes and values all peoples in their cultural and ethnic diversity. Within the particularity of ethnicity, God loves all peoples and invites all to faith in Jesus Christ, each in their own special cultural and ethnic makeup. Whether they respond or not, God still loves all peoples.

> For God so loved the world that he gave his one and only Son that whoever believes in him shall not perish but have eternal life (Jn. 3:16).

So the first affirmation that the Bible calls us to make has to do with a complementarity between cultural particularity and God's missional universality. Throughout the Scriptures, we find the people of God stressing God's careful sensitivity to particular cultural differences, recognizing the existence of different peoples and people groups. The "nations" are not just an amorphous amalgam of individuals caught in various webs of political dominance. Rather, they are "families, tribes, languages," each special in their particularity. However, at the same time, we find affirmed time and again that God loves *all* peoples—that God's desire to be in covenant extends an invitation to all the peoples. So all the peoples will be blessed in and through Abraham. Here, then, we can recognize McGavran's insistence on people groups—but we must also see here a profound re-definition of "receptivity" and "resistance."

The words of Jesus to Nicodemus focus the biblical narrative of God's universality of love for all peoples—and God's particularity of loving a plurality of specific and different peoples. One need only trace the theme through Scripture to see how very important it is in understanding God's mission. Risking belaboring the point, I will simply point out a few illustrative biblical references that may help us see God's mission as the outworking of the universality of God's love of all peoples in their cultural and historical particularity.

Genesis

Three times in the first eleven chapters of Genesis we are told that God is the creator and judge of all peoples. All people are created in Adam and Eve; all people descend from Noah; all people have their languages confused and are then spread out over the entire earth after the Babel episode. In each case, there is a recognition of the particularity and difference of various peoples—as is signaled by the inclusion of the Table of Nations in Genesis 10—yet in each case this multiplicity of peoples are collectively and unitedly said to be the object of God's concern.

Abraham

When God calls Abram, his call involves being a blessing to a plurality of nations—but through the particularity of one clan whose origins are traced back to Nahor and Terah from the Ur of the Chaldeans. They are particular instruments of God's mission, chosen with the intention of being a blessing to many particular peoples within the universality of God's concern, care, love, and judgment of all peoples.

Deuteronomy and 2 Chronicles

God's love of all peoples is repeated in Deuteronomy and, for example, also in 2 Chronicles. 1 Peter 2 draws from Deuteronomy 10:14–22. The creator Lord God (to whom "belong the heavens, the earth and everything in it") chose Israel out of all the nations, and now calls Israel to exhibit compassion and care for the fatherless, the widow, and the aliens who represent the plurality of particular nations. Thus many years later, even at Solomon's dedication of the Temple, the symbol of the most centralized form of Israel's faith—even here, Solomon prays, when

> the foreigner who does not belong to your people Israel but has come from a distant land because of your great name ... comes and prays toward this temple, then hear from heaven ... and do whatever the

foreigner asks of you, so that all the peoples of the earth may know your name and fear you . . . (2 Ch. 6:32–33).

Jesus and Isaiah

So it is no accident that Jesus, the messiah of Israel, would use Isaiah's language in speaking of Herod's temple as "a house of prayer for all nations" (Isa. 56:7; Mk. 11:17). In fact, the complementarity of universality and particularity is very strong in Jesus' ministry. Jesus at one point sends his disciples "to the lost sheep of Israel (Mt. 10:6). Yet this is the same Jesus and the same gospel of Matthew that will very strongly emphasize that the disciples are to meet him in the cosmopolitan, multicultural setting of Galilee. There he will say, "All authority in heaven and on earth has been given to me. Therefore go and make disciples of [*ta ethne* ...]"—the nations (Mt. 28:18–19).[3] The gospels strongly support the vision articulated by Simeon at the time of Jesus' dedication in the temple: Jesus is the Lord of lords and the messiah of Israel and he is "[God's] salvation, which you have prepared in the sight of all people, a light for revelation to the Gentiles, and for glory to your people Israel" (Lk. 2:31–32). Later, when Jesus describes his own mission, drawing from Isaiah 35, 49, and 61, he will proclaim his mission in Nazareth, speaking of it as a mission of preaching good news to the poor, freedom to the prisoners, recovery of sight for the blind, to release the oppressed and to proclaim the year of the Lord's favor in global, universal terms that have specific, local contextual significance in Galilee (Lk. 4:18–19; 7:22–23).

Paul

Paul emphasized God's love of all peoples. Even in the oft-cited universal passages like Galatians 3:28 ("There is neither

---

3 This combination of universality and particularity, with special emphasis on the Gospel of Matthew was the subject of Paul Hertig's Ph.D. dissertation done at the School of World Mission at Fuller Theological Seminary. His work will be forthcoming from Mellen Biblical Press as *Galilee in Matthew's Narrative: A Multicultural and Missiological Journey*.

Jew nor Greek, slave nor free, male nor female. . . .") and Colossians 3:11 ("Here there is no Greek or Jew, circumcised or uncircumcised, barbarian, Scythian, slave or free. . . .") the cultural distinctives are not erased. The particularity of ethnicity, sexuality, and socio-economics is not ignored. Yet, in the midst of such specific forms of homogeneity, there is a universality of union (not uniformity of culture)—a universality of oneness in Jesus Christ: "you are all one in Christ Jesus" (Gal. 3:28); "but Christ is all, and is in all" (Col. 3:11). Thus, in Ephesians, Paul's ecclesiology recognizes the distinctive differences of being Gentile or Jewish ("This mystery is that through the gospel the Gentiles are heirs together with Israel, members together of one body, and sharers together in the promise of Christ Jesus" (Eph. 3:6). Yet Paul also affirms that they are brought together into one new family in Jesus Christ (Eph. 3:15). This does not mean that Jews must live like Gentiles, neither must Gentiles live like Jews. Paul follows the dictum of the Jerusalem Council in Acts 15 in affirming the cultural differences yet creating a new oneness in Jesus Christ. In Acts 21, Paul participates in a Jewish rite of purification in the temple in Jerusalem, knowing he will be arrested, but making a public statement that Jews who are now believers in the messiah may still follow Jewish custom. Thus, even though "there is no difference between Jew and Gentile—the same Lord is Lord of all" (Rom. 10:12), yet the proclamation of the gospel, according to Paul, is "first for the Jew, then for the Gentile" (Rom. 1:16). In this regard, I have offered an outline of Paul's missiology in Romans in "The Effect of Universalism on Mission Theology" in *Mission on the Way* (Van Engen 1996:159–168).

John in Revelation

In Revelation, John echoes the same kind of complementarity of particularity and universality. Peppered all through the Revelation, John keeps emphasizing the fact that Christ is bringing together people "from every tribe and language and people and nation" (Rev. 5:9; 7:9). In Revelation 21, in the vision of the New Jerusalem, which is a picture of the church, there is a plurality of "nations" that will "walk by its light, and the kings of the earth will bring their splendor into it. . . . The glory and honor of the nations will be brought into it . . ." (Rev. 21:24, 26). Thus there is a recognition and celebration of the differences and distinctives of a plurality of different peoples and cultures—yet a oneness in their coming into the same New Jerusalem, to be in the presence of the one Lamb of God who takes away the sin of the world. In *Mission on the Way* I spoke of this as a missiology that is "faith-particularist" (in Jesus Christ), "culturally pluralist" (dealing with all the various peoples of the earth), and "ecclesiologically inclusivist" (all peoples are invited to the marriage supper of the Lamb) (Van Engen 1996:183–184).

This brief review of the complementarity of universality and particularity may seem unnecessary and perhaps even redundant to some readers. However, I believe it is of utmost importance that this biblical orientation strongly influence the rest of our reflection concerning resistance and receptivity. The way we understand God's love of all peoples will influence our missiological orientation to the issues facing us today in mission around the world, among peoples, some of whom are responsive, and some that are resistant. Too strong an emphasis on universality will drive us toward uniformity and blind us to cultural distinctives—and the differences in the particular response/resistance represented by a particular people group. Too strong an emphasis on particularity will push us to narrow our mission endeavor to only certain groups of people whom we have tagged "receptive," ignoring or neglecting others. Either option has serious consequences for following Christ in mission.

As I read Scripture, I see God affirming cultural distinctives. I see Babel as judgment, yes, but also as grace. The beauty of resplendent creativity shines forth in the wonderful multiplication of families, tribes, tongues, and peoples of humanity. Rather than destroy humanity (which in the Noahic covenant God had promised not to do), God chooses to confuse the languages. This confusion, although an act of judgment, mercifully preserves all humanity in its cultural and ethnic distinctives, differences so significant that we are given a Table of Nations to enumerate the civilizations known to the compilers of the Pentateuch. These differences are so significant that when the Holy Spirit comes at Pentecost one of the first extraordinary acts of the Holy Spirit is to enable people of many different languages to hear the proclamation of the gospel *in their own language*. Yet these distinctive features of multiple cultures are not allowed to divide humanity's relation to YHWH, nor to support the concept of a national or ethnic plurality of gods. There is one God, creator and sustainer of *all peoples*. Oneness in plurality, plurality in oneness. Particular universality, universal particularity. How can we give concrete, lived out shape to this biblical view of reality as God sees it? Should this theology of humanity not be normative for us as we consider the meaning of the concept of "resistant peoples"? I believe it should.

We could compile a long list of valid theological, missiological and strategic motivations for mission among specific "responsive" peoples, and why it is legitimate to "occupy lightly" areas where "resistant peoples" live. However, I would suggest that the most basic and pervasive of all our missional motivations must derive from the universal scope of God's mission as depicted in Scripture and spoken by a particular messiah (Jesus) to a particular Jewish teacher of the law (Nicodemus): "*For God so loved the world [of many peoples, tribes, tongues and nations] that he gave his Son . . .*" (Jn. 3:16). God loves all peoples and wants to develop a covenantal relationship with all peoples.

All Humans Are Receptive: They Have a Profound Spiritual Hunger to Know God

The affirmation that God loves all peoples has a complementary side in the spiritual hunger evident in all humans. As the continued multiplication of religious systems and forms over the centuries and in every culture attests, human beings are incurably religious. Even in the face of materialistic atheism like that which was prevalent for so long in the former Soviet Union (or in post-Christian atheistic secularism in the West, or the Cultural Revolution in China), even in these environments one can see evidences of profound spiritual hunger that eventually stimulates major social upheaval. Whether we relate this to "General Revelation" or to "Prevenient Grace" or to "Common Grace," this is something very basic in affirming that all peoples are receptive in their desire and need for an encounter with the divine.

What I have in mind here is not Roman Catholic natural theology in the train of Thomas Aquinas. I do not mean, either, a vague human construction of religion as an expression of the highest value of culture. Nor do I mean the European nineteenth century Protestant natural theology against which Barth spoke so forcefully. Nor do I mean a pluralist approach either through comparative religions, phenomenology of religion, religious psychology, or a theocentric pluralism, all of which draw in some way from the assumption of a common thread of humanity's interest in the nouminous. Nor do I mean exactly the "point of contact" between reason and revelation that Emil Brünner advocated when he spoke of

> humanity [having] within itself "a capacity for revelation" or "a possibility of ... being addressed," which enables a person to apprehend and receive God's revelation (Brünner 1946 cited in Bloesch 1992:153).

Nor do I mean a too-easy, revelatory approach to "General Revelation" about which John Calvin, Hendrik Kraemer, Karl Barth, G. C. Berkouwer, Hendrikus Berkhof, Donald Bloesch, Millard Erickson, Stanley Grenz, and Alistair McGrath, among others, have expressed anxiety and discomfort.[4]

---

4 Donald Bloesch has given us a very helpful overview of this discussion in Bloesch 1992:161–165. Donald Bloesch was probably on the right track when he wrote,

> Revelation as I conceive it yields real knowledge of God, but knowledge that is personal and concrete, not speculative and abstract. I agree, moreover, that revelation, even understood as occurring exclusively in Christ, does not necessarily entail the acceptance of salvation, but what it does bring us is the reality of salvation. . . .

> I am coming to agree with Hendrikus Berkhof that "general revelation" is a term that should probably now be abandoned because of its ambiguity and imprecision [referring to Berkhof 1979:74–77]. If revelation is essentially a personal encounter, general revelation would seem to contradict this essential dimension of revelation. If revelation is defined as God's effectual communication of his will and purpose to humanity, then we have no revelation in nature that can be positively conjoined with the biblical meanings of "unveiling" *(apokalypsis)* and "manifestation" (from *phanero¯*). . . . It is probably better to regard this general working of God as an exhibition or display of his power and goodness than as a revelation that effectively unveils or conveys his plan and purpose for our lives. Through his general working in nature and conscience, we are exposed to the mercy of God as well as to his wrath and judgment, but God's light and truth are disclosed to us only in the encounter with Jesus Christ as presented in Holy Scripture.
>
> It is appropriate to speak of a general presence of God in nature and history, but this general presence does not become a revelation of his grace and mercy until it is perceived in the light of Jesus Christ. Only in the light of Christ, Karl Barth contended on the basis of Psalm 39:9, can we properly discern God's general light in nature. Yet the light in nature is a reflected or derivative light. It is not a source of the light of Christ but a witness to it, a witness recognizable only to the eyes of faith. . . .
>
> In short, while the wonders of nature manifest God's deity and power, because of human sin they fail to give us real knowledge. They do bring us a deep-seated awareness of God—sufficient, however, to condemn us, not to save us (Bloesch 1992:164–165).

These considerations led Bloesch to disagree with prevailing conservative Protestant views of natural theology as exemplified by Bruce Demarest when Demarest says,

> Only when one sees himself as a sinner before the God of Creation does the offer of reconciliation in the gospel make sense. If intuitional and inferential knowledge of God were not present, God's gracious communication to man in the form of special revelation would remain a meaningless abstraction. Special revelation, then, begins at the point where man's natural knowledge of God ends. Natural theology is properly the vestibule of revealed theology. . . . Special revelation completes, not negates, the

Rather, what I am speaking of is, in Alvin Plantinga's words, that "God has implanted in us all an innate tendency, or nisus, or disposition to believe in God" (Plantinga 1992:67). John Calvin referred to this disposition as a *sensus divinitatis* or a *semen religionis* whereby, in Calvin's words,

> There is within the human mind, and indeed by natural instinct, an awareness of divinity. . . . God himself has implanted in all [persons] a certain understanding of his divine majesty. . . . As experience shows, God has sown a seed of religion in all [people] (1960:43, 47; *see* also Plantinga 1992:67–68).

Or as G. C. Berkouwer expresses it,

> The *sensus divinitatis* is not an organ of the knowledge of God which transcends the corruption of human nature; it is an unavoidable impression left on [humans] by the prevailing power of God. . . . All [people] have a sense of religion, and there is "no nation so barbarous, no race so savage as not to be firmly persuaded of the being of God" (citing Calvin 1960:44).

Further, Berkouwer says,

> The *semen religionis* is preserved by God in the human heart. This does not relieve the darkness, but it does help explain how it is that religions still arise in a fallen world and how it is possible that these false religions bear a marked resemblance of order (1955:152, 169).

---

disclosure of God in nature, providence, and conscience (citing Demarest 1982:250–251).

Donald Bloesch rejoins:

> Against Demarest I contend that to posit prior human receptivity to the gospel is to make salvation contingent on the human will as well as on divine grace. And to suggest that we can see ourselves as sinners before we are awakened to the truth of God's reconciliation for us in Christ is to attribute to human beings power that is simply not countenanced by the biblical witness or by the witness of the Reformation. I also disagree that special revelation completes the knowledge of God derived from nature and conscience, for this conveys the misleading impression that the two kinds of knowledge are of the same nature and therefore can be joined together (1992:162).

Psalm 19 and Romans 1 are commonly-mentioned passages in Scripture understood to speak of this disposition to believe in God. Psalm 19:1–4 says,

> The heavens declare the glory of God; the skies proclaim the work of his hands. Day after day they pour forth speech; night after night they display knowledge. There is no speech or language where their voice is not heard. Their voice goes out into all the earth, their words to the ends of the world.

Paul stated in Romans 1:19–20,

> What may be known about God is plain to [humans]... For since the creation of the world God's invisible qualities—his eternal power and divine nature—have been clearly seen, being understood from what has been made ...

Paul articulated this concept even more thoroughly in his well-known sermon at the Areopagus in Athens, applying it to the Athenian worship of the "Unknown God," one whom Paul claims to know and to proclaim.

Thus even Donald Bloesch, with his deep discomfort regarding "general revelation," speaks of this:

> general working of God as an exhibition or display of his power and goodness. . . . Through his general working in nature and conscience, we are exposed to the mercy of God as well as to his wrath and judgment. . . . It is appropriate to speak of a general presence of God in nature and history (1992:164)

Stanley Grenz says,

> We share a common dependency on something external to, or beyond, any shape that we can give to our "world." The God-shaped vacuum within us, to which this dependency bears silent witness, is a testimony in the human heart to the reality of God. . . . By virtue of the fact that we are created beings, God had directed each of us to a common human destiny. Just as our common human dependency bears witness to the reality of God, so also the residue of the divine image within us is a dimension of [what he calls] general revelation. Our awareness that we are directed beyond the present stands as a silent witness to the reality of God for whom we are created (1994:179).

In McGrath's words,

> God has endowed human beings with some inbuilt sense or presentiment of the divine existence. It is as if something about God has been engraved in the heart of every human being. Calvin identifies three consequences of this inbuilt awareness of divinity: the universality of religion (which, if uninformed by the Christian revelation, degenerates into idolatry), a troubled conscience, and a servile fear of God (1994:160).

I like the way Hendrikus Berkhof speaks of this innate disposition.

> The first thing we will then have to say is that man [*sic*] is apparently a being who is made to encounter God, to respond to his Word. Man is a responding creature. . . . I want to describe man as a "respondable" being. . . . From the point of view of theology it must be said that man had only become fully man when he became aware of God's presence and learned to pray.
>
> By describing man as "respondable" we delimit him from the outset in his maturity and autonomy. The first word does not come from him. He is made man by an initiative from the outside and from above. His creativity is based on re-creativity. And no less important is that with this description we have found that man's essence lies in a relationship, namely the relationship with God. From the standpoint of the Christian faith it is out of the question to regard man as a self-contained being who later happens to enter into relationships with other beings. Man is that creature who is made to live with God. . . .
>
> Meanwhile, by labelling man "respondable" we have given only a formal description. He is made to respond to the Word of God. But the content of that Word is the holy love with which God beneficially turns to his human creatures. Man is not made just for responding-as-such, but for responding to this Word, that is, to God's love. Love can only be responded to with reciprocal love. Man is made for *love*. He cannot do without that nurturing love from the outside, nor without responding to that love. . . . In this relation of receiving and giving love, man heeds his most central calling and actualizes his true essence. In love, man becomes himself (1979:181–185).

The importance of this innate disposition cannot be underestimated in its influence as a working assumption in much of our Evangelical missiology. Let me briefly mention four related missiological arenas where this assumption seems to be operative. First, Donald McGavran's theories of group conversion, indigenous church forms, and cultural appropriateness assume this innate disposition. McGavran's axiom was, "[Women and] men like to become Christians without crossing racial, linguistic and class barriers" (McGavran 1970:198; *see* also Hunter 1979:121; Gibbs 1981:117; McGavran 1984b:100; Zunkle 1987:100; Rainer 1993:254). Based on this assumption, McGavran developed an extensive analysis of the *Bridges of God* (1955), advocating the intentional use of natural relational, cultural, and social networks for gospel proclamation. "The faith spreads most naturally and contagiously along the lines of the social network of living Christians, especially new Christians," McGavran wrote.

> Receptive undiscipled men and women usually receive the possibility [of faith in Jesus Christ] when the invitation is extended to them from credible Christian friends, relatives, neighbors, and fellow workers from within their social web (McGavran and Hunter 1980:30).

The assumption behind McGavran's axiom is that once we can get beyond social, cultural, and relational barriers, people will be disposed to receive the gospel. Their innate hunger for God will come into play.

Second, the assumption of this innate disposition toward God is also built into theories of indigenization, contextualization, and communication in Evangelical missiology. As Charles Kraft has pointed out in *Communication Theory for Christian Witness* (1983, 1991), meaning in communication is ascribed by the hearer, not by the speaker. "The key participant [is] the receptor" (1991:ch. 6). Thus, if we can learn the art of listening well, and can begin to develop receptor-oriented communication, the innate desire for God will move the receptor to being open to a relationship with God in Jesus Christ. "To love communicationally," says Kraft, "is to put oneself to whatever inconvenience necessary to assure that the receptors understand" (1991:15). It is beyond the scope of this chapter to delineate the various models and approaches to contextualization by Protestant Evangelicals like David Hesselgrave (1978), David Hesselgrave and Edward Rommen (1989), Harvie Conn (1977, 1978, 1984), Paul Hiebert (1978, 1985, 1987, 1989, 1994), Charles Taber (1979a, 1979b, 1979c), Charles Kraft (1979, 1983), Dean Gilliland (1989), Krikor Haleblian (1982a 1982b, 1983), Daniel

Shaw (1988, 1989), and others. Contextualization theory follows this path, assuming that if one can present the gospel in a way (and with a biblical content) that is culturally appropriate to a people group—that the members of the group will then be free to be able to respond positively to the message, given their innate desire for God (*see*, e.g., Hesselgrave and Rommen 1989:211). This foundational assumption may be found in contextualization theory, no matter whether the model is one of "communication, cultural relevance, liberation, interfaith dialogue or knowing God in context" (Van Engen 1996:74–75).

Third, people's innate disposition toward God is also presupposed in the search for the various factors of receptivity and resistance as these have been developed in Evangelical missiology (particularly in church growth theory). Here it is assumed that certain experiences will bring people to be more responsive to their innate desire and need for God. C. Wayne Zunkel, for example, lists one hundred ninety-one "stress-causing situations in life" that may be times of greater receptiveness to the gospel (1987:149–156). We will return to this when we ask *to what* certain people may be resistant or receptive.

Fourth, the commonly-used language in Evangelical missiology concerning "redemptive analogies" to be found in a receptor culture also seems to assume that present in all cultures are what Karl Barth called "lights" that witness to God's existence, power and provision. The assumption that one can find such analogies in a given cultural context and then use them as "contact points" or communicational bridges for gospel proclamation presupposes a desire on the part of the persons in that culture to know and be related to God.

So, given this innate predisposition, with reference to both the resistant and the receptive, we find a need to affirm that all humans are receptive. However, this immediately pushes us to a third major affirmation about resistance-receptivity: *all humans are resistant.*

Because of Sin and the Fall, All Humans Are Resistant to God All the Time

It is a mistake to think that General Revelation provides a natural knowledge of God apart from the work of the Holy Spirit by grace through faith in Jesus Christ. Paul's point in Romans 1 was not that there is revelatory knowledge of God apart from Jesus Christ—but rather that humanity is condemned and without excuse because of its rejection of the greatness and goodness of God that can be seen in creation. Thus General Revelation is a reason for judgment and a proof of the sinfulness of humanity, not a basis for inclusivist or pluralist approaches to theology of religion, contra Clark Pinnock, John Sanders and others (*see* Van Engen 1996:169–190). As I have demonstrated elsewhere (*see* Van Engen 1991b:191–194 and 1996:159–168), Paul's ultimate point in Romans 1–3 is that, although the Jews separated the world into two kinds of people (Jews and Gentiles), in the final analysis, "all have sinned and fall short of the glory of God" (Rom. 3:23). Thus a new universality and a new particularity is constructed by Paul in the first eight chapters of Romans, based not on ethnicity but on faith in Jesus Christ. In other words, the innate disposition toward belief in God which we saw above is very weak and limited precisely because of the pervasiveness of sin and the Fall. So John Calvin rightly distinguished between knowledge of God as creator and knowledge of God as redeemer.

As Stanley Grenz says,

> Although the concept of general revelation is valid and helpful, it is also limited. It is restricted in scope. What God has made available to all persons through general revelation does not provide the complete self-disclosure of God. On the contrary, general revelation functions only as a testimony to the presence of the God who is the reality standing both behind and within the world. . . .
>
> The limited use of the concept is evident in the Bible itself. Paul's main purpose is not to set forth the thesis that creation testifies to the reality of God. Rather, his point is that sinful humans suppress even the testimony heralded by the natural creation. Because of human sin, people do not in fact give ear to this available testimony. . . . All humans stand justly condemned before a holy God (1994:180–181).

McGrath says,

> A natural knowledge of God serves to deprive humanity of any excuse for ignoring the divine will; nevertheless, it is inadequate as the basis for a full-fledged portrayal of the nature, character, and purposes of God. . . . Knowledge of God the redeemer—which for Calvin is a distinctively *Christian* knowledge of God—may only be had by the Christian revelation, in Christ and through Scripture (1994:161).

Donald Bloesch comments,

> While the wonders of nature manifest God's deity and power, because of human sin they fail to give us real knowledge. They do bring us to deep-seated awareness of God—sufficient, however, to condemn us, not to save us (1992:165).

G. C. Berkouwer emphasized Karl Barth's perspective at this point. Barth drew a very sharp distinction between revelation and religion. "[Barth] has reacted violently," Berkouwer explains,

> against almost every theory of psychology of religion and religious historicism. His reason is that they all seriously impugn the absoluteness of revelation. Far from paying honor to human religion, Barth speaks of religion as unbelief. Revelation is the abolition of religion. . . . "Religion is . . . an affair, yea rather, *the* affair of the godless man." All religion is cut off sharply from faith. Religion is nothing but the attempt to know God by way of man's own abilities, an attempt that is unmasked by revelation as resistance to revelation and grace. It forms an enterprise of man by which he encroaches with his own means and power upon what God wills to do and does in his revelation. . . . Since natural religion is the religion of fallen man, it accounts for the normalcy of unbelief, of resistance to revelation and grace (1955:158–159).[5]

As Berkouwer demonstrates, one need not necessarily accept Barth's radical differentiation between religion and revelation to still understand that human beings have and do continue to rebel and reject the light that God offers. In the words of John,

---

5 Berkouwer citing Karl Barth *Kirchliche Dogmatik* I,2, 327. Berkouwer cites Barth as saying, "Through religion we perceive that men have rebelled against God and that their rebellion is a rebellion of slaves" (1933:246).

"He came to that which was his own, but his own did not receive him." So John Calvin affirmed that human beings "do not . . . apprehend God as he offers himself, but imagine him as they have fashioned him in their own presumption" (1960:47).[6]

There are several very important implications that can be drawn from this third major reflection about "resistance." First, any theology of conversion in Evangelical missiology must begin by speaking of the miraculous work of the Holy Spirit by grace through faith in Jesus Christ. No amount of effectiveness in relation to contextualization can promise that humans will say *yes* to God. Quite the contrary. Even if—or precisely *when*—humans come to understand the gospel being offered to them—even if they understand it in very appropriate cultural, relational, and social forms—humans will still say *no* to God, apart from the working of the Holy Spirit. Thus, we must listen carefully to those who have been emphasizing the matter of spiritual issues in church growth and missiology, for conversion is not promised, much less guaranteed simply on the basis of good contextual methodology.

Second, the fact that all humans are sinful and resistant should heighten our awareness and care in relation to some contemporary emphases on spiritual warfare. Just as we see the lie in the perspective of Enlightenment Humanism that all humans are good and holy, so we also need to understand the inaccuracy of presenting humanity as a neutral battle ground on which opposing spiritual forces wage their warfare. If all humans choose against God, if all humans have sinned and fallen in Adam and Eve, then humanity is not neutral. Thus mission is not simply a matter of throwing our weight toward the right side of the conflict. Instead, our mission involves proclamation in word and deed that Jesus Christ is Lord, calling all humans to radical conversion and total transformation so that, in the

6 Calvin follows this with a series of comments on Ps 14:1 and 53:1 to the effect that human beings, "after they have become hardened in insolent and habitual sinning, furiously repel all remembrance of God. . . . But to render their madness more detestable, David represents them as flatly denying God's existence. . ." (1960:48).

words of John's Gospel, "all those who [receive] him, to those who [believe] in his name, he [gives] the right to become children of God—children born not of natural descent, . . . but born of God" (Jn. 1:12). We are involved in spiritual warfare. But that warfare includes transforming the human heart from death to life (which only the Holy Spirit can do), from rebellion against God to loving faithful obedience to God (Rom. 7).

Third, the fact that "all have sinned and fall short of the glory of God" means that a biblical understanding of "resistance" is no longer a sociological term simply referring to the fact that few churches have grown among a particular people. Rather, the term now takes on a biblical meaning that "resistance" entails saying *no* to God's covenantal initiative. This is a matter of faith. God is the "self-disclosing God," using Hendrikus Berkhof's term (Berkhof 1979:105). God is the God of the covenant, a loving God who comes to all humans and says, "I will be your God and you will be my people" (Van Engen 1989; 1996). "Resistance" is refusing the invitation that God extends. If "resistance," then, represents a negative faith response to God's initiative, this points us to the next two reflections: (1) *some humans are resistant all the time* and (2) *some humans are resistant some of the time to some things.*

Some Humans Are Resistant All the Time, to All Missional Approaches

If "resistance" is understood biblically and theologically as humans saying *no* to God's gracious invitation, then to understand "resistance" more deeply we need to re-examine the parable of the sower (Mt. 13:1–23; parallels in Mk. 4:1–12, Lk. 8:4–10). This parable most specifically addressed the matter of varying responses to the word of God. As we saw earlier, this parable has been used by many to support the concept of selective targeting in evangelization. I would suggest that the matter of selective targeting is not at all what the parable is about. But the parable *is* about recognizing that, given the same gracious invitation on the part of God, different persons will respond differently.

The parable of the sower appears in all three synoptic Gospels. Without getting into the details of the particular redaction of each gospel writer and the place and emphasis which each gives to the parable, it is enough to note here that the context of the parable is strongly missiological. All three gospels mention that the parable is told by Jesus while surrounded by large crowds, the audience of Jesus' mission (Mt. 13:2). Yet the explanation of the parable is addressed to the disciples (Mt. 13:10–11). Now although a detailed exegetical treatment of the parable is beyond the scope of this chapter, let me suggest the basic emphases that I believe are to be found in this parable. [7]

Contrary to those who would use this parable as a foundation for selective targeting of mission endeavor (renaming it the "parable of the soils"), I would suggest that the parable of the sower is in fact about the sower, about Jesus' mission, and by extension the mission of the disciples. And as such, it is actually an explanation by Jesus of why he speaks in mysterious parables and not plainly—and why some respond positively (are receptive) and why others respond negatively (are resistant). The parable speaks of the fact that Jesus presented his message *to everyone alike*, but that some were willing to hear and others were not. The difference in soils may have something to tell us about receptivity. But if this is so, it will *not* tell us to concentrate on the good soil. That may be good farming, but it is totally extraneous to the text of the parable.

The parable of the sower speaks about those who are too blind to see, too deaf to hear, and whose hearts are too dull to respond (*see* Mt. 13:14–15 where Isaiah's prophecy is mentioned which harks back to Dt. 29:4 and can be found in Isa. 42:19, 20; Jer. 5:21; and Eze. 12:2). The problem which the parable addresses is this: in view of the people's blindness, deafness, and hardness of heart, why does Jesus speak in mysterious parables and not in plain language (Mt. 13:10)? The different soils are the key to the answer given (Mt. 13:11). What is being presented is the "mystery" of the kingdom of God which is to be perceived by faith (as did the prophets of old, including Isaiah), not by sight (Mt.

---

7 The following section is adapted from Van Engen 1981:356.

13:17). Faith is recognized in the one who "hears the word and understands it; who indeed bears fruit ..." (Mt. 13:23, NASB). So, given the word that is being proclaimed by Jesus to everyone, why do some receive that word, and why do some reject it?

Now here we must at least take note of the socio-cultural context of the parable. And we can see it in our mind's eye. There is a field, surrounded by cactus (thorns) that serves as a fence around the outer perimeter of the field. There is a path that cuts through the field where people walk to get from one end to the other. Over in one part of the field there is a section that, although it looks excellent on the surface, has a ledge of flat rock just six inches or so below the surface of the tilled soil. And there is part of the field that has rich loam, deep and fertile. The farmer, in the method of that day, has plowed the field with a wooden plow that only tills a few inches of top-soil. Now the farmer takes his bag of seed, slings it over his shoulder, and begins to walk back and forth across the field. His sowing of the wheat seed is done by reaching into the bag and then broadcasting the seed out of his hand to let it fall where it will, all over the field. Jesus' teaching and ministry were like that. In Luke's words, Jesus went about the towns and villages, preaching the gospel of the kingdom and healing (*see*, e.g., Lk. 4:43; 8:1).

Now, given this mental picture, it is clear that the parable does not have to do with selective sowing—but with differences in reaping. If anything, the parable is a command to universal, all-inclusive, indiscriminate proclamation, knowing that the "field" (the world, or possibly a particular people group in a particular context) contains many kinds of "soils" all mixed together. The farmer's assessment is that of a critical realist. He knows that some of the seed will "bear fruit," but others will not. The farmer in the parable does not restrict his sowing to the "good ground." The farmer in the parable may not know what is good ground (since his wooden plow cannot go deep enough to find the shallow rock bottom). The path where people walk through the field is an inevitable hard spot where the scattered seed, which was not planted one at a time in that day, or with modern planters, will surely fall. For the farmer to try to restrict his sowing to only "good ground" would be not only difficult but absurd, for he would have to stay a long way away from the cactus hedge, he would have to try to avoid having seed fall on the path that cuts across the field, and he would have to spend a great deal of time digging deeply under the surface to know where the stone layer is located. In order to do all of that, he would end up also neglecting much good soil.

In other words, if something is crystal clear about this parable, it is the *indiscriminate* sowing of the seed, not the selective proclamation of the gospel.

But there are four other very important lessons that I believe Jesus wanted the disciples to learn. First, the farmer sows indiscriminately, *in spite of knowing that the responses will vary*. The farmer understands his field, and he knows (in fact he expects) differences in response. Second, the response of the seed is not to the sower, but rather consists in growing, developing, giving fruit—it is response to the word, to the kingdom, and to God. Third, notice in Jesus' explanation of the parable (Mt. 13:19–23), there are a variety of agents that create heightened resistance in addition to the conditions of the field. One thing is the condition of the field (the human heart), which itself contributes to a variety of responses. But there are others in this picture. The "evil one" is here. Trouble and persecution are here. And the worries of this life and the deceitfulness of wealth are here as well. In other words, the world, the flesh and the devil all contribute to the lack of response (that is, to "resistance") on the part of the hearers. Fourth, there is a background to this parable that deals with God's *providence*. Paul would later say, "I planted the seed, Apollos watered it, but God made it grow. So neither he who plants nor he who waters is anything, but only God, who makes things grow" (1 Cor. 3:6–7). In the providence of God (who, all through the Scriptures, is the one who gives the harvest of grain) the seed that falls on good ground (and the one who hears the word and understands it) "produces a crop." It is not in the seed to become a "hundred, sixty or thirty times" what was sown. Rather, God, in God's mysterious, providential, and loving fashion makes it grow and multiply (like the "mustard seed" in the parable that follows this one in Matthew).

This matter of other agents that exacerbate the resistance, that is, that lower the receptivity, directs us naturally to our final proposition: *some humans are resistant some of the time to some things.*

But before we move on, let me add a caveat. Please do not misunderstand me here. Although I do not believe the parable of the sower can be used legitimately to support selective targeting of mission, this does not mean I am opposed to selective targeting. To direct our mission resources to a specific audience at a particular time in an intentional and concerted fashion is not only good mission planning, it also demonstrates a high degree of contextual and receptor-oriented sensitivity. But there are other ways to provide biblical support for selective targeting. Some possible texts might include: Matthew 9:37–38 (workers in the harvest); Matthew 10:11–14 ("shake the dust off"); Matthew 10:6 ("go ... to the lost sheep of Israel"); Matthew 15:24 ("only to the lost sheep of Israel"—with reference to Jesus' mission). Jesus' ministry is focused on specific people and places. In John 4 he "had to go to Samaria," for example. And Paul's mission is highly targeted and specific. Selective targeting is also important if one considers *to what* a particular group of persons is resistant or receptive.

Some Humans Are Resistant Some of the Time to Some Things

With the story of Abraham in Genesis 12, we are informed of God's decision to use humans agents or instruments (*missio hominum*) for God's mission (*missio Dei*) of self-disclosing, covenantal love that reaches out to humanity to re-establish the broken relationship between humans and God. God chooses Abraham so that through him all the nations of the earth will bless themselves. But *missio hominum* makes things fuzzy with regard to "resistance" and "receptivity." In choosing to use human agency, God has chosen to use sinful, fallible humans with their mixed motivations, mixed methods, mixed goals, and mixed authenticity to extend God's invitation. But precisely because of such human agency, the receptor's response to God's invitation (now extended through other humans) may be less a matter of saying *yes* or *no* to the divine initiative, and be more a matter of response to the particular human instrument. There may be times, therefore, when "resistance" to God's invitation is decreased or increased on account of the human agents, the messengers of God's invitation. So when we think of the "resistance" in relation to mission theology, we must consider it not only in terms of the receptor's response to divine initiative—but also the receptor's response to the human instrument. And we must be careful not to confuse the two. Just because there is a negative response to my particular approach or message may not necessarily mean the receptor group is "resistant" in the sense of saying *no* to God. Their negative response to my instrumentality may, in fact, be more a commentary on my own ineffectiveness, sinfulness, foreignness, or inappropriateness as a bearer of the Good News. My church or agency and I may be bad news, rather than Good News. This issue forces us to ask, *to what* may humans be "resistant"?

Roy Pointer framed this issue in two complementary questions. He wrote,

> When there is no [favorable] response to the preaching of the gospel there are two basic questions that need to be asked. "Is the group resistant?" and "Is the group receptive, but we are evangelizing them wrongly?" (1984:159).

Referring positively to Pointer's work on this matter, C. Peter Wagner affirmed,

> Because of the crucial need to balance tests for correct methodology over against presumed resistance, it is helpful to distinguish, as Roy Pointer, between emic resistance and etic resistance, (Pointer 1984:159), or to use more familiar terms general resistance and specific resistance. General (or emic) resistance is caused by factors within the group or individual we are trying to reach. In many cases there is little or nothing we can do about such resistance. But specific (or etic) resistance has to do with the individual or group doing the evangelizing. It is here that we can exert some control by changing the evangelizers or by changing the methods. If wise adjustments are made, the resistance may dissolve (Wagner 1987:92).[8]

---

8 This is part of a chapter entitled, "Testing the Soil."

It is beyond the scope of this chapter to review the multitude of factors that church growth theory has discovered over the past forty years as contributing to a group's resistance or receptivity to gospel proclamation. The resistance/receptivity axis, shown below as a three-dimensional construct, consists of many complex interwoven factors that impact a group's openness (or lack thereof) to God's invitation.

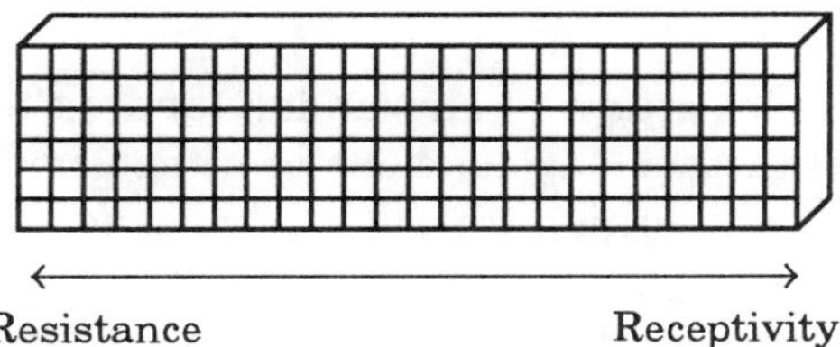

Resistance Receptivity

Because the matter of human instrumentality affects our theology of "resistance" so deeply, let me simply make mention of four major blocks of factors affecting a group's resistance/receptivity to the gospel and briefly comment on the theological issues they represent:

a. factors found within the receptor group and its culture (emic, general, intrinsic to the group—includes national and local contextual factors)
b. factors found within the church and mission agents (etic, specific, extrinsic to the group—includes national and local institutional factors)
c. factors involved in the way the receptor group perceives the church's witness, and
d. spiritual factors affecting both the missionary agent and receptor group.

Some Groups Are Resistant Because of Contextual Factors

One of the most helpful products of church growth research during the last forty years has been to identify the myriad contextual (both national and local) factors that impinge on the resistance/receptivity of a particular people group. These include worldview, religious, socio-economic, political, and historical factors. There are a number of changes that can occur in the historical development of a people group that will begin to make the members of the group receptive to hearing the gospel and willing to respond positively to that which they hear. And a developed theology of the "resistant" will be very sensitive to developing an appropriate hermeneutic of the context, reading carefully the signs of the times as they impact a particular people group, and then responding to the opportunity as it presents itself.

However, besides studying and understanding the contextual factors, we need further development of a theology of contextual analysis (I mean something different here than "contextualization"). Such a theological analysis of the context would include a theology of culture that opens itself to all the elements to be found in the group's worldview that may be consistent and coherent with biblical revelation. This involves a theology of culture that re-examines the contextual factors in light of the knowledge of God that God may have placed in the context and which provides bridges for incarnational proclamation. Second, such reflection on the context would call for a full-blown theology of providence, where one seeks to understand what God is doing in the world in terms of drawing a group through historical and creational means from resistance to receptivity. This, however, will call, third, for a careful theology of suffering, for we must never excuse oppression and suffering by subsuming it to a utilitarian view that accepts suffering because it is producing greater openness to our mission endeavors. Fourth, a theological hermeneutic of the context of resistance would also entail a profound re-examination of the ministry of the Holy Spirit and the presence of the church as being agents through whom God, in God's providence, may be able to call a group from resistance toward receptivity. Fifth, there is a theology of intercessory prayer involved here that calls on God, in his providence, in the midst of the already/not yet rule of Christ the King, through the operation of the Holy Spirit, to give a particular people group a "heart of flesh" rather than a "heart of stone" (Eze. 11:19; 36:26).

Some Groups Become Resistant Because of Factors within the Church

A second group of issues has to do with the internal or intrinsic institutional factors inside the church. And there are related issues of theology of mission. First is the issue of the spirituality of the church itself. Down through the centuries, I believe the nominalism and secularization of the church itself has been one of the greatest obstacles to world evangelization, and one of the factors that I believe has contributed greatly to resistance on the part of groups outside the church. This has been the case with state churches in Europe, old-line denominations in North America, the traditional Roman Catholic hierarchy in Latin America, and the colonially-ghettoized churches in Africa, for example. When the church has nothing new or different to offer a particular group, or when the church is part of the problem in oppressive contexts, I believe resistance is increased on the part of the receptor group.

Second, the churches in the context may have lost their missional intention. They may have turned inward to such a degree that they have no commitment to presenting a credible gospel to a particular people group, whether that is across the street or around the world. Again, older churches in Europe and North America exhibit this loss of commitment to an alarming degree. Then to label a particular group "resistant" is quite inaccurate. It may be more accurate to speak of their being "ignored" with particular reference to the church's intentionality, rather than to the receptivity of the receptor group. For example, the emphasis in North American church growth circles on planting upper-middle-class, white, suburban churches tends to give the impression that groups of people in the center-cities of North America are "resistant" to the gospel. Nothing could be further from the truth—they are simply being ignored by a movement whose primary focus has been the white, Anglo-Saxon, upper-middle-class suburban ghetto.

In both of the above situations of nominalism and loss of mission vision, renewal and reformation become important keys to issues of resistance and receptivity. This has been borne out in so many instances down through the history of the church. But this is also beyond the scope of this chapter. Suffice it to say that renewal and revitalization of the church internally might be one of the most significant factors in helping a particular people group be open to saying *yes* to God. And this issue is a significant one everywhere in the world today.

Third, our theology of conversion may itself create resistance. As McGavran and Pickett pointed out decades ago, typical Western expectations of a particular form of conversion may create an unnecessary barrier. Such expectations of conversion may include a host of cultural issues that are not intrinsic to the gospel. Thus, McGavran's axiom comes into play: "[women and] men like to become Christians without crossing [unnecessary] racial, linguistic, or class barriers" (1970:198). This issue is central to the Gentile mission in the book of Acts. Too often modern churches and missions have insisted on superimposing a particular kind, style, or form of conversion upon those who would say *yes* to God. We need much more careful missiological work in reflecting upon a theology of conversion: individual or multi-individual? punctiliar, process, or series of transforming moments? only vertical in relation to God or also including reconciliation to self, others, and the world? only rational/mental assent to a series of propositions, or including profound experiential, participatory events? These are but a few of the questions we must ask ourselves if we are to avoid creating unnecessary resistance.

Fourth, the relation of the church to its surrounding culture and political structures must be carefully studied if the church is not to increase resistance. A church that insists on being strongly countercultural may create resistance. I believe this is one of the most significant background issues in the tense and sometimes conflictive discussion about worship styles in the churches of North America and Europe.

I suspect this has been part of our difficulty in the evangelization of Japan, for instance. The insistence of the older churches in Japan on basing their theological reflection and ministry formation on German theology, coupled with their heavy use of an educational model of being church, together with their strong avoidance of interacting theologically with issues of Shinto shrines, holy places, family theology, and the world of the unseen—all of these have, it would seem, contributed to the sense of foreignness of the older churches in Japan, as seen through the eyes of the Japanese people. Thus, at a time of profound religious searching, especially on the part of Japanese young people, the older churches in Japan seem isolated and out of touch—possibly increasing resistance rather than aiding receptivity.

Another example of this, in relation to Islam, may be the church's strong insistence over the centuries that our predominant theory of atonement must derive from a form of Anselmian satisfaction theory and a forensic understanding of justification by faith, based on legal assumptions. This theological construct on the part of churches and missions—evident in Evangelical missiology as well—creates a built-in difficulty for Muslims to accept the gospel. Yet as I study the words of Jesus and the preaching and teaching of Paul and the first Century church, I find a rather wide range of ways to present God's covenantal invitation, "I will be your God and you will be my people," presentations that do not necessarily need a satisfaction theory of atonement to be valid forms of conversion and reconciliation.

Thus "resistance" may in fact be the result of unexamined, unresolved, and unnecessary theological and cultural issues within the church itself. Notice I say "unnecessary." There is also the "scandal of the cross," a scandal which must never be ignored or downplayed in calling sinners to repentance. But let us make sure the difficult barriers to conversion have to do with the "scandal of the cross" and not unnecessary cultural and historical walls of our own making. Mission vis-à-vis the resistant should begin by examining the beam in our own eyes before we try to extract the sliver in the eye of the receptor.

Some Groups Become Resistant Because of the Lack of Cultural and Spiritual Interface between the Church and the Receptor Group

Increased resistance may also be the product of an inappropriate cultural or spiritual interface between the church and the receptor group. Here we are dealing with neither the group as such, nor with the church only. Rather, we must examine the issues that may raise the boundary between the church and the receptor group because of the lack of an appropriate interface between them. Such lack will create unnecessary resistance.

The first element we might point to in this missiological interface has to do with the particular history of the encounter of the church with a specific people group. Everywhere in the world today, wherever the church is involved in mission, there is a historical background (some immediate, some more remote) of the receptor group's encounter with the church. We ignore this historical data to our peril. I could list hundreds of illustrations here. Obvious cases-in-point might be the encounter of Islam with Christianity, the conquest by Spain of the pre-Colombian peoples of Latin America, the European colonial baggage surrounding the encounter of the peoples of Africa with European churches, the story of Aleut Christianization by early Russian Orthodox missionaries (compared today with Aleut encounter with the government of the United States), and the encounter of the peoples of Hawaii with early Christians, missionaries and otherwise, and more recently the place of Christianity in western capitalism as that interfaces with peoples of Eastern Europe and China. We need much more careful, repentant, self-critical and prayerful reflection on these histories if we are to understand more deeply how "resistance" may involve not so much a particular people saying *no* to God, but rather rejecting the way Christians have interacted with them throughout the centuries.

This may also include issues of long historical and cultural animosities that need reconciliation and redemption before gospel proclamation may take place. Some months ago, for example, I was speaking with a Brazilian missionary who in the last eleven years has planted four churches in Paris among French Parisians. When he told me about his successful church planting, I expressed great surprise, since I have always assumed the French people to be rather "resistant" to the gospel. With a wide grin of joy, the Brazilian missionary remarked, "You American, English-speakers can't do this, but we

Brazilian Portuguese-speakers can." The Tower of Babel is always with us in one way or another.

A second element of this interface between the church and its context has to do with the church's own missional intentionality in relation to a particular people. As David Liao pointed out twenty-five years ago, it may be that a people is not so much "resistant" as "neglected." Too easily we are tempted to label a group that does not respond to our form of evangelization as "resistant," when in fact it may be the church's lack of cultural and spiritual sensitivity that has increased resistance through neglect.

In 1972 David Liao studied the situation of the Hakka Chinese in Taiwan, a people whom some had labeled "resistant." The product of Liao's study is a marvelous case study to show that those whom some would call "resistant" may in fact simply have been *neglected* by the church. "The thesis of this book," wrote Liao, "is: Many seemingly resistant peoples in the world, like the Hakkas, are really being neglected" (1972:15). In his introduction to the book, Donald McGavran wrote,

> As the church carries out the mandate of her Lord to disciple the nations, she continually meets unresponsive peoples. As missionaries carry the good news to the two billion who have yet to believe, they often encounter indifferent or resistant populations.
>
> Sometimes unresponsiveness is due to hardness of heart, pride, or aloofness; but more often than we like to think, it is due to neglect. The gospel has been presented to an "unresponsive" ethnic unit in the trade language, not its mother tongue. The only church its members could join was one made up of people of a different culture. The only pastors its congregations could have were those from another ethnic unit or subculture. . . .
>
> It is a great merit of David Liao's book, *The Unresponsive: Resistant or Neglected?* that it focuses attention on this church problem, commonly found in all six continents. . . . Mr. Liao is convinced that failure of the church to grow among the Hakkas is best explained by the fact that the Hakkas have been neglected, their language has not been learned, and they have had to join Minan- or Mandarin-speaking congregations. Consequently to them "becoming Christian" has come to mean "leaving our beloved Hakka people" (citing Liao 1972:7).

Liao is most thought-provoking when he deals with the issue of ancestor worship in relation to the evangelization of the Hakka and of Chinese in general. A careful, culturally-appropriate, biblically-faithful, and missiologically intentional theology of ancestor veneration still cries for development. In many parts of Latin America, Africa, Asia, Oceania, and even North America (among Native Americans, especially), a theology of those who have gone before us, of the "living dead," of the ancestors (whatever you may call them) is desperately needed if we are going to address one very important element of gospel proclamation that the church has essentially neglected. It is too easy to label a group "resistant" when in fact its lack of response may be due more to the church having lost its missionary vision, its commitment to gospel proclamation, or its willingness to pay the price of self-examination, repentance, and transformation that may be called for in order to be appropriate agents of God's mission in a specific context.

Third, the interface between the church and a particular people group may be strongly impacted by the authenticity of the church's witness as that is perceived by a receptor group. Lesslie Newbigin, writing from a context of the church's evangelization of the post-Christian and post-Christendom West, called this the church's role of being a "hermeneutic of the gospel" for the people in the surrounding context. "The primary reality of which we have to take account in seeking for a Christian impact on public life," writes Newbigin,

> is the Christian congregation. . . . The only hermeneutic of the gospel is a congregation of men and women who believe it and live by it. . . . This community will have, I think, the following six characteristics: It will be a community of praise. . . . It will be a community of truth. . . . It will be a community that does not live for itself. . . . It will be a community . . . sustained in the exercise of the priesthood in the world. . . . It will be a community of mutual responsibility. . . . It will be a community of hope (1989:222–233).

In this picture we have the receptor group looking in, into the life of the church. This is centripetal, "show-case" mission, as is strongly developed in parts of Scripture, for example in Deuteronomy and the Psalms. It is the kind of mission Jesus referred to when he said, "By this all [people] will know that you are my disciples, if you love one another" (Jn. 13:35).

I believe the sinfulness of the church is one of the most powerful factors creating resistance among those who are not yet Christian in North America and Europe, as well as other parts of the world. The divisiveness, the shameful ways Christians too often treat one another in the church, and the lack of authenticity on the part of the church and its leaders contribute to those outside being resistant to hearing God's loving invitation extended in word and deed. Particularly in the West, I believe the church's lack of authentic witness may be too easily excused or ignored by simply labeling those outside the church as being "resistant." Once again, matters of spiritual renewal, revitalization, reformation, and refreshment of members and leaders in Christ's church must be re-examined carefully in order to see how they may or may not be contributing to the supposed "resistance" of a particular receptor group.

Fourth, and finally, the cultural appropriateness of the church's identity, means and message may also affect the resistance/receptivity of a target group. In Pointer's words,

> Etic resistance (or receptivity) is determined by factors introduced by the evangelising agent. In this case the group or individuals are or would be responsive to the gospel but the methods used fail to communicate it effectively, so that no disciples are made or churches planted. Cultural distance between the missionary or church and the unevangelised group is often the cause. In many British churches there is also the self-imposed exile of the church from the people (1984:159).

What Pointer has called "the self-imposed exile" of the church has been termed "the distant church" by folks in Denmark, for example. In fact the church has become so removed from those whom it would evangelize—culturally, socially, relationally, structurally, liturgically distant—that the church-created chasm makes evangelization impossible. In such a case, it is too easy to label those outside the church as being "resistant" when in fact the difficulty lies in the gulf which the church itself has created. This, I believe is what Luke seeks to convey in the story of Peter's conversion in Acts 10. In terms of the mission of Israel of that day, it was far easier to label others "unclean" than to accept the commission of God's mission for Israel's witness among the peoples surrounding it. Yet the God of Abraham, Isaac, and Jacob, the God who is worshipped by Cornelius the centurion, says to Peter, "Do not call anything impure that God has made clean" (Ac. 10:15).

This need for the church's own conversion is where I think prayer movements today have much to offer us. Movements like those led by Edgardo Silvoso and others that call for all of the pastors in a city to begin to pray together on a regular basis, or for church members to participate in prayer marches—these movements affect not only the spiritual climate of the context but also the transformation and renewal of the church, as well as the dynamics of the interface between the church and the people groups in the context. Maybe the "resistant" are thus because we have not prayed in such a way that the Holy Spirit may convert us to be fit instruments of gospel proclamation.

Yet we must remember what we have said earlier in relation to the parable of the sower. After all is said and done, even when humans in a people group may understand completely the message brought to them by a spiritually authentic and appropriate agent of God's mission—even then, some humans may (and probably will) choose to say *no* to God's gracious invitation in Jesus Christ through the operation of the Holy Spirit.

Conclusion

Now, I want to conclude with some good news.

Just a few weeks ago my oldest daughter called me to ask my advice on some issues she was facing with some personal relationships there at Boulder, as well as matters relating to her study program. As I was talking with her, she suddenly exclaimed, "Dad! It's happening!"

"What?" I asked, surprised.

"You really are! You really are getting smarter! It's just like you said!"

Well, this afternoon I want you all to know that my problem is beginning to find a remedy. I am getting smarter—and my children are getting receptive. That is, at least my daughters are! My sixteen-year-old son has grave doubts about my sanity! But his sisters are reassuring him that there is hope for me yet.

Theological reflection with regard to the resistant? I do not know. All I know is that we need desperately to examine ourselves and call on the Holy Spirit to transform us in order to make us appropriate and useful agents of God's mission in the midst of God's providential invitation to all peoples. God does not want "anyone to perish, but everyone to come to repentance" (2 Pe. 3:9). Maybe you and I can mostly stay out of the way, and as our Lord Jesus Christ's love compels us, may we be transformed by the Holy Spirit, new creations, ambassadors of reconciliation, calling to a fallen world loved by God, "We implore you on Christ's behalf: Be reconciled to God" (2 Cor. 5:14, 17, 20).

Then we will see a miracle happen: the "resistant" become "receptive"—they say *yes* to God's gracious invitation.

References

Barth, Karl. 1958. *Church Dogmatics*. Edinburgh: T & T Clark.

Berkhof, Hendrikus. 1979. *Christian Faith: An Introduction to the Study of the Faith*. Sierd Woudstra, trans. Grand Rapids: Eerdmans.

Berkouwer, G. C. 1955. *General Revelation*. Grand Rapids: Eerdmans.

Bloesch, Donald G. 1992. *A Theology of Word and Spirit: Authority and Method in Theology*. Downers Grove: IVP.

Brünner, Emil. 1946. "Nature and Grace." In *Natural Theology*. John Baillie, ed. London: Geoffrey Bles.

Calvin, Jean. 1960. *Institutes of the Christian Religion*. Ford Lewis Battles, trans. Philadelphia: Westminster.

Coggins, Wade. 1980. "COWE: An Assessment of Progress and Work Left Undone." *Evangelical Missions Quarterly* 16(October):225–232.

Conn, Harvie. 1977. "Contextualization: Where Do We Begin?" In *Evangelicals and Liberation*. Carl Armerding, ed. Pp. 90–119. Nutley, NJ: Presbyterian and Reformed.

______. 1978. "Contextualization: A New Dimension for Cross-Cultural Hermeneutic." *Evangelical Missions Quarterly* 14:1(January):39–46.

______. 1984. *Eternal Word and Changing Worlds: Theology, Anthropology, and Mission in Trialogue*. Grand Rapids: Zondervan.

______, ed. 1984. *Reaching the Unreached: The Old-New Challenge*. Phillipsburg, NJ: Presbyterian and Reformed.

Dayton, Edward R. 1980. *That Everyone May Hear*. 2nd edition. Monrovia, CA: MARC.

Dayton, Edward R. and David A. Fraser. 1990. *Planning Strategies for World Evangelization*. Monrovia, CA: MARC/Grand Rapids: Eerdmans.

Demarest, Bruce A. 1982. *General Revelation*. Grand Rapids: Zondervan.

Douglas, J. D., ed. 1975. *Let the Earth Hear His Voice*. Minneapolis: World Wide Publications.

______. 1980. "Lausanne's Extended Shadow Gauges Evangelism Progress." *Christianity Today* 8(August):43–44.

Gibbs, Eddie. 1981. *I Believe in Church Growth*. Grand Rapids: Eerdmans.

______. 1986. "The Power behind the Principles," In *Church Growth: State of the Art*. C. Peter Wagner, Win Arn and Elmer Towns, eds. Pp. 189–205. Wheaton: Tyndale.

Gilliland, Dean S., ed. 1989. *The Word Among Us: Contextualizing Theology for Mission Today*. Waco, TX: Word.

Grenz, Stanley J. 1994. *Theology for the Community of God*. Nashville: Broadman.

Haleblian, Krikor. 1982a. *Contextualization and French Structuralism: A Method to Delineate the Deep Structure of the Gospel*. Unpublished doctoral dissertation, Pasadena, CA: Fuller Theological Seminary.

______. 1982b. "Evaluation of Existing Models of Contextualization." In *Contextualization and French*

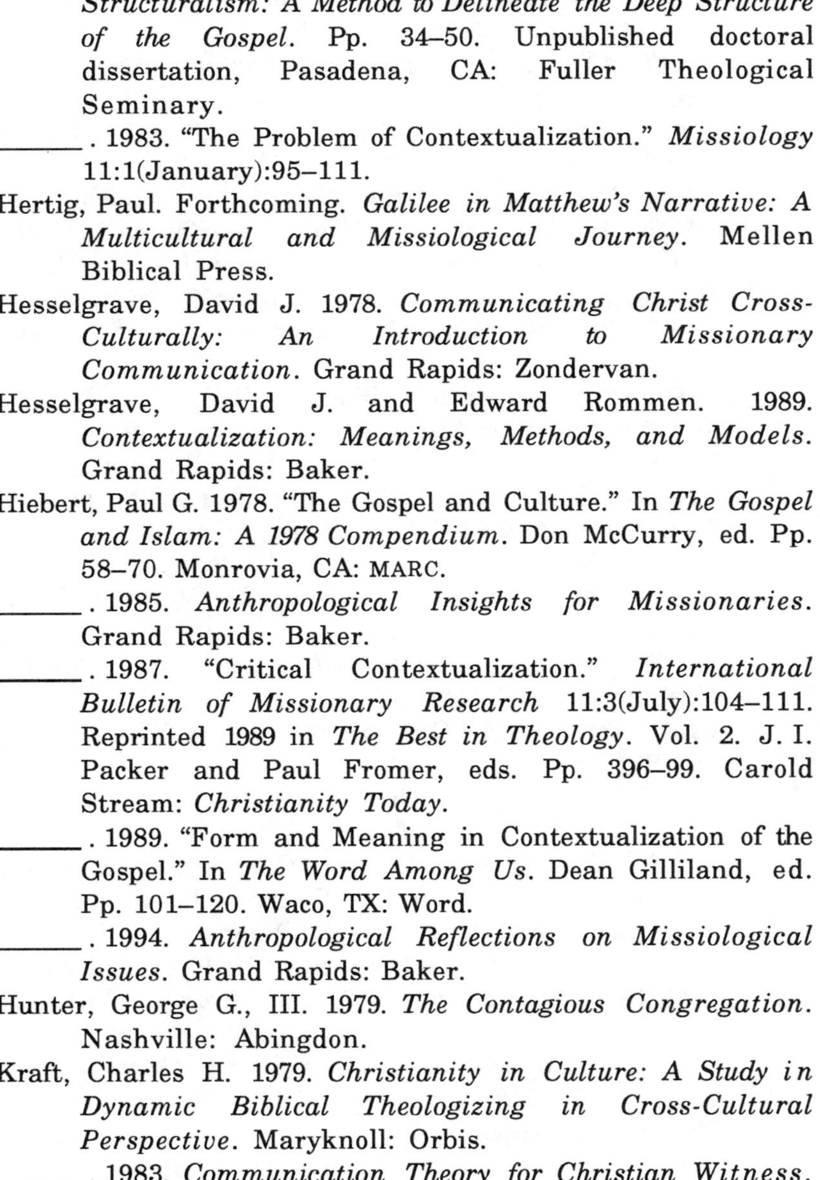

Structuralism: A Method to Delineate the Deep Structure of the Gospel. Pp. 34–50. Unpublished doctoral dissertation, Pasadena, CA: Fuller Theological Seminary.

______. 1983. "The Problem of Contextualization." *Missiology* 11:1(January):95–111.

Hertig, Paul. Forthcoming. *Galilee in Matthew's Narrative: A Multicultural and Missiological Journey*. Mellen Biblical Press.

Hesselgrave, David J. 1978. *Communicating Christ Cross-Culturally: An Introduction to Missionary Communication*. Grand Rapids: Zondervan.

Hesselgrave, David J. and Edward Rommen. 1989. *Contextualization: Meanings, Methods, and Models*. Grand Rapids: Baker.

Hiebert, Paul G. 1978. "The Gospel and Culture." In *The Gospel and Islam: A 1978 Compendium*. Don McCurry, ed. Pp. 58–70. Monrovia, CA: MARC.

______. 1985. *Anthropological Insights for Missionaries*. Grand Rapids: Baker.

______. 1987. "Critical Contextualization." *International Bulletin of Missionary Research* 11:3(July):104–111. Reprinted 1989 in *The Best in Theology*. Vol. 2. J. I. Packer and Paul Fromer, eds. Pp. 396–99. Carold Stream: *Christianity Today*.

______. 1989. "Form and Meaning in Contextualization of the Gospel." In *The Word Among Us*. Dean Gilliland, ed. Pp. 101–120. Waco, TX: Word.

______. 1994. *Anthropological Reflections on Missiological Issues*. Grand Rapids: Baker.

Hunter, George G., III. 1979. *The Contagious Congregation*. Nashville: Abingdon.

Kraft, Charles H. 1979. *Christianity in Culture: A Study in Dynamic Biblical Theologizing in Cross-Cultural Perspective*. Maryknoll: Orbis.

______. 1983. *Communication Theory for Christian Witness*. Nashville: Abingdon.

______. 1991. *Communication Theory for Christian Witness*. Revised edition. Maryknoll: Orbis.

Liao, David C. 1972. *The Unresponsive: Resistant or Neglected?* Chicago: Moody.

McGavran, Donald A. 1955. *The Bridges of God*. London: World Dominion.

______. 1959. *How Churches Grow*. New York: Friendship.

______. 1965. "Homogeneous Populations and Church Growth." In *Church Growth and Christian Mission*. Donald A. McGavran, ed. Pasadena, CA: William Carey Library.

______. 1970. *Understanding Church Growth*. Grand Rapids: Eerdmans.

______. 1972a. "Wrong Strategy, the Real Crisis in Mission." In *The Conciliar-Evangelical Debate: The Crucial Documents, 1964–1976*. Pp. 97–107. Pasadena, CA: William Carey Library. Reprinted from *International Review of Mission* 54(October 1965):451–461.

______. 1972b. *The Conciliar-Evangelical Debate: The Crucial Documents, 1964–1976*. Pasadena, CA: William Carey Library.

______. 1974. *The Clash Between Christianity and Culture*. Washington, D.C.: Canon.

______. 1977. *Ten Steps for Church Growth*. New York: Harper and Row.

______. 1980. *Understanding Church Growth*. Revised edition. Grand Rapids: Eerdmans.

______. 1981a. "Why Some American Churches are Growing and Some are Not." In *The Complete Book of Church Growth.*.Elmer Towns, John N. Vaughan and David J. Seifert, eds., Pp. 285–294. Wheaton, IL: Tyndale House.

______. 1981b. *Back to Basics in Church Growth*. Wheaton: Tyndale.

______. 1984a. "Ten Emphases in the Church Growth Movement." In *Unto the Uttermost: Missions in the Christian Churches/Churches of Christ*. Doug Priest, Jr., ed. Pp. 248–259. Pasadena, CA: William Carey Library.

______. 1984b. *Momentous Decisions in Missions Today*. Grand Rapids: Baker.

______. 1990. *Understanding Church Growth*. 3rd edition. Grand Rapids: Eerdmans.

McGavran, Donald A. and Win Arn. 1973. *How to Grow a Church: Conversations about Church Growth*. Glendale, CA: Regal.

______. 1977. *Ten Steps for Church Growth*. New York: Harper and Row.

McGavran, Donald A. and George G. Hunter III. 1980. *Church Growth Strategies That Work*. Nashville: Abingdon.

McGrath, Alister E. 1994. *Christian Theology: An Introduction*. Oxford: Blackwell.

McQuilkin, J. Robertson. 1973. *How Biblical Is the Church Growth Movement?* Chicago: Moody.

Miles, Delos. 1981. *Church Growth: A Mighty River*. Nashville: Broadman.

Newbigin, Lesslie. 1989. *The Gospel in a Pluralist Society*. Grand Rapids: Eerdmans.

Peters, George. 1981. *A Theology of Church Growth*. Grand Rapids: Zondervan.

Plantinga, Alvin C. 1992. "The Reformed Objection to Natural Theology." In *Major Themes in the Reformed Tradition*. Donald K. McKim, ed. Pp. 66–75. Grand Rapids: Eerdmans.

Pointer, Roy. 1984. *How Do Churches Grow? A Guide to the Growth of Your Church*. London: Marshall, Morgan and Scott.

Rainer, Thom. 1993. *The Book of Church Growth: History, Theology and Principles*. Nashville: Broadman.

Reeves, R. Daniel and Ronald Jenson. 1984. *Always Advancing: Modern Strategies for Church Growth*. San Bernardino, CA: Here's Life.

Scott, Waldron. 1981. "The Significance of Pattaya." *Missiology* 9(January):57–75.

Shaw, Daniel R. 1988. *Transculturation: The Cultural Factor in Translation and Other Communication Tasks*. Pasadena, CA: William Carey Library.

______. 1989. "The Context of Text: Transculturation and Bible Translation." In *The World Among Us*. Dean Gilliland, ed. Pp. 141–159. Waco, TX: Word.

Starling, Allan, ed. 1981. *Seeds of Promise*. Pasadena, CA: William Carey Library.

Taber, Charles. 1979a. "Hermeneutics and Culture: An Anthropological Perspective." In *Gospel and Culture*. John Stott and Robert Coote, eds. Pp. 129–130. Pasadena, CA: William Carey Library.

______. 1979b "Contextualization: Indigenization and/or Transformation." In *The Gospel and Islam*. Don McCurry, ed. Pp. 143–154. Monrovia, CA: MARC.

______. 1979c. "The Limits of Indigenization in Theology." In *Readings in Dynamic Indigeneity*. Charles H. Kraft and Tom N. Wisley, eds. Pp. 372–399. Pasadena, CA: William Carey Library.

Tippett, Alan R. 1972. "The Holy Spirit and Responsive Populations." In *Crucial Issues in Missions Tomorrow*. Donald A. McGavran, ed. Pp. 77–101. Chicago: Moody.

Towns, Elmer, ed. 1995. *Evangelism and Church Growth: A Practical Encyclopedia*. Ventura, CA: Regal.

Van Engen, Charles E. 1981. *The Growth of the True Church*. Amsterdam: Rodopi.

______. 1989. "The New Covenant: Knowing God in Context." In *The Word Among Us*. Dean Gilliland, ed. Pp. 74–100. Waco, TX: Word. Reprinted in *Mission on the Way: Issues in Mission Theology*. Pp. 71–89. Grand Rapids: Baker, 1996.)

______. 1996. *Mission on the Way: Issues in Mission Theology*. Grand Rapids: Baker.

______. 1991b. "The Effect of Universalism on Mission Effort." In *Through No Fault of Their Own? The Fate of Those Who Have Never Heard*. William Crockett and James Sigountos, eds. Pp. 183–194. Grand Rapids, MI: Baker. Reprinted in *Mission on the Way: Issues in Mission Theology*. Pp. 159–168. Grand Rapids: Baker, 1996.

Wagner, C. Peter. 1971. *Frontiers in Mission Strategy*. Chicago: Moody.

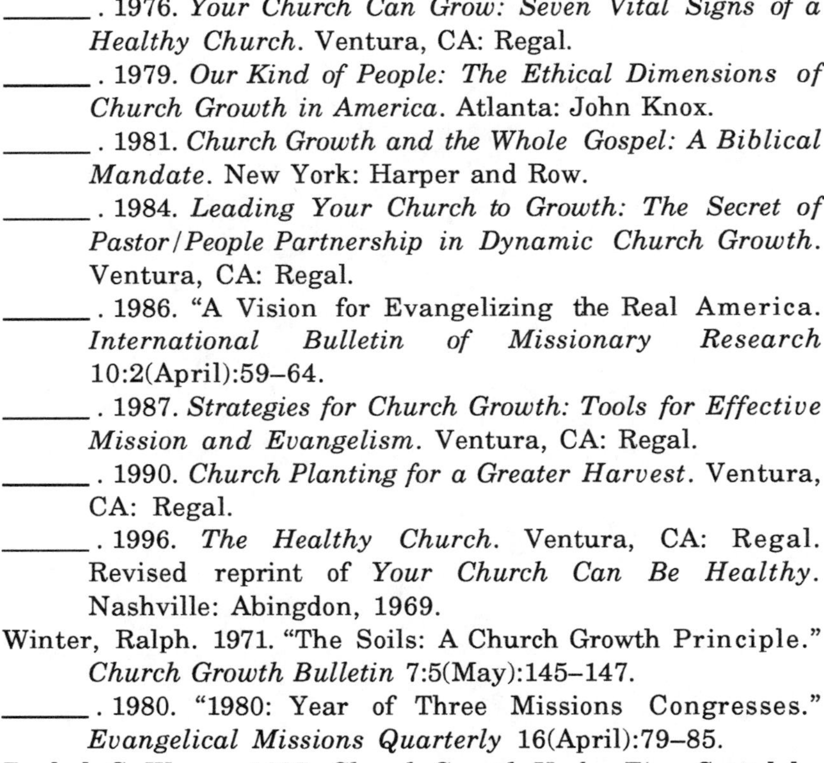

______. 1976. *Your Church Can Grow: Seven Vital Signs of a Healthy Church*. Ventura, CA: Regal.

______. 1979. *Our Kind of People: The Ethical Dimensions of Church Growth in America*. Atlanta: John Knox.

______. 1981. *Church Growth and the Whole Gospel: A Biblical Mandate*. New York: Harper and Row.

______. 1984. *Leading Your Church to Growth: The Secret of Pastor/People Partnership in Dynamic Church Growth*. Ventura, CA: Regal.

______. 1986. "A Vision for Evangelizing the Real America. *International Bulletin of Missionary Research* 10:2(April):59–64.

______. 1987. *Strategies for Church Growth: Tools for Effective Mission and Evangelism*. Ventura, CA: Regal.

______. 1990. *Church Planting for a Greater Harvest*. Ventura, CA: Regal.

______. 1996. *The Healthy Church*. Ventura, CA: Regal. Revised reprint of *Your Church Can Be Healthy*. Nashville: Abingdon, 1969.

Winter, Ralph. 1971. "The Soils: A Church Growth Principle." *Church Growth Bulletin* 7:5(May):145–147.

______. 1980. "1980: Year of Three Missions Congresses." *Evangelical Missions Quarterly* 16(April):79–85.

Zunkel, C. Wayne. 1987. *Church Growth Under Fire*. Scottdale, PA: Herald.

Part II

Case Studies: Encountering the Barriers

Chapter 4

ENCOUNTERING JEWISH RESISTANCE

David Brickner

INTRODUCTION

An oft told joke within the Jewish community opens with four Russian Jews on a train. It seems that each one has converted to Christianity. The first says that he changed his religion to escape persecution. The second explains how he desperately wanted to attend the university, and since Jews were not admitted, he became a Christian. The third tells how he fell madly in love with a beautiful Gentile who would not have him unless he converted. The fourth says, "I became a Christian because I saw the light and was convinced that it was true," to which the other three disdainfully respond, "Tell that to your Gentile friends."

That joke reflects a deep seated truth: within the Jewish community it is deemed unthinkable that a well-informed Jew could actually believe the gospel. In fact, Jewish resistance to the gospel is so deeply entrenched that one who pretends to be a Christian in order to escape censure or receive benefits is still less contemptible than one who actually claims to believe that Jesus is the son of God.

Celebrated Yiddish linguist Leo Rosten gives a definition for the Jewish people when he quotes the anonymous saying,

"Jewish people are just like everyone else . . . only more so" (Rosten 1968:xxxix). Jewish resistance to the gospel certainly fits this definition. Jews are certainly not the only people to resist the gospel yet my Jewish people have the longest history of opposition to the gospel, as well as the best documented, most prolific and comprehensively strategic opposition to the Christian message of any people group.

In approaching the subject of Jewish resistance to the gospel, I intend to deal with foundational as well as strategic factors. By foundational factors, I mean the historical, spiritual, and social issues that contribute to Jewish resistance. By strategic factors, I am referring to the well-defined efforts by Jewish community leaders to perpetuate resistance to the gospel. Finally, I would like to suggest appropriate Christian responses to Jewish resistance.

Foundational Factors

Many writers of material on "resistance and receptivity" focus on sociological factors. Many missiologists limit the role of theology: they allow the Bible to say why it is important to go into all the world and preach the gospel, but they rarely consult it concerning the manner in which to proceed. Missiology should be an interdisciplinary study between theology and the social sciences. The Bible not only defines our imperatives, but also provides the foundational understanding of receptivity. It is through that theological grid that we must interpret the data of the social sciences and develop a strategic response.

Spiritual

As I minister in churches on behalf of Jews for Jesus, many Christians ask me, "Why don't more of your people believe in Jesus when he is presented so clearly in their own Bible? Can't they just read Isaiah 53?" Yet a more biblically informed position recognizes that fallen human nature rebels against God. Rather than expressing surprise at those who reject the gospel, we, like the disciples, might well exclaim, "Who then *can* be saved?" (Mt. 19:25b, emphasis mine). The Bible teaches us that the most pressing reasons to resist the gospel are spiritual. This is true for Jews and Gentiles alike. Humanity's sinful condition is what made the gospel necessary, and it is also the condition that causes people to resist the gospel.

Sin is not merely our outward failure to resist one temptation or another. It is the ingrained reality of every human soul. Ever since Adam and Eve sinned in the Garden of Eden, all of humanity has been shaking its fist at the heavens, declaring to God, "We will not have you rule over us." The rabbis reject the doctrine of total depravity, citing it as one of the differences between Jewish and Christian theology. Yet it is a Jewish doctrine from the standpoint that the sinfulness of the human condition is clearly taught in the Jewish Scriptures:

"The Lord looks down from heaven on humankind to see if there are any who are wise, who seek after God. They have all gone astray, they are all alike ... perverse; there is no one who does good, no not one" (Ps. 14:2–3, trans. from Heb.). "The heart is devious above all else; it is perverse—who can understand it?" (Jer. 17:9, trans. from Heb).

It should come as no surprise that any people, including the Jews, resist the gospel. Jesus himself experienced in his own body the full force of rejection by his own people. He did not cry out in amazement, "What's wrong with you people? Don't you know who I am? Can't you just read Isaiah 53?" As he wept over Jerusalem, he cried out, "Oh, Jerusalem who kills the prophets and stones those who are sent to her." He did not see his own rejection as an isolated event in the history of Israel but as the culmination of a long history of resistance and rejection of the messengers of God. The apostle Paul understood this when he declared that "the man without the spirit does not accept the things that come from the Spirit of God, for they are foolishness to him, and he cannot understand them, because they are spiritually discerned" (1 Cor. 2:14). There is no difference between Jews and Gentiles when it comes to the sinfulness of the human heart which is the first and primary reason for gospel resistance.

We must also recognize the place of satanic deception in gospel resistance. The apostle John declared, "We know that we are ... of God and that the whole world is under the control of the evil one" (1 Jn. 5:19). The apostle Paul referred to Satan's role in deceiving individuals with regard to the gospel when he said, "the god of this age has blinded the minds of unbelievers, so that they cannot see the light of the gospel of the glory of Christ, who is the image of God" (2 Cor. 4:4).

All too often, we give mere lip service to this spiritual reality. We fail to include a proper awareness of spiritual power in our evangelistic strategy. I believe that the Jewish people are the particular target of satanic attack. Ever since Abram left Ur of the Chaldees, his descendants, the Jews, have been a people of destiny. And that destiny has been wrapped up with the supernatural. God elected to convey his truth to the world through the Jews. "Salvation is from the Jews" (Jn. 4:22). No wonder the enemy of God has, throughout history, attempted to destroy the Jewish people.

The very integrity of God, the trustworthiness of the Bible, and the future promises concerning world redemption will be demonstrated not only through the survival of the Jewish people, but also through their salvation in Christ (Rom. 11:12 and 15). That is why,

> With every fiber of his depraved sinister being, Satan despises the Jews. He hates them with a perfect hatred. Their total destruction is his goal. He is the author of the spirit of anti-Semitism. There is no other way to explain the venomous hostility that has been directed against the Jews by so many people and so many countries for so many years (M. Brown 1992:155).

As we consider the spiritual factors of Jewish resistance to the gospel, we cannot afford to underestimate the special attention the adversary pays to God's ancient people. It takes the power of the Holy Spirit to come against the power of the unholy spirit.

There is a third spiritual factor that we must confess is a mystery though the Scriptures speak openly of it. There exists a special blindness which is unique to the Jewish people. Paul himself calls it a mystery when he says, "I do not want you to be ignorant of this mystery, brothers, so that you may not be conceited: Israel has experienced a hardening in part until the full number of the Gentiles has come in" (Rom. 11:25). The veil is a scriptural metaphor for this hardening: "Even to this day when Moses is read, a veil covers their hearts. But whenever anyone turns to the Lord, the veil is taken away" (2 Cor. 3:15).

This hardening of the Jews' hearts remains a mystery but must be factored into our understanding of Jewish resistance to the gospel. Some missiologists and pastors have concluded that Jewish evangelism is not a primary concern at this time. One well-known pastor said,

> I don't have a great burden for Jewish evangelism. I believe that God will evangelize them when He is ready. In the meantime, God has poured out His grace, His spirit upon the Gentiles and thus I like to fish where the fish are biting. I really feel that for the most part [Jewish evangelism] is a waste of church finances that can be better used to evangelize the Gentiles at this time.[1]

In light of this divine hardening, perhaps we should apply to Jewish evangelism esteemed missiologist Donald McGavran's suggestion to "hold lightly" the work in resistant fields.[2] But there is a danger of misconstruing what the Scriptures teach regarding Jews and Jewish evangelism. Paul describes the hardening as partial and temporary. Yes, there is an eschatological element to consider with respect to the receptivity of the Jewish people as a whole, but meanwhile, Paul affirms that the veil can be lifted from individuals when "they turn to the Lord." Paul did not "hold lightly" to Jewish evangelism. Despite his own calling to the Gentiles and despite his several pronouncements that, "From now on I will go to the Gentiles" (Ac. 18:6), Paul maintained a fundamental commitment to the primacy of Jewish evangelism (Rom. 1:16).

Paul recognized that God had preserved a remnant according to the election of grace (Rom. 11:5). This understanding of the continuing remnant must shape our thinking with regard to Jewish evangelism, especially in the face of Jewish resistance to the gospel. If our goal were to see the majority of Jews accept

---

1 From a transcription of a radio message by Chuck Smith (Calvary Chapel, Costa Mesa CA) on KFAX, December 30, 1992.

2 "Correct policy is to occupy fields of low receptivity lightly.... Resistant lands should be held lightly" (McGavran 1980:262).

Christ now, then I would agree with Chuck Smith that the church had better concentrate on evangelizing Gentiles. But we must remember that humanity in general will not accept the gospel en masse: "Small is the gate and narrow the road that leads to life, and only a few find it" (Mt. 7:14). Unless we apply this biblical understanding to our theories of gospel resistance, we will inevitably wring our hands and despair of the task. Instead, we can rejoice with the angels that God is indeed saving some. We certainly see this in Jewish evangelism today. Though the level of official resistance is greater than ever and though the strategies to prevent a gospel witness among the Jewish people abound, we are still seeing Jewish people receive the gospel. In fact, more Jews today are coming to faith in Christ than at any time since perhaps the first century when those first Jews for Jesus, Peter, James and John were preaching the gospel.

Our understanding of Jewish resistance to the gospel requires an awareness of spiritual factors, but there are other factors to consider.

Historical

Jewish history is replete with persecution in the name of Christ. It has been said that the sad saga of Jewish-Christian relations could be written in blood and punctuated with violence. It is not the purpose of this chapter to catalog this history, but certainly a few examples are in order. Czar Nicholas I ordered conscription in the Russian army: twenty-five years for all boys, unless they happened to be Jews. Jews were to serve for thirty-one years. Those extra six years were designed to convert Jewish boys to Russian Orthodoxy (Sachar 1977:86–87). One account of Czar Nicholas I tells how a group of Jewish children were brought to the Volga River to be baptized—and at the command of Nicholas, all were plunged under, never to come back up" (1977:86–87).[3]

The Crusades, although not aimed specifically at Jews, provide another poignant example of persecution in the name of

---

3 Sachar's wording suggests that this may have been a suicide chosen in preference to conversion.

Christ. The Crusaders, upon reaching the city of Jerusalem, found that the Moslem invaders had passed on through, and all that was left was a defenseless group of Orthodox Jews. They rounded up those Jews into the great synagogue and then burned it to the ground. As the people inside perished, those outside marched round and round with their crosses, singing "Christ We Adore Thee" (Mayer 1972:99–100 cited in Rausch 1984:27).

These and other shocking historical facts appear as mere blips on the screens of most people's understanding of history. Yet, for Jewish people, these facts are huge on the horizon of Jewish-Christian relations. These and so many other historical facts that show Jews suffering at the hand of Christians form the cornerstone upon which Jewish historical identity is based.

Jewish people do not distinguish between those who call themselves Christians and those who actually practice the Christian faith. Most Jews have concluded that Jewish survival is based upon their own historic resistance to the Christian flood. Christian mission is seen as synonymous with persecution and anti-Semitism. From most Jewish people's understanding, there are two types of people—the Jews and the Christians. "Christian" has become synonymous with non-Jews who have persecuted Jewish people throughout the ages.

Therefore, Willie Mays, Billy Graham, Adolph Hitler, and the Pope all fall into the same category. They are Christians.

Social

The third foundational factor in Jewish resistance to the gospel is social. Issues of individual and group identity have a profound bearing on Jewish resistance to the gospel. This is where the more recent theories of resistance and receptivity are most helpful. Jewish people are rooted and grounded in the biblical narrative, yet the historical split between synagogue and church has led to a highly developed social identity within the Jewish community. The leaders of this community have designed this identity to provide plenty of cultural distance between the Christian church and the Jewish community.

In speaking of Japanese resistance to the gospel message, Peter Lundell introduces the concept of "Nihonkyo." The concept actually speaks to one's ultimate loyalty. Loyalty is not to a particular belief or even to a nation, "but rather to one's identity and obligations as a Japanese person" (Lundell 1995:409). Similarly, there is an expectation of loyalty on the part of individual Jews despite their religious convictions. Part of that loyalty is defined as not believing in Jesus.

Jewishness is defined broadly within the Jewish community. It is a fact of birth, a product of social development, education, and identification, and lastly, a matter of religious affiliation. Yet when it comes to the specifics of Jewish identity, even the leaders of the community disagree. In fact, the question of who is a Jew is one of the most hotly contested issues in the state of Israel today. Israel is a largely secularized state, but the religious minority has a very prominent voice.

The majority of Jews in Israel and elsewhere minimize the religious aspect of identity. That is Jewish identity broadly defined. But there is a more narrow definition of Jewish identity that is widely accepted, a definition that gives the appearance of religious or spiritual content. That definition amounts to identity by negation. "We are Jews because we don't believe in Jesus." "We are Jews because we celebrate Passover, *not* Easter." "We are Jews because we celebrate Hanukkah, *not* Christmas."

Because Jewish identity comes in the form of a negation which precludes faith in Christ, resistance to the gospel is a given. It is an indoctrination that comes with mother's milk. Montgomery rightly points out that,

> receptivity toward an outside religion will be low if adherence to it is regarded as bringing about a sense of loss of a valued aspect of social identity, such as ethnic or national identity and perhaps a religious identity closely associated with them.... Becoming attached to a religion, coming from the outside, is perceived as rejecting one's own ethnic group or cultural heritage (Montgomery 1986:292).

Christians need to know that Jewish people do not see Jewish believers in Jesus as those who have followed their convictions. They see Jewish believers in Jesus as traitors to themselves, their family, their people. They see them as traitors to their very survival. And survival is paramount in the Jewish community.

The facts of Jewish history have combined with the forces of secularization to transform Judaism into a religion of survival. Preservation of Jewish identity has become the highest and the only non-negotiable religious ideal. Couple that fact with the conviction that Jews cannot believe in Jesus and remain Jewish, and the syllogism leads to the highest possible form of gospel resistance in the social realm.

Robert Priest rightly points out,

> people refuse to convert because of the implication that conversion is a conversion from one culture—their own, which they are familiar with, successful in terms of, and believe is good—to the missionary's national culture—which is alien and may even seem immoral. The resistance ... may have little to do with resistance to the Holy Spirit and rejection of Christ, and a great deal to do with allegiance to one's own culture and society in the face of an invitation to a disloyal conversion to an alien culture (Priest 1994:304).

For Jews, the invitation to Christ appears to come, not from merely an alien culture, but from a culture that is perceived as hostile. Moreover, Jewish identity and faith in Jesus are considered mutually exclusive by the Jewish establishment. That means that for a Jew to accept Christ he or she must violate that part of his or her conscience that has always accepted the equation that becoming a Christian equals betraying the Jewish people.

Strategic Factors

Jewish community leaders recount with great passion the historical and social factors that help maintain the collective conscience—and the commitment to identity by negation as described above. This leads to our second set of factors in Jewish resistance to the gospel: strategic factors. These factors are highly developed, well organized, and intended to produce a negative commitment to the person of Christ.

Theology

Many Christians assume that Judaism today is much like it was in the time of Jesus, or that Christianity and Judaism are alike except for faith in Jesus. This is simply untrue. Today's rabbis teach a Judaism vastly different from that of Jesus' day. Contemporary Judaism is thoroughly polemical in its construct—and it was not constructed in a vacuum. It developed within the context of a particular challenge: that of an emerging sect of Jews whose hearts were committed to Jesus.

With the destruction of the second temple by the Romans in 70 A.D., the success of the Jewish Christian sect in winning converts grew at what was, for the rabbinical authorities, an alarming rate. Some scholars have estimated that by the turn of the first century as many as one third of the Jews in Palestine had professed faith in Christ. Jewish authorities felt they had to do something to staunch the flow of Jews who were coming to Christ. Their efforts to deal with this have been well-documented by Jacob Jocz, James Parkes, and others (Jocz 1979, esp. ch. 5; also Parkes 1981, esp. chs. 2 and 3). Shifts in theology have helped to keep the Jewish religion separate from Christianity. The differences in theology are real enough, but they are rendered even more intense by false impressions that many Jewish people have of Christian beliefs and/or practices. Following are three examples of such theological shifts in Judaism with attendant misunderstandings that many Jews have regarding Christian theology.

Sin: Rabbis have embraced an ethical dualism and have established the belief that each soul is endowed with a good inclination (*yetzer ha tov*) and a bad inclination (*yetzer ha ra*). Each person is responsible to follow the good inclination and reject the bad. While this emphasis on responsibility and the continual choice to do good or evil parallels Christianity to some extent, the Jewish religion veers away in its teaching that human beings are born morally neutral. In contrast to the doctrine of original sin, Judaism recognizes no human condition which would prevent people from doing good and rejecting evil. Part of the morning liturgy recited each day from the Jewish prayer book illustrates this: "O my God, the soul Thou gavest me is pure; Thou didst create it, Thou didst form it, Thou didst breathe it into me. Thou preservest it within me, and Thou wilt take it from me, but wilt restore unto me hereafter" (Hertz

1961:19). Sin is seen as individual acts and not as a natural condition. While most Jews will admit that they have made mistakes, few would identify themselves as sinners. Sinners are those who have stolen, murdered, sold drugs, and so forth.

Further, most Jewish people do not understand what Christians mean by original sin. For many, it comes down to another "we" and "they" distinction. We (meaning the Jewish people) believe that people are good and created in God's image as the Scriptures teach. They (meaning the Christians) have little respect for humanity; they teach that all people are evil from birth and punished for something that others did. The concepts that sin has marred humanity's ability to reflect God's image and that God treasures humanity so much that he came to suffer and die for our redemption are alien to most Jewish people.

Salvation: The Exodus from Egypt, or deliverance from national calamity, is the paradigm of salvation in the Old Testament. Add to that the fact that Jewish theologians do not believe that people are born separated from God, and it is not surprising that they do not see a need for personal salvation. Salvation is viewed as a corporate, not personal, concern. In addition, there is the concept of *tikkun olam*, whereby the Jewish people see themselves in partnership with God to create a better world. Many Jews do not believe in an afterlife, or assume that if there is one, they will naturally have a place in heaven. Christianity is viewed by many as a religion that is only concerned with what happens to people after they die.

Savior: Judaism has been forced to evolve since the destruction of the second temple. Prayer, repentance, and good deeds have been substituted for the temple sacrifices. Whereas Judaism was once a redemptive religion, it is now a moralistic religion. Rabbis rarely speak of atonement for sin, or how to have a relationship with God. Instead the concerns are "horizontal"—how to treat one another and how to live as a good Jew. The idea that Israel needs a savior to die for their sins is no longer a part of mainstream Jewish thinking. Therefore, the response to the gospel might sound something like this: "Judaism teaches every man dies for his own sins. Even if there was to be a savior, we would not worship him—that is idolatry."

A common misunderstanding among Jews is that Christians believe a human being became God rather than vice versa.

These are just a few examples of many ideas which developed in opposition to Christian teaching and ultimately Old Testament doctrine as well.

Education

Many Jewish leaders view education as the answer to most ills within the Jewish community. And since Jewish "defection" to Jesus is viewed as an "ill," many suppose that a defective Jewish education is to blame. The answer to this apparent defect is more rigorous education which actually amounts to indoctrination. That indoctrination takes two forms: first, the development and study of literature designed to refute the New Testament and second, the use of Jewish identity and history to maintain a we/they mentality.

While local rabbis are entrusted with the responsibility to provide such education, their efforts are bolstered by national and international organizations. Groups like the Jewish Community Relations Council Task Force on Missionaries and Cults, Jews For Judaism, and a host of other groups exist solely for the purpose of preventing the gospel message from penetrating the Jewish community. While these organizations have limited personnel actively involved in "anti-missionary work," they provide resources for rabbis, parents, and other educators to refute Christian evangelistic efforts.

This kind of organized opposition is not a recent phenomenon. The history of Jewish polemics and refutation literature is as old as the Talmud itself. One refutation document which is still in use is a sixteenth-century document entitled *Faith Strengthened*, by Isaac Troki (1970). Other recent attempts to discredit the gospel, such as Gerald Sigal's little book, *You Take Jesus, I'll Take God: How to Refute Christian Missionaries* (1980), are more intemperate. A tape series, *Let's Get Biblical*, by Rabbi Tovia Singer (1995) has grabbed the attention of many evangelicals simply because it has been so widely distributed.

In evaluating this disputation literature, it is important to realize that its purpose is not to engage Christian scholars in debate or to persuade them to abandon Christianity. Refutation literature is a purely defensive measure, designed to discourage Jewish people from considering the claims of Christ. In some cases, authors make honest attempts to weigh evidence and present a credible argument against the gospel. More often than not, this material is characterized by such logical fallacies as making straw men, question begging, and misrepresentation of the facts.

The first line of attack is to contradict the New Testament claims that Jesus fulfilled the Hebrew Scriptures. For example, Matthew's Gospel quotes Isaiah 7:14 concerning the virgin birth. This is refuted as a mistranslation of the Hebrew word *almah* which means "young woman" not virgin. The predicted child is said to be the son of the prophet Isaiah.

Attempts to identify Jesus as the suffering servant of Isaiah 53 are rejected on the basis that they do not depict a person at all but rather the nation of Israel. Since Israel is elsewhere identified as the servant, it is presumed that Isaiah is again speaking of Israel in Isaiah 53.

A second attack on the New Testament borrows heavily from the form criticism of liberal Protestantism. These presume late dates for the authorship of the gospels; they make much of "contradictions" in the Gospel narratives and they seek to demonstrate the roots of pagan mythology in Christian theology. While many Jewish leaders echo these critics, they do not seem to realize that the very approach they borrow to attack the veracity of the New Testament can be applied to undermine the authority of the Hebrew Scriptures as well.

A further aspect of the indoctrination of gospel resistance is the notion that Jewish identity—by definition and based on historical perspective—precludes Jesus as an option for Jews. Some have accused Jewish leaders of fostering a "victim mentality" in the Jewish community. This mentality allows the strategic use of shame to prevent Jewish people from considering ideas which they perceive as the special property of those who have persecuted them.

The term "victim mentality" is problematic because to some it implies that the victimization is purely imagined, and this has certainly not been the case for Jewish people. In fact, Jewish people have suffered enormously at the hands of so-called Christians. Nevertheless, little effort is made in the Jewish community to present other relevant facts. Instead there has been a systematic spin on history to create the widest chasm possible between Jews and Christians. Martin Luther illustrates the point. This luminary of the Reformation, scholar, and prolific author is known to Jews only as the author of the book, *Concerning the Jews and Their Lies* (1971:121–306). This vitriolic polemic against the Jews is terrible indeed. But it is not the sum of Luther's life and ministry. Nor is it embraced by Christians today. Yet it is deemed all that is necessary or relevant for a Jewish understanding of Luther. And for many, it is regarded as proof that Christians and Christianity are hateful.

Another interesting distortion of history in Jewish education is the notion that the Inquisition was launched by Catholics seeking to persecute Jews. In reality, the Inquisition was a case of Christians persecuting other Christians.

The Holocaust has dominated the Jewish perspective of history to the point where some within the Jewish community are beginning to call for balance.[4] Yet the horrors of the Holocaust are compounded by the inference—and often outright accusation—that Hitler's diabolical plan was the logical

---

4 "There is almost nothing more sacred or more sensitive for Jews living in the generation after the Holocaust than the memory of the six million martyrs of the Nazi genocide. The poignant question, 'Where was God?' rather than being a theological provocation, is more likely a reflection of the abiding pain that lingers from the staggering losses. After all, what could possibly be more important than sanctifying the memory of those who died—except ensuring a future for those who wish to live as Jews? There is great justification for the continuing obsession with the Holocaust. . . . But obsession with the Holocaust is exacting a great price. It is killing America's Jews. An obsession with victimization leaves no room for the joy of the faith and is driving many away" (Buchwald 1992).

conclusion of accepted Christian theology. Scant attention is paid to those valiant Christians who resisted the Nazis. Well developed and heavily funded Holocaust studies that are an integral part of Jewish education neglect names like Bonhoeffer and Ten Boom, and the Barman declaration is virtually unknown.

This unbalanced view of history is designed to place any consideration of Christianity on a par with the highest form of disloyalty and betrayal of the Jewish people. Honest intellectual inquiry about Christianity is impossible from within the Jewish community since the very question brings with it the specter of the highest form of community censure.

Further, anti-Jewish attitudes of the past are often imputed to present-day Christians. The idea that Christians hope to destroy the Jewish people by converting them to Christianity is common. Many Christians are so horrified to learn this that they are too intimidated to tell Jewish friends about Jesus. Thus distorted education regarding Christians and Christianity has its desired effect. Jewish people learn prejudices regarding Christianity, and many Christians, wishing to prove those prejudices untrue, are unwilling to say anything that might be taken amiss by Jewish friends or acquaintances.

It is difficult to level an accusation of prejudice at the Jewish people, who have been the objects of so much prejudice. Nevertheless, the prejudice people experience does not necessarily keep them from prejudging others. In fact, prejudice tends to be a vicious cycle, as people form judgments and poorly informed opinions of those whom they feel have judged them.

Creating Distance

This leads to the third strategic response within the Jewish community: the estrangement of vocal Christians—and particularly of Jews who believe in Jesus—from the Jewish community. Jews who profess faith in Christ often meet with tremendous outrage and hostility from other Jews. Jewish community leaders do everything possible to encourage this outrage.

In the past Jews who professed faith in Christ were publicly excommunicated. Families held funerals for the son or daughter who had "gone astray," and they became social outcasts. With the secularization of the Jewish community, this occurs infrequently. Other methods of censure have been developed. Jewish Christians are labeled *meshummad* which means a destroyer. The most pervasive response is for Jewish leaders to simply say to the believer in Christ, "You are no longer Jewish." Yet the weight of Jewish literature teaches that a person born Jewish can never become a non-Jew. It is possible to be a bad Jew, but no Jew can become a non-Jew.[5] Nevertheless, the public stance of Jewish leaders is that a Jew who believes in Jesus no longer is a part of the Jewish community.[6]

By ruling of the Israeli Supreme Court, December 25, 1989, any Jew who professes faith in Jesus Christ is no longer eligible for Israeli citizenship as a Jew under the Law of Return. Jewish Christians are refused access to any formal Jewish community

---

5 For example, in the Babylonian Talmud, Sanhedrin 44a, we read: "R. Abba b. Zabda said: Even though [the people] have sinned, they are still [called] 'Israel.'" The *Encyclopaedia Judaica* remarks that, "Throughout the ages the rabbinical authorities have been concerned with the problem of a person who is technically a Jew but subscribes to another religion ... the majority of decisors have always felt that such a person must halakhically be considered a Jew" (1972:24). *See further* Robinson 1996:33–40. Even counter-missionaries David Berger and Michael Wyschogrod assert that a Jewish believer in Jesus commits idolatry but "does not thereby cease to be a Jew, since a Jew always remains a Jew," albeit a sinful one (1978:66).

6 For example, consider these quotes:

> No Jewish organization, religious or secular, acknowledges the Jewishness of Messianic Jews. Furthermore, we find them to be abhorrent. . . . Why should these people have to masquerade as Jews when their spiritual life is based upon belief in Jesus as their Christ? (Miller 1997).

> So for a Jew to say, "I believe in the Christian Messiah," is to be a Christian. That's the equation. Any Jew who says, "I believe in the Christian Messiah, and I am still a Jew," is lying to themselves—and it is lying to every other Christian (Lennick cited in Hinson 1996).

assistance, and they are denied the right to be buried in a Jewish cemetery.

Further, efforts to create as much cultural distance as possible between the Jewish and Christian communities are made by blurring the lines between social, political, and theological differences between the two. Jewish people tend to be more liberal than most Christians when it comes to politics and social mores. Jewish leaders make the most of those differences to present Christianity in as unappealing and alien light as possible to Jewish people. Unfortunately, many Christians contribute to this impression without realizing that using religious clout to tout a particular party line has convinced many Jews that a vote for Jesus is a vote for a political party they may not be inclined to endorse.

Dialogue

A further strategy to protect Jewish resistance to the gospel is dialogue. When Jewish leaders engage evangelical Christians in a dialogue, more often than not it is an attempt on the part of the Jewish community leaders to undermine the evangelical commitment to a forthright gospel proclamation. The ostensible goal of dialogue is understanding, but what Jews want Christians to understand is that Jews do not need Jesus. The dialogues become one-sided propaganda machines.

Many evangelical institutions, theologians, and pastors have participated in these dialogues with the expressed hope of building bridges of understanding between the two faith communities. But in order to do so, they must often agree to ground rules that preclude honest discussion of pertinent theological issues. Inevitably the Jewish leaders tell how destructive evangelistic efforts are, how the notion that Jews need Jesus is patronizing, and how the idea that there are Jews who do believe in Jesus is false.

Many dialogues are thinly veiled attempts to secure from evangelical participants statements deploring "deceptive practices" in evangelistic endeavors. Later on, these statements will be trumpeted as "evidence" that "mainstream evangelicals" are disavowing Messianic groups. So there is an effort to drive a wedge between evangelical leaders and Jewish evangelistic enterprise. What evangelical would not want to deplore deception of any kind? Yet the specific deceptive practices are not clearly defined in these discussions. What Christian participants would discover were they to push the point is that the very existence of Jews who believe in Jesus is considered deceptive, not on the basis of what they do, but because the Jewish community has decided that Jews cannot believe in Jesus. Anyone who dares to contradict this decision will be labeled deceptive. Sadly, many Christians have taken their Jewish friend's view of Jewish Christian groups without checking with their Jewish brothers and sisters in Christ to see if they have any basis in truth.

Friendships often serve as leverage in dealing with the perceived threat of Jewish evangelism. For example, a pastor will establish a friendship with the local rabbi. He grows to respect the rabbi, as well he might, and he enjoys having the rabbi's respect in return. As soon as this pastor invites a Jewish ministry into his church, he receives a call from the rabbi. "I thought we were friends," the rabbi might begin. "Perhaps you don't realize that having a group like this one is offensive to our community and will end up destroying the relationship you and I are trying to build." I do not know how many times Jewish missionaries have heard, "We believe in what you are doing but we can't have you speak in our church because we don't want to jeopardize the good relationships we are building with our Jewish neighbors." True dialogue can be worthwhile, but it will never substitute for evangelism. More often than not it runs counter to the evangelistic mandate.

What is most telling is the resolute commitment Jewish community leaders have to excluding Jewish Christians from the dialogue. When evangelical leaders agree to exclude Jewish Christians from the discussions, they do not realize that the very integrity of dialogue is violated in the process.[7] One theological

---

7 "Gerald Anderson, a United Methodist official with the Overseas Ministries Study Center, criticized the workshop's leadership for refusing to include a Messianic Jew on the panel.... I find an attitude

institution which sponsored such a dialogue agreed to the demand that a Jewish Christian who was one of their own faculty members be barred from participating in the dialogue. How sad that in an attempt to build trust between believers in Jesus and non-believers, many Christians have spurned their own brothers and sisters and have sown mistrust between believers, Jews, and Gentiles within the church.

CHRISTIAN RESPONSES

Church history is littered with examples of wrong responses to Jews and Jewish resistance to the gospel. These wrong responses have evolved from hostility and even violence to indifference and finally to cozy compromise. There have always been some right responses to the Jewish community, but those responses are becoming all too rare. It is time for evangelicals to reconsider their relationship to the Jewish community in the light of Christ's mandate from Matthew 28.

The growing presence of the remnant—that is, Jewish believers within the body of Christ—should serve to encourage evangelicals that Jewish people can be won to Christ. These Jewish believers can also be a tremendous resource to the larger body of Christ, helping Christian brothers and sisters understand how Jewish objections to the gospel can be overcome. Evangelical churches need to utilize the knowledge and experience of such Jewish believers. Christians who respond to the Jewish community without any regard to their own Jewish brothers and sisters in Christ are repeating the mistake some foreign missions have made in failing to consult and work through indigenous Christian leaders overseas.

Much of the "cozy compromise" that evangelicals have made with the Jewish community is a direct result of what is known as dialogue. Ideally, dialogue might afford evangelical leaders an opportunity to interact with and bear testimony to Jewish

---

toward Messianic Jews—or Hebrew Christians—that smacks of contempt, intolerance, lack of respect and theological denial" (Hinson 1996).

community leaders (*see*, e.g., Tanenbaum, Wilson, and Rudin 1978; Rudin and Wilson 1987). Unfortunately, it can just as easily be used to shame Christians into silence. Christian leaders must be willing to risk the displeasure of Jewish community leaders if there is to be honest interaction with no strings attached. Jews who believe in Jesus have traditionally been barred from the dialogue table, and evangelical leaders have been all too quick to comply. They need to question why they, as Gentiles, are to be accepted representatives of the Christian faith while Jews who believe the same thing are to be excluded. Christian leaders need to stand firm and insist that a fair dialogue will include local Jewish believers in Jesus providing there are such believers in the area.

Likewise, if a rabbi tells a minister that he stands to lose the respect and friendship of the Jewish community by welcoming a Jewish believer in Jesus to the pulpit, that minister needs to question the basis of the supposed respect and friendship. Ignoring, avoiding, or even politely refusing to hear from Jewish believers in Jesus for the sake of maintaining friendship with unbelievers is wrong. It is contrary to Scripture, hurtful to the body of Christ and ultimately, hurtful to the Jewish people who might have come to hear the gospel. Ministers who separate themselves from Jewish Christians and who eschew opportunities to tell Jewish people about Jesus out of respect and friendship for rabbis must ask themselves, "How good a friend am I to the cause of Christ?" He sacrificed all so that Jews and Gentiles could be saved. What sacrifices are ministers of his gospel willing to make?

Christians can rightly respond to Jewish resistance by reaching out and learning what they can from Jews who have embraced the gospel. Another right response to Jewish resistance to the gospel is simply to publicly acknowledge the existence of those Jewish believers. Literature, even Christian literature, traditionally presents Jews as non-Christians. If Christian journals, magazines, and even Sunday School lessons would recognize the presence of a Jewish remnant within the church, it would be an important step toward undermining the myth that Jews do not believe in Jesus.

Another way to acknowledge the existence of Jewish believers is to take a positive stance toward Messianic congregations. These local congregations provide Jewish-oriented institutions and houses of worship where Christ is central, but culture and community remain distinctly Jewish. Christians should be supportive of this movement whenever possible. Some questions remain to be answered and not all Messianic congregations are alike, but the ideal is worth striving for.[8] In fact, the majority of Jewish believers in Jesus worship in mainline evangelical denominations. Yet Messianic congregations do seem to meet a need for Jewish believers particularly as they are discovering their new identity in Christ.

From a theological perspective, certain trends within the evangelical community have undermined the case for the Messiahship of Jesus. Old Testament scholars need to reexamine their approach to the prophetic passages as well as to those passages that speak of God's covenants with Israel. Too many Christians have accepted the notion that these covenants could somehow affect atonement for sin and personal salvation for Jewish people when in fact God's irrevocable promises had to do with land, the perpetuation of a people, and the reign of David's seed. To use the covenants which actually predict the messiah Jesus to say that Jews need not believe in him is ironic indeed. The church needs to develop new scholarship that takes into account the Jewish need for Christ and deals with objections to his Messiahship head-on.[9]

On a historical and sociological level, it is important for Christians to understand and to deal honestly with the horrors of

---

8 One of the earliest publications on messianic congregations was Goble 1974. *See also* Schiffman 1992. The movement is young, and on questions of ecclesiology and practice a wide variety of viewpoints can be found.

9 The last book-length compendium to respond in a fairly comprehensive way to Jewish objections to the gospel was Williams 1919—nearly eighty years ago! However, the various Jewish missions and umbrella agencies such as the Lausanne Consultation on Jewish Evangelism have produced numerous articles and smaller studies of Christian apologetics for Jewish people.

anti-Semitism. Yet there must be a balanced approach to this history. The Scriptures teach, "No longer will it be said the fathers have eaten sour grapes and the children's teeth are set on edge" (Jer. 31:29, trans. from Heb.). Christians do not bear responsibility for past horrors of anti-Semitism any more than Jews today bear responsibility for the crucifixion of Christ. Christian leaders must not be ashamed of sins they did not commit. When they are confronted with Jewish prejudices toward the gospel, they must be willing to refute those ideas rather than politely accepting them as a difference of opinion. A loving and gracious offer of friendship should be extended with integrity. This means a willingness to speak of Christ when it is convenient and when it is not convenient as well as a commitment to train leaders and laymen alike in the task of sensitively bringing the message of the gospel to Jewish people they encounter.

The church has been most comfortable with the mission enterprises that allow us to meet a need in addition to the need for salvation. For example, we go to India and build a clinic or hospital which we staff with medical missionaries and nurses. As we tend to the physical needs of the people we seek to tell them about the Great Physician who can heal the sickness of the soul. Or maybe we will send our agricultural specialists to Africa where subsistence farming and drought have wreaked havoc on the population. As we teach them to provide for themselves through modern agricultural techniques, we hope to sow the precious seed of the gospel. These are fine avenues to travel so long as they lead to the gospel proclamation which they very often do. But what if these avenues are not available?

What does the church have to offer the Jews? Many Christians seek medical help from Jewish physicians. Jewish people do not need our medical expertise. Christians who have visited Israel and have seen the way the Jewish people have made the Negev to bloom know that Jews do not need our agricultural help, either. So what can the church bring to the Jewish people? The simple, unadorned, life-changing gospel message.

This puts Jewish evangelism on the cutting edge of missions. In our seeker-sensitive culture we prefer to offer people those things for which they immediately recognize their need. We do not like to risk rejection, and we particularly do not like to present the gospel in the context of dispute. But that is exactly the context within which Jewish evangelism will by definition take place. The best possible Christian response to Jewish resistance to the gospel is loving confrontation that is willing to risk offense, willing to be vulnerable, and willing to give a gentle yet firm answer for the hope that is within us.

Finally, the power of prayer works miracles in overcoming Jewish resistance to the gospel. A dear Christian couple prayed for my father's family every day for seven years without seeing any openness to the gospel. Suddenly, within a period of two weeks, my father and his entire immediate family came to faith in Christ. I am a bit skeptical when I hear someone describing miracles coming down as abundantly as rain in the spring, but after eighteen years of ministry I am fully convinced that God is still performing miracles. Paul tells us, "Jews require a sign." God has been gracious to provide those signs time and time again. I have met too many Jewish people who have been gloriously saved and forever changed by the miraculous power of God to dismiss such events as merely anecdotal information. The Christian who seeks to be effective in Jewish evangelism must be willing to pray with an expectation that God will answer with a miraculous demonstration of his power.

Some miracles are more obvious than others. One person awoke at three a.m., his room filled with an orange glow, and whereas he had never been inclined to accept the gospel, he suddenly knew it was true. Fred Wertheim, a survivor of the Holocaust, is now a Christian because, as he tells it, "Jesus visited him in his home." Other miracles are more subtle.

I was handing out gospel tracts in front of Macy's department store one bright sunny day in New York City. The big bold four inch letters on my T-shirt proclaimed, "Jews for Jesus." A well-dressed woman in her mid- to late sixties approached me and began to yell, "You should be ashamed of yourself. Do you know what you are doing? Does your mother know you're doing this?" Then she spat out words that cut like a knife. "You are trying to complete the work that Hitler began." She rolled up the sleeve of her dress to show me the numbers tattooed on her arm. Ruth is a survivor of Auschwitz. I understood Ruth's anger, but there seemed very little I could say to her at the time.

Weeks later, an older woman walked into the Jews for Jesus Friday evening chapel service. I recognized her immediately but could not remember where we had met. After the service I approached her and Ruth reminded me where we had met. I asked, "So what brings you here tonight?" She replied, "I have an open mind." Indeed. Ruth returned week after week and eventually it was my privilege to pray with her to receive Jesus as her messiah.

How can someone who is totally opposed to the gospel, so resistant and so hardened, turn and receive God's grace through faith in Jesus Christ? It is simply this: the same power that raised up Jesus from the grave is at work in the world today. God's power to save is the only real hope we have of overcoming anyone's resistance to the gospel—Jewish or otherwise. The good news is that God is as mighty to save today as he ever was and he can cut through any amount of resistance in the blink of an eye. The question is, will we be conduits for that saving power?

REFERENCES

Berger, David and Michael Wyschogrod. 1978. *Jews and "Jewish Christians."* New York: Ktav.

Brown, Michael. 1992. *Our Hands Are Stained with Blood.* Shippensburg, PA: Destiny Image.

Buchwald, Ephraim, "The Holocaust Is Killing America's Jews." *Los Angeles Times*, April 1992.

Encyclopaedia Judaica. 1972. "Jew." In *Encyclopaedia Judaica.* Vol. 10. P. 24. Jerusalem: Encyclopaedia Judaica/New York: Macmillan.

Goble, Phillip E. 1974. *Everything You Need to Grow a Messianic Synagogue.* Pasadena, CA: William Carey Library.

Hertz, Joseph H. 1961. *The Authorized Daily Prayer Book.* Revised edition. New York: Bloch.

Hinson, Keith. 1996. "Phil Roberts Defends SBC Stance in Christian-Jewish Panel Session." Southern Baptist Conference press release concerning the Fifteenth National Workshop on Christian-Jewish Relations, October 27-30, (October 31).

Jocz, Jakob. 1979. *The Jewish People and Jesus Christ: The Relationship between Church and Synagogue.* 3rd edition. Grand Rapids: Baker.

Lundell, Peter. 1995. "Behind Japan's Resistant Web: Understanding the Problem of *Nihonkyo*." *Missiology: An International Review* 23:4(October).

Luther, Martin. 1971. *Concerning the Jews and Their Lies. Luther's Works.* Vol. 47. Franklin Sherman, ed. Pp. 121–306. Philadelphia: Fortress.

Mayer, Hans Eberhard. 1972. *The Crusades.* John Gillingham, trans. New York: Oxford University Press.

McGavran, Donald. 1980. *Understanding Church Growth.* Revised edition. Grand Rapids: Eerdmans.

Miller, Jonathan. 1997. Letter to the editor. *The Birmingham News*, April 1.

Montgomery, Robert L. 1986. "Receptivity to an Outside Religion: Light from Interaction between Sociology and Missiology." *Missiology: An International Review* 14:3(July).

Parkes, James. 1981. *The Conflict of the Church and the Synagogue: A Study in the Origins of anti-Semitism.* New York: Atheneum.

Priest, Robert J. "Missionary Elenctics: Conscience and Culture." *Missiology: An International Review* 22:3(July 1994).

Rausch, David. 1984. *A Legacy of Hatred: Why Christians Must Not Forget the Holocaust.* Chicago: Moody.

Robinson, Richard. 1996. "Who Was a Jew?" In *Jewish Identity and Faith in Jesus.* Kai Kjær-Hansen, ed. Pp. 33-40. Jerusalem: Caspari Center.

Rosten, Leo. 1968. *The Joys of Yiddish.* New York: McGraw-Hill.

Rudin, A. James and Marvin R. Wilson, eds. 1987. *A Time to Speak: The Evangelical-Jewish Encounter.* Grand Rapids: Eerdmans/Austin, Center for Judaic-Christian Studies.

Sachar, Howard Morley. 1977. *The Course of Modern Jewish History, Updated and Expanded Edition.* New York: Delta.

Schiffman, Michael. 1992. *Return of the Remnant: The Rebirth of Messianic Judaism.* Baltimore: Lederer. (Originally titled *Return from Exile: The Re-Emergence of the Messianic Congregational Movement*).

Sigal, Gerald. 1980. *You Take Jesus, I'll Take God: How to Refute Christian Missionaries.* Los Angeles: Hanorah.

Singer, Tovia. 1995. *Let's Get Biblical.* Monsey, NY: Outreach Judaism.

Talmud, Babylonian. 1935–48. Sanhedrin 44a. I. Epstein, trans. and ed. London : Soncino.

Tanenbaum, Marc H., Marvin R. Wilson, A. James Rudin, eds. 1978. *Evangelicals and Jews in Conversation on Scripture, Theology, and History.* Grand Rapids: Baker.

Troki, Isaac. 1970. *Faith Strengthened.* New York: Ktav.

Williams, A. Lukyn. 1919. *A Manual of Christian Evidences for Jewish People.* London: Society for Promoting Christian Knowledge.

Recommended Reading

Anti-Semitism

Brown, Michael. 1992. *Our Hands Are Stained with Blood.* Shippensburg, PA: Destiny Image.

Parkes, James. 1981. *The Conflict of the Church and the Synagogue: A Study in the Origins of Antisemitism.* New York: Atheneum.

Jewish History

Johnson, Paul. 1987. *A History of the Jews.* New York: Harper and Row.

Sachar, Howard Morley. 1977. *The Course of Modern Jewish History, Updated and Expanded Edition*. New York: Delta.

The Movement of Jewish Believers in Jesus

Elgvin, Torleif, ed. 1993. *Israel and Yeshua: Festschrift Celebrating the Tenth Anniversary of Caspari Center for Biblical and Jewish Studies, Jerusalem*. Jerusalem: Caspari Center for Biblical and Jewish Studies.

Goble, Phil. 1974. *Everything You Need to Grow a Messianic Synagogue*. Pasadena, CA: William Carey Library.

Jocz, Jakob. 1979. *The Jewish People and Jesus Christ: The Relationship between Church and Synagogue*. 3rd edition. Grand Rapids: Baker, © 1949.

Kjær-Hansen, Kai, ed. 1996. *Jewish Identity and Faith in Jesus*. Jerusalem: Caspari Center.

Riggans, Walter. 1995. *Yeshua ben David: Why Do the Jewish People Reject Jesus as Their Messiah?* Crowborough, UK: MARC.

Rosen, Moishe. 1974. *Jews for Jesus*. Old Tappan, NJ: Revell.

Schiffman, Michael. 1992. *Return of the Remnant: The Rebirth of Messianic Judaism*. Baltimore: Lederer.

Counter-Missionary Books and Responses

Berger, David and Michael Wyschogrod. 1978. *Jews and "Jewish Christians."* New York: Ktav. Counter-missionary.

Fruchtenbaum, Arnold G. 1974. *Jesus Was a Jew*. Tustin, CA: Ariel Ministries. Messianic Jewish apologetics.

Levine, Samuel. 1980. *You Take Jesus, I'll Take God: How to Refute Christian Missionaries*. Los Angeles: Hanorah. Counter-missionary.

Singer, Tovia. 1995. *Let's Get Biblical* [15-tape cassette set]. Monsey, NY: Outreach Judaism. Counter-missionary.

Troki, Isaac. 1970. *Faith Strengthened*. New York: Ktav. Counter-missionary.

Williams, A. Lukyn. 1919. *A Manual of Christian Evidences for Jewish People*. London: Society for Promoting

Christian Knowledge. Messianic Jewish apologetics (by a Gentile Christian).

Evangelical-Jewish Dialogue

Rudin, A. James and Marvin R. Wilson, eds. 1987. *A Time to Speak: The Evangelical-Jewish Encounter*. Grand Rapids: Eerdmans/Austin: Center for Judaic-Christian Studies.

Tanenbaum, Marc H., Marvin R. Wilson, A. James Rudin, eds. 1978. *Evangelicals and Jews in Conversation on Scripture, Theology, and History*. Grand Rapids: Baker.

Tanenbaum, Marc H., Marvin R. Wilson, A. James Rudin, eds. 1984. *Evangelicals and Jews in an Age of Pluralism*. Grand Rapids: Baker.

Chapter 5

ENCOUNTERING MUSLIM RESISTANCE

Kevin Higgins

From one point of view, the history of Christian attempts to communicate with Muslims is also a history of the search for ways to diminish Muslim resistance to the gospel message. Various approaches have been advocated and used, including an increasing interest in "contextualization" as a means of lessening resistance.

For the purposes of this chapter, I would like to use a working image of contextualization rather than a definition per se. In literary criticism (and biblical exegesis) a staple ingredient in the "mix" of tools for properly understanding a text is the requirement that it be taken in "context," that is, seen in the light of the surrounding literary terrain. Without this step, it is very easy to misunderstand a writer completely.

So too with the gospel. I will use the word "contextualization" in this chapter to refer to the process of seeking to so communicate the gospel that it is seen in the light of the "hearer's" surroundings (culture) in such a way that there is an "aha" experience, an authentic cognitive and emotive grasp of what the message means.

There is not much space in this setting for a full treatment of this subject. I will focus on three points, making reference to several context-specific examples along the way.

Message and Contextualization

A reading of the history of Muslim/Christian encounters leaves me with the impression that an underlying assumption of most approaches to communicating with Muslims has been the idea that if we can just explain the message more clearly and sweep away Muslim misunderstandings of the message (e.g., that the Trinity does not include Mary, etc.) then our Muslim friends will understand and believe. We can see this behind the early work of John of Damascus and in the more recent and more sympathetic works of Zwemer and Cragg.

My first year in the country of my primary concern was largely spent in applying this unspoken philosophy of ministry. Simply put, I believed that if I could help Muslims understand the message, then they would not be resistant to it. My studies of Islamics and the Qur'an and the uses I made of those studies were directed towards this end—the clearing up of misunderstandings.

I suppose I still hold to this, but I am learning that to "understand" is far more complicated and nuanced than the usual intellectually oriented assumptions would lead one to think.

It is not merely the explanation of the message that is needed, but the setting of the message within a context, a conceptual and emotive universe, so that it makes sense inside of that world.

This issue of message and context of course has at least two dimensions. It is not only the context of the hearer (in this case Muslim hearers) but the message's own context as well which needs careful attention and wholistic understanding.

I do not have the space here to deal with the latter dimension in any depth, but it is important to note that it is simplistic to assume that my particular understanding of the gospel is truly the gospel message in its own context. Suffice it to say that we are all in danger of merely preaching to others that facet of the gospel which converted us. So nineteenth century evangelicalism spawned a movement of men and women who went forth with "hearts warmed" by the rediscovery of justification by faith. Roman Catholic missionaries in the past have had other gospel themes burning in their hearts (e.g., the vision of the body of Christ as an organically and historically connected community linked to the head and supplying life to the world through its members). High church Anglicans have tended to emphasize the incarnation in a way similar to, but distinct from, their Roman colleagues.

These are all (I would contend) true as *facets* of the gospel, but none can be equated with the gospel. A fuller understanding of the full range of themes found in the New Testament proclamation of the gospel will help to preserve us from the danger of equating any single facet with the whole. But contextualization requires more. When the message crosses cultural lines, it needs to be communicated in such a way that not only is it authentically the actual gospel, but also in such a way as to have integrity or congruence with the new context. An example will illustrate this.

I had the privilege to be invited to help coordinate a major study of a reported people movement among Muslims in a particular south Asian country. This was a fairly controversial and highly contextualized effort. I had been working alongside some of the national leadership for nearly a year when the project began and so had ample access to observe and learn.

It had been reported that tens of thousands of Muslims had become followers of Jesus while remaining Muslim. In some missionary circles, controversy raged over what it meant to be Muslim, what it meant to be Christian, what it meant to be a follower of Jesus, whether the reported "followers" had actually accepted and understood the gospel, and so forth.

Working closely with a major seminary (which gave the training and oversaw the development of the whole study process to ensure proper standards) we designed, implemented, and collected the results from the study. My point here is not to defend or deny the reported numbers (more than many expected, fewer than reported), or to pass judgment upon the "validity" of the faith expressed among those involved in the "movement" (we found a wide mix ranging from very articulate "Christian" expressions to very "confused" conglomerations of terminology. The latter I found encouraging as it gave evidence that people were not trying to give "expected" answers.)

I am also not going to wrestle here with the controversial particulars about continued attendance at mosque prayers (some did continue, some did not; some met for what we can only describe as pietist study groups outside of the mosque setting but still saw themselves as Muslim), or views of the Qur'an and Bible (again, a wide range).

What I do want to point out from the results of the study is that the message of the gospel was presented in a "setting," a context, which seemed to hit home with a large number of hearers, and the context was the culture of the hearers.

In the country in question, the social fabric includes a pattern of patronism and intermediaries in which jobs, selection for certain schools, positions in government, and so forth, all depend upon being linked to the right patron, and the right "go between," the right, if you will, intercessor.

The role of Jesus as intercessor is a theme of Scripture of course. And it is a theme important to many Christians. But it is probably *not* the first title of Jesus that a western pastor considers for his sermon series on the work of Christ. The western church (I mean this in the historic sense of the Latin church, through the Reformation and down to today) has tended to be impressed and shaped in terms of soteriology, largely by the concept of atonement and substitution. This can be seen in the Latin fathers, and is reflected in popular tracts today (e.g., the Four Spiritual Laws).

But this is only one facet of the New Testament proclamation. How did the movement described above come up with the facet "intercessor"? Was there a western missiological genius who stepped outside of his/her own cultural stream and objectively selected the right theme and then "presto," plugged it in and it worked?

No. The proclamation of Jesus as Intercessor Par Excellence seems to have been the collaborative insight of several national leaders, or bridge people, who had learned a good bit of missiology (a "western" science) but were free thinking enough to find their own expression and not merely mime the missionary. It seems likely too that similar ideas were floating around the Christian and missionary community within that country, but found powerful expression through national believers from a Muslim background who had been exposed to these ideas.

So, the message in context is the first theme we touch on in this chapter. This relates to the vital task of facilitating the "aha" experience, in which the gospel is seen and heard and felt to make sense inside of a specific cultural setting. I would argue that this has two dimensions. There is a need for explanation through which the gospel is constantly looked at and understood. There is also contextualization through which the gospel is "set" within a new context so that others within that context may understand and believe it.

But already we have begun to move to the next point, for the placing of the message into a new cultural context begins to raise questions about who it is that does the placing. If the message is to fit into the context, how does the messenger relate to that context?

Messenger and Contextualization

In the first sections I have sought to illustrate two major points. First, the gospel "in context" means the gospel communicated so as to have congruence within a specific setting. Second, I began to hint at the fact that the best vehicle for accomplishing this may not be (I would want to say, very likely will not be) a true outsider, a foreigner.

Yet I acknowledge the fact that in true frontier settings only a foreigner (though not necessarily a western foreigner) will be available to be the messenger. Yes, I acknowledge this and even preached it fervently during deputation visits, but I want to raise issues here not about how the message fits into the cultural context but also about how the messenger fits.

In my experiences with both practical contextualization (i.e., the full range, from adopting local Muslim dress, to vocabulary, to praying in mosques, to assuming the label "Muslim," to experimenting with *tawiz* and other expressions of folk Islam, etc.) and tentmaking, I am becoming more and more convinced that both are leading me to ever deeper reflections on the issue of having integrity, which is bigger than a mere commitment to honesty and faithfulness. Integrity for me means a wholistic congruence between my heart, my worldview, my job, my organizational ties, my roles in society, and more.

How does a messenger from the outside fit enough into a new cultural context to get the message into that context as well? Is contextualization (becoming Muslim to Muslims) the answer? My own journey has lead me in that direction, but not blindly, and I have learned some things along the way.

I was asked in one Muslim country where I had been resident for some time whether I might let a young couple from another western country come and stay with me to observe our philosophy of ministry and ways of integrating business and ministry among Muslims. I agreed.

I had been told by the couple themselves that they were convinced that radical contextualization was the mode of ministry to which God was leading them. This fit my own sense of calling. But I was alarmed within a few hours of our first meeting to realize how little this well-meaning couple knew about anything Islamic: the Qur'an, *namaz/salat*, Muhammad, and so forth.

They wanted immediately upon arrival to go visit a local mosque for prayers. I did not allow them to go and explained to them that until they could demonstrate that they knew what they were talking about I would not allow them to go, unless they explained to all that they were observers.

I know it is popular in some circles to affirm "yes, I am a Muslim" under the rubric that the word merely means one who is submitted. But this is not putting the messenger in context. It lacks a deeper integrity, though it is true enough semantically.

I will push it still further. I used to advocate that we foreigners in frontier settings, in order to be "in context" should become Muslim in the sense of acting, talking, smelling, praying, and preaching like Muslims (with the distinction that Jesus—Isa-al Masih—would be the focal point of our spirituality and life).

For many hearing or reading this that will be a hard position to stomach and I sympathize. I now reject it in most cases, but not for theological reasons. I am instead more and more convinced that it lacks integrity to receive a missionary income via donations from Christians, and to itinerate among supporting churches on furloughs, but claim to be a Muslim and act like a Muslim "in the field."

For the messenger to be properly "in context" means that he/she really fits, really connects to, the cultural setting in an appropriate way. This is more than dress, language, vocabulary, or even ritual. There must be integrity, congruence. I do not think there are many non-Muslim-background Christians, whether western or national, who would pass the integrity test for claiming to be Muslim to Muslims. (I hesitate to use the word national because, as one of my Asian friends is always ready to point out, westerners are nationals too; they just have different nations!)

So, what is the relationship of messenger to context? There needs to be some sort of getting near, drawing alongside, learning, and so forth, if for no other reason than to find the bridge to people from within that culture who can with integrity speak the new message from inside the culture.

One common means of gaining such access to a culture is to seek a business visa, or student visa, or some other alternative means. My own personal history has included the attempt to gain and maintain a business visa.

But integrity crops up again. My first business visa was exactly what most business visas (or student visas or whatever) are to most missionaries: my key to the country. Now I was "in." I did it. Now I could get on with being a missionary.

Surprise. The government actually wanted to see proof that I was in business, and since it was only a visa, I had no such proof (though I had honestly tried to export some fish). I was gone within ten months of my arrival.

I came back, dug in, learned about business, started to learn a new trade (aquaculture), started a company, made a business plan, raised financing for the venture (mostly our own money went into it), took more time in another country to learn more about the new trade, and went back to our target country. Now, I thought, "I have integrity."

But we still received our personal support from churches, and this enabled us to live in the artificial situation of not really having to have the business make a go of it in order to eat.

These two points are somewhat theoretical issues, but the problem got extremely practical pretty quickly.

We had been operating a hatchery in a village. God blessed the work spiritually (though we still have not seen many fish come out alive!) A local business colleague somehow heard about the spiritual dimension of the work, did some digging, and discovered the truth: this Kevin Higgins is really a missionary. The attempt at overcoming resistance via contextualization and tentmaking actually ended up generating more resistance.

Were I to do it over again (and we are still at it), I think I would work harder at raising enough financing and the right team to run the business as a business, including paying the employees through the business, not through separate mission-governed accounts. Tentmaking is not an entry strategy! It is a lifestyle and a role one can choose to adopt for any of a number of reasons (only one of which should be the issue of access). But if chosen, the tentmaker better actually make (and sell!) some tents! The same principle applies to any other form of access.

So, I have argued that the contextualization of the message is not merely an issue of explanation, but involves placing the message inside the cultural context so that it "fits" and can be understood from the inside of the culture. I have hinted that this can only finally be done by an insider, and I have examined the issue of integrity related to outsiders trying to become insiders (practical contextualization) or alongsiders (via tentmaking). This is all begging the question of what the aim and object of all this is.

If, as I have argued, only insiders will really contextualize the gospel, and if, as I have hinted, the foreigner's role is to get near enough to find the first insiders (the bridge people), what does this say about the end result we should be aiming at? And what model might we find in Scripture to help point the way for us?

MODEL AND CONTEXTUALIZATION

Historically, missionary movements have tended to look to Paul as the model missionary. Paul has been the inspiration for thousands to go boldly where no gospel was preached before.

There is something natural about this. The New Testament is largely a Pauline set of texts. He is a central figure in the theology and missiology of the early church. His character is captivating and real. He is a towering personality, full of courage and yet somehow possessing sensitive emotions. His adventures spark the wanderlust of many readers.

But is he really a model for missionaries in the sense of cultural outsiders who seek to get the gospel inside a culture to which they themselves are strangers? Was Paul really a cross-cultural missionary? We need to recall that he was born a Jew and so could with integrity *truly* be a Jew to the Jew. But he was also born into the Greek language and culture and worldview of the god-fearing Greek, the slice of Greek culture which seems to have formed the target for much of his direct ministry. He could thus with integrity also truly be a Greek to the Greek.

There is another New Testament figure, closely related to Paul's ministry, who would seem to be a model for cross-cultural mission. This man was in the right place at the right time and recognized in Paul the gifts and calling needed to minister to Greeks. He served to link Paul with the suspicious leadership of the Jerusalem church and defended Paul to them. He stood alongside Paul in ministry at Antioch and accompanied Paul on itinerant ministry, though always taking an apparent back seat to Paul's leadership. And in the end, this man simply fades into oblivion so that the story of the people movement among the Greeks is largely a story of Paul's ministry, not his own (though without him it is doubtful that Paul would ever have been what we know).

This man Barnabas seems to me to be the model, or at least a model, after which we need to pattern our ministries. If we do, we will find ways to come alongside others. We will have eyes to see whom God may be raising up as a new Paul, no matter how difficult the new Paul may be for other Christian leaders to accept. We will have the humility to stand in the background.

And in the end we will have the grace to face the fact that our role is really to disappear. If Barnabas is our model, we can trust God to raise up his messengers to voice his message in the contexts of the remaining cultures among which we long to see his kingdom come.

Chapter 6

ENCOUNTERING JAPANESE RESISTANCE

Stan Conrad

INTRODUCTION

Some years ago while in Japan, I was very challenged by this topic and read David C. E. Liao's book *The Unresponsive: Resistant or Neglected?* Donald McGavran wrote the foreword in which he stated, "Sometimes unresponsiveness is due to hardness of heart, pride, or aloofness, but more often than we like to think, it is due to neglect" (Liao 1972:7). By using the word "neglect," the meaning is that the language had not been learned and that there were not Hakka-speaking congregations for their fellowship. Mr. Liao's contention is that people "reject the Christian religion, not because they dislike it, but because they do not want to be swallowed up by another culture" (1972:14), and he substantiates this premise by showing how the Hakkas were treated in the Minan- and Mandarin-speaking congregations.

A more recent personal experience had to do with our son's employment by a large corporation involved in trade with Japan. When he returned after his first visit and showed them all the sales he had made, he said that his superiors were amazed and told him that they had been trying to do that for years. He said it was not difficult for him because he was raised in Japan and understood the sensitivity of the culture in areas of business negotiations which those who had been sent before did not. In fact, that company has now sent him there to set up a branch office to penetrate further the Japanese market.

Drawing upon thirty-five years of cross-cultural church planting in Japan, our position is that the title of this chapter might better be "Japanese Resistance: Fact and Fiction." This can be demonstrated both from the analytic and from the experiential viewpoint. It was our privilege to be involved in the planting of eleven churches of which eight were from scratch, and we give praise to God that all are functioning today as his lights in that needy land.

THE FACT OF JAPANESE RESISTANCE TO THE GOSPEL

Anyone with a minimal amount of exposure to missions in Japan has probably heard that Christians in Japan number just one percent of the population. Not only that, but the ratio of churches to population is around one for every seventeen thousand people. Probably one of the questions most asked of missionaries to Japan is, "Why is the response between Korea and Japan so different?" In order to understand more fully why Japan is a "resistant" land, we need to understand some of the historical and cultural factors which have moved Japan in that direction.

Historical Factors

I believe that there are two main historical factors which have caused great harm to the spread of the gospel in Japan. As is fairly well known, the initial entrance of Protestant missions saw a response in which "every three years the membership of the church doubled" (Drummond 1971:192). The years from 1859–1890 were called the "golden years," but something happened in 1890 that would change all of that. It was the issuance of "The Imperial Rescript on Education."

In the very year that this Rescript was declared as the law of the land, the gain in membership dropped from 5,677 new members in 1888 to 1,199 in 1890 (Thomas 1959:183). While seeking to affirm ancient Confucian virtues, the law made the "ancestors" into "divine emperors" and ultimately the veneration of them became the test of State Shinto (Holtom 1943:80). One missionary to Japan refers to the "Rescript" as "the most damaging blow ever struck the Christian cause in Japan" (Young 1958:44). Of course it needs to be pointed out that the "unequal treaties" also did much to stir the development of nationalism, but as Drummond points out, "A focus of this nationalism was the cult of veneration of the emperor which took on more and more the elements of religious faith" (1971:243). This nationalistic spirit spread to the churches and resulted in great controversy concerning the status of churches receiving mission aid. At one point, in 1897, the very validity of the concept of a foreign mission organization carrying out ecclesiastical function was called into question, and Iglehart comments that, "It is probable that at this time no such question had been raised anywhere else in the foreign missionary world" (1959:122).

In addition to nationalism, another contributing historical factor to Japan's resistance to the gospel has to be liberalism in the church. Yanagita points out that actually liberalism arrived early in Japan and that among the three large theological groups (liberal, sub-orthodox, and orthodox) even the orthodox group was not truly orthodox (1957:51–57). The liberal school emphasized Christ as teacher and example (Drummond 1971:218) whereas the sub-orthodox group held to the orthodox view of Christ (1971:219) but was not favorable to a strong creedal statement or the view of verbal inspiration of the Bible (Young 1958:35–37). The interesting thing is that the leader of the orthodox group, Kanzo Uchimura, was captured by syncretism and made such statements as "Is Buddhism an enemy of Christianity? On the contrary, is there not the common ground upon which the two stand side by side?" (1958:58). He also capitulated to an extreme nationalism, as is seen in his most famous statement, "I love two J's and no third; one is Jesus and the other is Japan. I do not know which I love more, Jesus or Japan" (1958:48). I have treated the historical factors in more detail in my doctoral project, "The Relationship of the Japan Evangelical Free Church Mission and the Japan Evangelical

Free Church Conference: A Survey and an Analysis" (pp. 124–149), and it seems evident that the historical factors of liberalism and nationalism profoundly affected the receptivity of the gospel in Japan.

Cultural Factors

In 1989 a book of over six hundred pages entitled *The Enigma of Japanese Power* by Harold van Wolferen was written and is illustrative of many that seek to explain the "enigma of the Japanese mind" to westerners. The basic distinction between the two can best be understood in terms of worldview in that the Japanese are concrete relational thinkers, as contrasted with westerners, who believe in universal absolutes that are abstract in nature (Hesselgrave 1978:207–208). Another description of this phenomena in Japan is what Takie Lebra calls its "social relativism" which is at the core of its mentality (1976:2–9).

This brings us to a consideration of the psychological characteristics of the Japanese people that contribute to their resistance to the gospel. In the doctoral project referred to previously, I have treated four of these as crucial and exemplary of this mindset. The four include: the concept of selfhood, ethnocentricity, irrationalism, and dependency. Because of space limitations I will only treat the first one, but all are important in dealing with the Japanese mind.

Any person with experience in the Japanese culture will readily acknowledge that individuality in Japan has much less emphasis than in the West and is approached in a much different manner. Minami, a respected Japanese writer, acknowledges that even after the Meiji period, "there was no social foundation on which the Japanese could establish a free and individual self" (1971:17). The effects of this are considerable. For instance in the area of law, Kawashima Takeyoshi notes that there is "no room for the existence of the image of an individual who is 'equal' to every other on the ground that he is 'independent' of every other" (cited in Moore 1967:263). Ozaki points out that a person "who doggedly pursues his rights of private property ownership is considered selfish and avaricious—a foe to society" (1978:129). It can readily be seen how the emphasis on self-denial and submission of the individual causes resistance to a gospel that emphasizes personal salvation and deliverance from sin. In discussing the matter of self-negation in favor of the group and loyalty to the group over personal rights, Moore comments that "this emphasis has seemed stronger in Japan than in any other major tradition" (1967:299). It cannot be denied that there are psychological aspects of Japanese culture that are strongly resistant to the entrance of the evangelical gospel.

This is also true of some sociological aspects as well. In the doctoral project referred to earlier, I examined three of these: the concept of the vertical society, the concept of reciprocity, and the concept of harmony. In one sense all of these are related to each other, but they can also be examined separately. We will only treat the concept of harmony since this best illustrates how these sociological considerations present obstacles to the free entrance of the gospel to all.

The word and Chinese character for harmony in Japan is the simple *wa*, but the fact that Andrew Nelson lists sixty-four different combinations of this character with other Chinese characters shows how powerful a concept it is (1962:664–665). The famous expert on Japan, Edwin Reischauer, states that

> The key Japanese value is harmony, which they seek to achieve by a subtle process of mutual understanding, almost by intuition, rather than by a sharp analysis of conflicting views or by clear-cut decisions" (1977:135).

Ozaki states, "The theme of harmony runs deep in Japanese history" (1978:138).

The support for harmony has a long history and in fact goes back to Article 1 of Prince Shotoku's Constitution which states, "Japan, unlike other countries where rights and duties prevail, must strive to solve interpersonal cases by harmony and compromise" (Moore 1967:278). In addition, Hajime Nakamura reminds us that, "One reason for the central emphasis in Japan on harmony is, 'The peculiarly Japanese conception of the prestige of the emperor and the Emperor Institution'" (cited in Moore 1967:152). The pervasiveness of harmony is well illustrated in the Japanese language by the use of the word *ne* which translates as "isn't it." In ordinary conversation, this expression is used profusely to prevent any kind of disagreement from the listener (Lebra 1976:39).

There are other areas of life where the emphasis on harmony is extremely important, and one of these is the matter of litigation. While there is one lawyer for every three hundred sixty people in the USA, there is just one for every 9,294 in Japan (van Wolferan 1989:281). When people have to resort to litigation in place of a harmonious resolution of conflicts, it is considered to be a loss of face in Japan. In order to reinforce the practice of harmony, the Japanese have a proverb that states, "The nail that sticks up gets pounded down." In other words, to insist on one's rights at the expense of group harmony is considered a breach of culture.

In 1965 Robert Whiting wrote a very interesting book entitled *You Gotta Have Wa*. It listed the Ten Commandments for foreigners playing baseball in Japan, and one of these is, "Do not disturb the harmony of the team" (1989:85). Whiting claims that if you ask a Japanese manager what is the most important ingredient for a winning team, he would assert it to be harmony. He claims that most of the same managers would consider the hiring of an American as beginning on the road to destruction (1989:78). Our experience in Japan has verified this as we have seen great baseball stars come from the West only to fail in the Japanese setting while others who were less known do very well because they learned the importance of team unity and harmony.

Certainly more needs to be said to treat fully the subject of Japanese resistance to the gospel, but these few insights into the history and culture of Japan demonstrate the deep-seated nature of this opposition. We must also remember that the high degree of homogeneity in Japan gives great reinforcement to this worldview, and the task of missions, in every sense of the word, becomes a true battle.

THE FICTION OF JAPANESE RESISTANCE TO THE GOSPEL

At this point some may feel that what has been said only confirms the views of people who question the necessity for sending missionaries to Japan in light of its resistance and cost. Is such a conclusion valid? I for one would strongly disagree. Years ago I read Shusaku Endo's famous novel *Silence*, in which he questioned the power of the gospel to penetrate Japan. His famous statement, "You were defeated by the swamp of Japan," (1969:12) refers to the fact that the swamp "sucks up all sorts of ideologies, transforming them into itself and distorting them in the process" (1969:13). The story is based on the early Roman Catholic mission in Japan, which was crushed by severe persecution. I remember sharing my impressions of the book with my co-worker pastor at the time, and hearing his strong reply that the novel was only one part of the picture. This co-worker left our largest church to become a home missionary to what was then our smallest church, and he was committed to showing that there was a sizable area of fiction associated with the understandings that many had regarding the gospel taking root in Japan. Some of these so-called "obstacles" that confront the missionary often are reinforced by a fictitious understanding rather than a true understanding of the situation.

Internal Obstacles to Church Growth

Of these internal obstacles, I can think of none greater than that of the image of the church in Japan. Since the church has been small for so long, it is assumed that this is a given and that we should not expect any change to occur. I remember the pastor of one of our larger churches chiding a fellow pastor at a ministerial gathering because he was only preparing one thousand flyers for distribution instead of ten thousand. He was only thinking of the immediate surroundings of the church and the number of people who could be involved in distribution rather than using the newspapers for extensive coverage. It is actually true that there are Japanese pastors who do not want their churches to exceed fifty in number because this is the number that they can handle and that can support a pastor financially. Toru Takakura comments on this by stating,

> Once a church building is built and the local congregation is able to stand on its own feet, all its energies are poured into maintaining itself, and it ends in the establishment of a small, in-grown, self-satisfied clique (1970:19).

One thing that is helping to overcome this problem is a dynamic evangelical ecumenicity where Christians unite in citywide or area-wide efforts. After a large united effort in the city of Nagoya, one of our believers said to me in surprise, "I never dreamed that there were so many Christians in this city."

Another problem related to church image is perhaps related to the word for church in Japanese (*kyookai*) which literally means, "a place of studying together." Of course the study of the Bible is of paramount importance, but the emphasis should not be on trying to create a society of the learned. The picture of the early church in Acts 2 places great emphasis on fellowship in prayer and sharing. The pastor of the large church who was previously mentioned introduced our Free Churches to the concept of having simple noon meals together on Sunday, and this greatly enhanced the image of the church. A balance between truth and life began to be seen by many.

Finally, there is the matter of Western influence in the church. Since the church entered Japan from the West, the impression was left that it must therefore be western to the point where one writer comments, "Even the style of architecture of Christian Churches is alien, resembling more the New England meeting house than anything Japanese in flavor" (Lee 1967:162). In the area of communication, Hesselgrave must have been thinking of Japan when he wrote, "Messages prepared by Western authors in Western idiom, for Western audiences are hastily translated, printed, and distributed in Latin America, Africa, and Asia" (1978:407). The organizational pattern of the Western church is also followed, in contrast to a more indigenous pattern as is used by the Soka Gakkai organization. Yamamori asserts that the vertical, horizontal, and diagonal organizational web framework of that group has prevented membership leakage, which is a major problem in the church in Japan (1974:151). I can still remember attending a watch night service in Japan which our pastor was desirous of having since he had attended these while studying in America. He did not give much attention to the fact that our church would also have a New Year's Day service because this is a very important holiday in Japan, whereas in America it is reserved primarily for football. Only as true efforts are made in contextualization will the church be able to shed the label of a "Western religion."

A second internal obstacle has to do with the matter of church leadership. Here we need to consider both pastoral and lay ministry. It is apparent, from a general view of the Japanese church, that it has followed Western models with rare exception. One leader expressed his concern by saying, "The present practice of taking a young inexperienced person and placing him in a position of leadership after training in an isolated academic atmosphere is detrimental to church growth (Vanderbilt 1972:6). Again, the high importance given to intellectual attainment, as over against a pastoral ministry, is counter-productive. One survey of pastors revealed that, in terms of usage of time, theological study rated fourth and evangelism sixth! (Jacobsen 1977:12–14). This occurs in a land that is only one percent Christian.

Not only the area of intellectualism, but the matter of pastoral hierarchy needs to be addressed as well. As pointed out earlier, Japan has a vertical social structure so hierarchy cannot be avoided, but Dale makes a point of distinction "between hierarchical authoritative leadership and single-handed autocratic leadership" (1975:158). It is interesting to note that even authoritarian organizations like Soka Gakkai have been able to incorporate multiple leadership into their structure. Braun has correctly pointed out that "Japan has a higher ratio of clergy to churches, than any other country in the world" (1971:34). This is not only indicative of how central the pastor is to the life of the church, but how dependent the believers are upon him. In Japan even the women's meeting is dependent upon the pastor's presence! This unhealthy dependence needs to be altered.

While it is true that the hierarchical pastorate can be a factual representation of cultural resistance, it does not have to be so. It was my privilege to work with experienced pastors in the Kinki (Osaka, Kyoto, Kobe area), Nagoya, Tokyo, and Sendai areas. These men were all serving as home missionaries of the denomination when we teamed up, and though all exerted their leadership, it was a servant leadership which resulted in successful church planting. The last effort (Sendai) was in northern Japan, which is considered very resistant, but by using a team approach and much prayer, we saw a self-supporting church planted in two years, and that church has now given birth to its first daughter church. God did some extraordinary things in answer to prayer, and pastoral leadership was not a negative, but rather a positive factor in the success of that work.

Lay leadership is a difficult subject in Japan because of the time demands put upon corporation workers. There is, however, a move in Japan to increase the amount of time that an average worker can have for leisure time, so the church needs to be resourceful at this point. I remember a lady who had been a Christian for fifteen years, and who began attending our church membership group in the new church we were planting. When we began to study Christian doctrine, she said this was all new to her since her previous pastor had said that all that was expected of her was that she attend and contribute in the offering. Sincere efforts need to be made to train lay people to become leaders and evangelists if the number of Christians in Japan is ever going to change significantly. Again, if one looks at the extensive training that the Soka Gakkai gives their followers, it is not "fiction" to believe that this is possible within the structure of the church.

A third area of internal obstacles that is part of the fiction of resistance has to do with the area of church extension. The fact remains that Japan, with its well trained leadership, modern infrastructure, and financial capacity still has about one church for every seventeen thousand people. There are several contributing reasons for this dismal situation with one of them being that the average Japanese Christian feels that this is the task of the missionary. Apparently, early in the history of the church in Japan, this concept was sown and has not been replaced by one that is more missiologically correct.

Another aspect of the difficulty of church extension is that many churches are reluctant to sacrifice their believers so that they can become part of the nucleus for a new church. I am amazed at how many people are members of churches that they rarely or never attend because they live too far away but they send their contributions there and thus are considered members in good standing. To plant churches without having some believers who can demonstrate the Christian life is, to say the least, an arduous task.

A third hurdle to church extension is the high cost of land and building as well as the difficulty in finding suitable rental locations. Public schools are not available for religious use and Japanese homes are usually too small so kindergartens and other types of rentals must be procured. Obviously, this obstacle cannot be overcome without great sacrifice and commitment, but I believe a source of great strength can be found in the joint efforts of churches toward church planting goals. In 1994–1995 it was our privilege to return to Japan to fill a temporary need in our Tokyo office. Shortly after arrival, I was contacted by one of our leading pastors to assist in a church planting effort by his church and one in a neighboring city. These two churches had raised 1.5 million dollars to buy land and erect a three-story building. Each church contributed about ten members, and all of this would be ready by November 1994, but their pastor elect would not graduate from his Ph.D. studies until March 1995 so I was asked to work with the other two pastors until he arrived. By the time he arrived, the church had passed the thirty mark and thus was already larger than many Japanese congregations. It is amazing what can happen when the Body of Christ is committed and works together! This surely points out that the church extension obstacle is in reality "fiction" that needs to give way to reality.

External Obstacles to Church Growth

While most of you by now probably would agree that the internal obstacles to church growth can be addressed optimistically, you may feel that the external ones present a Herculean problem. I have selected the three which I consider to be the most formidable: the Japanese religions, the Japanese social structure, and the Japanese language.

Obviously the most difficult part of dealing with the Japanese religions is that they are considered to be indigenous to Japan. I remember the surprise and amazement of some of our Christians when they learned from a Christian lecturer that Japanese Buddhism and the "Danka System" (a method of registering all people at the Buddhist temple) was really forced upon the Japanese and that original Buddhism had nothing to do with the worship of the dead. The fact is that Buddhism has adapted to the Japanese people in their love of nature, aesthetic beauty, and festival celebrations. Generally held opinions change slowly in Japan, but if the church prepares its people to understand more fully the content of Japanese Buddhism and the need to contextualize the Christian faith in Japan, this would decrease the difficulty considerably. Robert Lee mentions a comment by a police officer who referred to the church building as "the big brown building with a funny tower on top" (1967:73). In contrast to this, one can see in the buildings of the new religions that they identify with the Japanese culture.

While there are many benefits that accrue from serious study and dialogue with the existent Japanese religions, including such strategic insights as have been noted from Soka Gakkai methodology, it is always necessary to be on one's guard. As David Hesselgrave reminds us,

> Any form of dialogue that compromises the uniqueness of the Christian gospel and the necessity that the adherents of other faiths repent and believe it should be rejected and supplanted by forms of dialogue that enjoin conversion to Christ (1978:237).

The second external obstacle that has been mentioned is that of the Japanese social structure. We have already noted that in Japan there exists a strongly knit group culture, whereas Yamamori tells us that, "The Christianity which was introduced to Japan for the first time in the mid-nineteenth century was highly individualistic" (1974:19). Susumu Akahoshi describes this "collectivist dependency mentality" as one that is developed from infancy (cited in Dale 1975:170–171) and thus extremely difficult to change. Instead of fighting this structure, however, would it not be wiser to use it for the kingdom? For instance, missionary Paul Boschman incorporated into his missionary work a strong emphasis on following the family lines of the Christians in the church as the most important potential for evangelistic growth. His premise was that "each member must become the gateway to his kin" (1968:70).

Another way to use the social structure is to use the neighborhood associations *tonarigumi* which are well developed, and whose social organizational patterns have been made use of by such organizations as the Soka Gakkai in Japan. The great benefit of this is that it breaks down the impersonal nature of formal religion and replaces it with a more personal and intimate type of relationship. David Hesselgrave lists four characteristics: a neutral location, a recognized leader, informal meetings with total participation, and open channels of communication (1978:360–364). As the church grows, this type of structure greatly facilitates the maintenance of feelings of belongingness and participation.

Finally, the last external obstacle that needs some attention is that of the Japanese language. Perhaps Lee best describes the dilemma that the Western Christian communicator faces when he says that "One has to understand the Japanese mode of communication which Westerners might think devious or circuitous, but which actually is subtle, symbolic, and sensitive to feelings" (1967:165). To be aware of this distinction as a "cultural pattern" and not a moral failure can help the missionary greatly in his or her communication.

A larger problem is actually the vocabulary itself. Charles Corwin describes the frustration he experienced after learning Japanese equivalents for Christian concepts and then after using them discovered that he made little impression upon his Japanese audience (1967:14). The only way I know of in Japanese to escape this problem is to use amplification. Instead of simply saying "God" in a mixed group of believers and nonbelievers, I always say "the God of the Bible." Since the word for

God (*Kami*) is the same word used for the myriad of gods worshipped in Japan, a distinction of this nature must be made. The solution to the problem of language can only come through meticulous study and the exercise of great care in the use of religious vocabulary.

Conclusion

Are the Japanese resistant to the gospel? "Yes" if we think in terms of the historical developments and cultural aspects of this great nation. "No" if we look at the obstacles to church growth, whether internal or external, as challenges that can be met if, and when, the needed sacrifice and commitment are made.

References

Boschman, Paul, ed. 1968. *Experiments in Church Growth Japan*. Kobayashii: Japan Church Growth Research Association.

Brannen, Noah S. 1968. *Soka Gakkai*. Richmond, VA: John Knox.

Braun, Neil. 1971. *Laity Mobilized*. Grand Rapids: Eerdmans.

Conrad, Stan M. 1993. "The Relationship of the Japan Evangelical Free Church Mission and the Japan Evangelical Free Church Conference: A Survey and an Analysis." D.Miss. Project, Trinity Evangelical Divinity School.

Corwin, Charles. 1967. *Biblical Encounter with Japanese Culture*. Tokyo: Christian Literature Crusade.

Dale, Kenneth. 1975. *Circle of Harmony*. Tokyo: Seibunsha.

Drummond, R. H. 1971. *A History of Christianity in Japan*. Grand Rapids: Eerdmans.

Endo, Shusako. 1969. *Silence*. Tokyo: Tuttle.

Hesselgrave, David J. 1978. *Communicating Christ Cross-culturally*. Grand Rapids: Zondervan.

______, ed. 1978. *Dynamic Religious Movements*. Grand Rapids: Baker.

Holtom, D. C. 1943. *Modern Japan and Shinto Nationalism*. Chicago: University of Chicago Press.

Iglehart, C. W. 1957. *Cross and Crisis in Japan.* New York: Friendship.

Jacobsen, Morris. 1977. *Japanese Church Growth Patterns in the 1970s.* Tokyo: Japan Evangelical Missionary Association.

Lebra, Takie S. 1976. *Japanese Patterns of Behaviour.* Honolulu: The University Press of Hawaii.

Lee, Robert. 1967. *Stranger in the Land.* Tokyo: Kyo Bun Kwan.

Liao, D. C. E. 1972. *The Unresponsive: Resistant or Neglected?* Chicago: Moody.

Minami, H. 1971. *Psychology of the Japanese People.* Translated by Albert R. Ikoma. Tokyo: Tuttle.

Moore, C. A., ed. 1967. *The Japanese Mind.* Tokyo: Tuttle.

Nelson, Andrew. 1962. *The Modern Reader's Japanese-English Dictionary.* Tokyo: Tuttle.

Ozaki, R. 1978. *The Japanese.* Tokyo: Tuttle.

Reischauer, Edwin O. 1977. *The Japanese.* Tokyo: Tuttle.

Takakura, Toru. 1970. "Issues Confronting the Japanese Church Today." In *Japan Christian Yearbook (1969–1970).* John E. Kummel, trans. Tokyo: Kyo Bun Kwan.

Thomas, W. T. 1959. *Protestant Beginnings in Japan.* Tokyo: Tuttle.

van Wolferen, K. 1989. *The Enigma of Japanese Power.* London: Macmillan.

Vanderbilt, M. 1972. "Breakthrough." *Japan Harvest* (Summer):4–9.

Whiting, Robert. 1989. *You Gotta Have Wa.* New York: Vintage Books.

Yamamori, T. 1974. *Church Growth in Japan.* Pasadena, CA: William Carey Library.

Yanagita, T. 1957. *Christianity in Japan.* Sendai: Seisho Tosho Kankokai.

Young, J. 1958. *The Two Empires in Japan.* Tokyo: Bible Times.

Chapter 7

Encountering Post-Christendom Resistance

David Bjork

Seventeen years of experience as an evangelist, disciple-maker, and church-planter in France has convinced me that ministry in post-Christendom[1] lands presents the missionary

[1] I use the term *Christendom* to indicate the visible, surface "forms of Christian civilization which have given Western peoples their spiritual values, their moral standards, and their conception of a divine law from which all human laws ultimately derive their validity and their sanction" (Dawson 1965:34). It is commonly agreed that Christendom began with the conversion of Constantine and the foundation of the new capital of the Christian empire. With the beginning of Christendom those living within the boundaries of the Roman Empire experienced a shift from existing in the tradition of the pagan (pre-Christian) past to embrace a new revelation and the promise of new life.

However, since the nineteenth century, it is Christianity which seems to many to be a thing of the past and part of the vanishing order of the old Empire. In spite of the fact that our modern Western civilization in Europe is the direct successor and heir of Christendom, our modern civilization is not a Christian one. It is the result of two hundred years of progressive secularization during which the distinctively Christian institutions and social standards have been gradually eliminated. Many contemporary missiologists and

community with challenges and opportunities that call into question the most widely accepted of our missional paradigms and many of our methodologies. This is particularly true for the evangelical community whose witness for Christ in Western Europe is often ineffective because our governing missional paradigm and our ministry methods, working in conjunction, tend to project a separatist image and isolate us from those we wish to reach for Christ.

My goal is to discover an effective missionary approach to post-Christendom peoples. As I attempt to combine elements from my own missionary experience and reflection, I sense that a tool can be developed to enable us to gauge the extent to which a given missionary endeavor is seen as "culturally appropriate" by the receptor culture. This level of "cultural appropriateness" can be correlated with the degree of resistance to our message by the people we are attempting to reach for Christ.

Recognizing that every missionary enterprise is delimited by the governing assumptions of its underlying paradigm and made visible to the receptor society by its methods, I suggest that we can measure the relative strength of these forces and identify four different types of missional ministry in post-Christendom lands resulting from their combination.

I will begin by reflecting on the two major missional paradigms that are available to us as we minister in post-Christendom France. The "church-centered paradigm" and the "kingdom of God paradigm" are the "poles" of a continuum along which all current ministries in France can be placed. I will demonstrate that these paradigms do indeed define the nature and goals of our ministries and determine their effectiveness.

---

sociologists have used the term *post-Christian* to identify this trend in contemporary Western European culture. I think that what they are referring to is, in reality, *post-Christendom*.

The term *post-Christendom* does not mean to imply that there is no church or valid Christian experience left in what once was Christendom. It is used in this article to indicate the dissolution of the historical phenomenon of Christendom (Hoekendijk 1950:138).

Ministry methods also decide the efficacy of our outreach. Ministry methods presently used by missionaries in France can be located on a continuum stretching between the two poles of "Formal" and "Relational."

PARADIGMS IN CONFLICT

On my arrival in France I felt that my ministry goal of leading French men and women to personal faith in Christ and banding them together to give birth to self-supporting, self-governing and self-propagating evangelical churches was the correct missional response to the French situation (Hodges 1971:128). I assumed that the church either did not exist in France, or that if it did exist, it was so weakened and compromised by its history that it should be replaced. The fact that Europeans recognized the need for missionaries in their lands strengthened my resolve. And, although the strategies developed by the church growth movement had met with very limited success in France, my commitment to the objective of planting independent evangelical churches was unshaken (Koop 1986:109).

At the same time I became aware of growing ferment within Francophone Catholic circles partly in response to the appeal of John Paul II for the "re-evangelization" of Europe. As my understanding of contemporary French society grew, I began to realize that a good number of Catholic leaders were deeply concerned by the nominal religious adherence of most of the French (Wessels 1994). I also learned that many of these men and women recognize that the community of faith needs to be "reborn" in many different localities in France and within most of the segments of French society (Suenens 1992; Carrier 1993).

Monsignor Gilson, the Bishop of Le Mans typifies these individuals. He once explained to me that, whereas in the past French people grew up in the Christian faith and discovered Christ because they were born within Christendom, today this is not the case. He stated his observation that French men and women were all too rarely brought to faith in Christ by the sacraments and liturgy of the church. His conviction, shared by a good number of French bishops, is that people must first be brought to faith in Christ before they can discover the church. He is deeply concerned by the areas in his diocese where the church has ceased to exist as a community of faith.

The discrepancies between the assumptions of my missional paradigm and the reality I discovered in France bothered me. I wondered: Is it really necessary for me to establish a "new church" in France? How seriously should I take the faith and witness of the ancient church in this land? What would be my most appropriate response, as the cultural "outsider" and "guest" in France, to the spiritual needs of the French? My inner turmoil was calmed only as my missional paradigm moved away from the church-centric model to an understanding of ministry in the light of the kingdom of God.[2] The kingdom of God paradigm, based on the simple statement of John 20:21, is different in many ways from the church-centered concept under which I had been operating. Whereas the church-centric model encourages individual groups of believers to assert and develop themselves,[3] the kingdom of God model stresses the cross. It is a

---

2 J. I. Packer gives the following description of the kingdom of God (1995:166):

> The kingdom of God exists wherever Christ reigns as king and God's revealed will is actually done. The life of the faithful disciple is the kingdom—that is, the rule of Christ—in individual manifestation; the life of the faithful congregation is the kingdom in corporate manifestation; the life of a faithful parachurch body is the kingdom in a form of executive manifestation, inasmuch as all the doings of such a body aim to be kingdom activities, gestures of obedience to Christ that express and extend his rule over human lives.

3 This is, in my opinion, the major difference between the two missional paradigms. The church-centered model encourages individual groups of believers to assert and develop themselves as Beyerhaus has noted: "The danger inherent in the individual's assertion of self also threatens the Church. It is possible for a church to affirm its human 'self' against God, and so to become odious to both God and man. The Church should therefore hesitate to apply to itself an ideal that stresses the affirmation of the self" (1979:26).

radical perspective that lives out the truth that "we do not preach ourselves, but Jesus Christ as Lord, and ourselves as your servants for Jesus' sake" (2 Cor. 4:5).

Rather than being "church-centric,"[4] the kingdom of God paradigm is centered in the person of Jesus, sent from the Father and empowered by the Spirit. It is in Jesus' crucifixion and resurrection that the missionary enterprise must take its start, find its methods, and define its goal (Jn. 20:21, 23). Missions, seen from the perspective of the kingdom of God, flow out from the cross of Christ, are characterized by the cross (Phil. 2:5–8; 1 Cor. 9:19ff.; 2 Cor. 4:5), and result in the application of the cross (Lk. 9:23; Rom. 12:1–2, 14:7–11; Gal. 2:20).

The kingdom of God paradigm, like the church-centered paradigm, requires that the sending church dispatch missionaries who are ready for the self-emptying of their westernness in order to plant churches that are a "thing of the soil." However, unlike the church-centric paradigm, the kingdom of God paradigm proposes that when missionaries are going to a post-Christendom land, such as France, their self-emptying must also include a stripping, or putting aside, of their ecclesiastical rights and privileges. The indigenous church-centric paradigm, as it is understood and applied today by many missionaries in France, serves to reinforce the ecclesiastical rights, theological distinctives, and self-awareness of each

---

4 Hoekendijk used the term *churchification* to identify the way in which evangelism is often corrupted to mean the extension of the numbers, influence and prestige of the church under the church-centered paradigm (1950:134). He contended that "Church-centric thinking" is bound to go astray because it revolves around what he labeled an "illegitimate center":

> When results are considered, it seems to make little difference whether independent, indigenous Churches, or popular or national Churches rooted in the soil, or the ecumenical world Church is regarded as the goal of missionary endeavor; in every case, wherever the missionary enterprise is dominated by a Church-centric conception, that is bound in the long run to end by imperiling its very existence (cited in Andersen 1955:39).

group of believers, whereas the kingdom of God calls us to willingly put the emphasis elsewhere.

THE POWER OF A PARADIGM

What we understand determines what we choose to do. And what we choose to do makes all the difference in the world in the missionary enterprise. The following table contrasts the practical ramifications of these two paradigms:

Church-Centered Paradigm	**Kingdom of God Paradigm**
Message Conversion is often understood as becoming a follower of Jesus and joining *our church.*	*Message* This paradigm recognizes that members of God's kingdom are to be found within the state churches; conversion involves becoming a follower of Jesus and joining *a community or network of believers.*
Focuses on the group's doctrinal distinctives, the observance of what the group considers to constitute the essential forms of worship, and its particular system of pastoral government.	Focuses on worldview allegiance to Jesus Christ as the central issue and allows for a certain amount of diversity within the boundaries of "supra-cultural" truth.
The convert changes his or her identity to "become one of us."	The goal is to change the convert's understanding of his/her previous identity (so that in France, for example, he or she would experience a "ratification" of his or her baptism).

Missions	*Missions*
Have the same goals for ministry in post-Christendom lands as they do for ministry in pre-Christian countries, i.e., the "Three-self formula."	Allows the goals to be determined by the particular needs of the church which already exists in post-Christendom lands.
The missionary agency is self-promoting in that it seeks to establish an indigenous church "after its kind" in foreign soil.	The missionary agency sees itself as the "servant" of the existing Body of Christ.
Reinforces a "fragmented" view of the kingdom of God based on the idea of ecclesiastical independence.	Reinforces the universal scope of the kingdom of God based on the ideas of inter-relatedness and interdependence.
Establish their own "indigenized" sacraments and liturgy.	Teach converts to appreciate the established (indigenized?) sacraments and liturgy of the existing church.
Adopts an analysis of the spiritual needs of the country based on the contemporary situation.	Adopts a broad view of the situation with appreciation for what God has been doing in the country through the ages.
Missionary Spirituality	*Missionary Spirituality*
The missionary tends to view himself/herself as "one who has arrived" at a better, more thorough, understanding of the truth than the one held by the leaders of the state church.	The missionary takes serious account of the believers who are already present in post-Christendom countries. The missionary is a "pilgrim" who has things to both offer to,

	and learn from, the existing church.
The emphasis is on the product.	The emphasis is on the process.
The missionary sees himself/herself as a church-planter who is beginning the true church in virgin soil.	The missionary sees himself/herself as one who proclaims the kingdom in word and deed, inviting men and women to submit themselves to the Lordship of Christ.

Formal Versus Relational Methods

It is often our choice of methods that determines how we are perceived by the members of the society we are trying to reach for Christ. The testimony of Tom Julien, Director of European Missions for Grace Brethren Foreign Missions, and missionary to France for twenty-eight years, illustrates this reality: "When we first came here," says Mr. Julien, "we spent three weeks with a team of thirty people. We put tracts everywhere; we visited every house in the area; we had a dozen or so meetings in rented homes; we had meetings in the streets." He continues, "and as a result of all this, we had nobody." Not only did his group not find open hearts, but they closed many doors of opportunity: "We probably created more barriers that we are still trying to break down. We created an image of a cult rather than allowing the glory of the gospel to shine through the life of a person" (1986:5).

Koop agrees that our formal, highly visible, activity-oriented ministries in France actually communicate the wrong messages to the French people, thereby making our mission exceedingly more difficult (1986:44–46, 86–87). The following table summarizes the major differences between relationship-oriented and formal, activity-oriented ministries:

Formal[5]	**Relational**
Evangelism	*Evangelism*
Something one "does." It becomes centered around special events like the Sunday Celebration or Evangelistic Meetings.	A lifestyle that influences everyday encounters with others. All of life's circumstances and situations become vehicles for the communication of our Christian hope.
Something that is done only by specially gifted members of the church. Anyone can witness, but it takes uniquely gifted individuals to introduce people to Jesus Christ. Hence the need to organize events where one brings friends to whom witness may or may not have already been given.	Something every member of the Christian community is involved in because that is how followers of Jesus live. It is always going on "behind the scenes" as lay-people are sharing their faith and their lives with their acquaintances and friends.
Discipling	*Discipling*
Takes place in a "Sunday School Class" environment where there is little in-depth one-on-one mentoring involved. The group is promoted and continues to exist even though the members may change.	Takes place in one-on-one mentoring relationships and in small groups. The group exists for the strengthening of the individual members and has no identity or life of itself.

---

5 I do not contrast this term with *informal*. Rather, I place it in contrast to *relational*. I use *formal* to denote the typical activist mindset and missionary outlook of English-speaking evangelicalism which tends to formalize relationships. In this perspective following Jesus and "being the church" is understood as things that one does (either individually or in community with others) rather than living relationships.

Group Identity The identity of the group is extremely important. The desire is to be "known" in the community as a "truly Christian" group (often in opposition to other groups). The highly visible activities are, more often than not, organized around a "Worship Celebration" (irregardless of the day or time of the week on which this group gathers).	*Group Identity* The individual Bible study groups do not have a name or identity of their own. They might exist either on the inside or outside of the existing parish structures. There is low visibility of the group with high visibility of the lives and witness of the individual members of the group.
The group is centralized around an established meeting place such as a community center, transformed garage, or church building. This "place" of worship and fellowship is tied to the identity of the group and hosts the most important of its activities.	The group is de-centralized in the sense that it grows out of the "street" or the "marketplace." The homes of the believers are the most important places where ministry takes place because that is where the most intimate of life's experiences are lived.
Growth Numerical growth is relatively easy to measure since it occurs as the Lord "adds to the group those who would be saved," and they, in turn, join in the activities of the group.	*Growth* Numerical growth is difficult to measure because it occurs as the converts reproduce their lives in the lives of others (2 Tim. 2:2). There is no centralized "gathering" of these converts to reinforce their ties to the missionary agency.

A Model for Analysis of Incarnational Ministry in Post-Christendom Lands

Now that we have considered the two dichotomous pairs of missional paradigms and methodologies, it is time to place them together to form our analytical tool (*see* Figure 1).

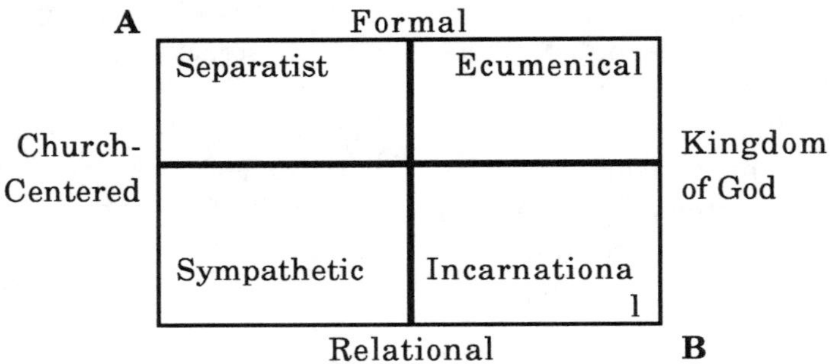

Figure 1
Analytical Model of Incarnational Ministry

As with any analytical tool, the missional paradigm/missionary methods model has inherent strengths and weaknesses. The application of this model is not intended to reduce the contextualization of the gospel in post-Christendom lands to a simple, four variant matrix but rather to enable missionaries ministering in such places to compare and contrast their own approaches to the other possibilities. The missional paradigm/missionary methods model provides conceptual glasses through which we may discover new perspectives on the incarnation of the gospel in countries marked by Christendom.

Separatist (Church-Centered/Formal)

These missionaries understand their mission in terms of individual conversions with the implied aim of gathering believers into self-supporting, self-governing, and self-propagating churches on the basis of a closely defined statement of faith.[6] One reason why this view of their mission makes perfect sense to these missionaries is their reluctance to acknowledge the legitimacy of the ancient church in de-Christianized lands (Koop 1986:22, 171). The following words, written by Jacques Blocher in 1966, express the commonly-held view of the evangelical community in France:

> We strongly emphasize the fact that churches may become apostate even if they retain the name of a Christian Church. In some of them the teaching of the Word of God has been adulterated to such an extent, that a born-again Christian can scarcely be expected to grow in grace and prosper and serve, *if he does not break away and unite with a church in which God's truth is effectively proclaimed.*
>
> The church of which the writer was pastor for many years in Paris has a majority of its membership composed of former Roman Catholics. For many of them *it was very difficult to leave their old church, but they could not do otherwise. I am certain that there are some real Christians within the Roman Church, but their difficult struggle for survival is a proof that their position is to be regarded as exceptional*. Our statement remains valid! The Roman Catholic system hinders the spiritual growth of a born-again Christian. And it is to be feared that Rome is not the only Church of which this is true.... We know that from the apostolic time until today proper missionary evangelism will inevitably involve change of religious adherence (1996:119–120, *emphasis mine*).

While their position makes sense to these missionaries, it often results in suspicion and real harm. For over three years I met once a week for a time of prayer with a French parish priest. One morning when I arrived at our appointed place of prayer I

---

6 Reinforcing the Pietist "individualism" was the thesis which gained widespread acceptance among conservative missionaries after World War I that the Scriptures clearly taught the obligation to separate from those with whom one disagreed. Hence the evangelical believers, who had developed a strong antipathy toward the views of other Protestants and toward Roman Catholicism in general and who found little indication that other Christians should be considered part of the church in any way, sought to establish indigenous churches of "sound faith."

found my friend visibly troubled. After I pressed him to tell me what was bothering him, he reached into his drawer and pulled out a tract which he slid across the desk to me. The tract had been placed in his mailbox (and in the mailboxes of all of his parishioners) by an evangelical group whose address was rubber-stamped on the back. The tract urged all its readers to "save themselves from hell and the Antichrist" by leaving the Catholic Church and joining the evangelical group. With tears in his eyes my Catholic brother asked, "Why do you evangelicals do this to us?" It is no wonder that many priests and bishops are wary of the evangelical missionaries they encounter and view their intentions with suspicion.

Reinforcing the sectarian and "cultist" image of these evangelical groups in the eyes of the receptor society is the activity-centeredness of their approach (Koop 1986:44–46). One example of this style is the attempt to replace Catholic mass with "worship" in the context of an evangelical style Sunday celebration which is projected as the focal point of the Christian experience. Koop has pointed out that the success of "planting" a small church centered on an evangelical Protestant Sunday celebration, in a place like France, will probably make evangelistic success unlikely (1986:86–87):

> The Americans were so anxious to get a church started, and so proud of their achievement once a tiny church was organized, that they failed to realize that their small success made greater success less likely. The Evangelical missionaries came from a culture which accepted and even took pride in small independent churches. Many midwestern towns supported a different church on each street corner. The French saw things differently. For them, there was only one church; or perhaps two in regions where Protestants were visible. Everything else was a sect. They lumped together all little religious groups no matter how divergent their beliefs: Adventists, Jehovah's Witnesses, Friends of Man, Mennonites, Brethren, Baptists, Salvation Army, Pentecostals, Christian Scientists, etc. In American history small dissenting sects had grown into major denominations. While not all sects became large churches, most large churches had started as sects. In France, the relationship between sect and church was antithetical, not evolutionary. Sects remained outside the center of traditional French religious culture, and so did the sectarian missionary churches.

Nonetheless . . . the search for strategy took most American missions in France to the policy of establishing small indigenous churches (emphasis added).

The separatist position fails to take seriously the European mentality which links their identity to the church.[7] This is something that North Americans have real difficulty understanding. Although the average Frenchman in the 1990s does not regularly practice his Catholic faith, it is an integral part of his identity. People are born Catholic or Reformed, and to ask them to give up this heritage is like asking them to give up their nationality:

> Everybody says that they are Catholic—that their roots are Catholic. But today, very few of the Catholics really adhere to their religion. They call themselves "Catholique non-pratiquant"—"I'm a Catholic that doesn't practice my religion." I was baptized a Catholic and I'll die a Catholic, but I don't go to church and I don't necessarily believe in God (Wilheim 1986:20).

ECUMENICAL (KINGDOM OF GOD/FORMAL)

Those missionaries who find themselves strongly influenced by the kingdom of God paradigm and who are deeply committed to formal, activity-centered ministries would experience the same kind of formalized relationship to the state churches as one sees between the French Reformed Church and the Roman Catholic Church.

Although those in this quadrant acknowledge the other as "truly Christian," there is a distance between "themselves" and the "others" which is measured by important theological differences, the observance of the essential forms of worship, and the various systems of pastoral government. These believers do feel that they can proclaim together with the state church the apostolic faith enshrined in the creeds and dogmas of the early church. They can also labor side by side in defending the religious heritage of Christendom in what has become a militantly

---

7 For a detailed description of this phenomenon see Boon 1982:15.

secularized environment. However, they work to maintain separateness.

These believers do not want to do anything that might be seen as a betrayal of their ecclesiastical heritage enshrined in their religious forms. They worry that if they get too close to other kinds of Christian believers they will be unduly minimizing the theological, doctrinal, and ecclesiastical battles fought by their forefathers. They fear that if they do not maintain a certain distance from others they will lose their distinctives.

Separatism does not only concern the missionary population. There are also leaders of the state churches who do not want missionaries crossing over the ecclesiological divide. Several years ago a French bishop told me that he would feel more comfortable with me if I would develop an "ecumenical" relationship with the Catholic Church. His analysis of my ministry was: "No one that I know of can do in the diocese what you are doing. You are ministering to people that we have been unable to reach for Christ. The church is strengthened by your presence. However, Catholics and Evangelicals are like oil and water; they don't mix!" This bishop urged me to start an evangelical church like other missionaries do. He was troubled that I had crossed over the gap and entered into a ministry of service which did not underline our distinctives and enforce "separateness" from each other.

Sympathetic (Church-Centered/Relational)

I have encountered a number of North American evangelical missionaries in France who find themselves in this position. These missionaries are not rigidly hostile toward Catholics since most French people make little more than a nominal commitment to the Catholic Church. However, although they realize that French Catholics who readily criticize their church are at the same time reluctant to leave it, those in this quadrant believe firmly that it is the presence of regenerate persons that properly constitutes a group as a church (Andersen 1955:15). Some of these missionaries press their converts to sever promptly and completely their connection with Catholicism because of doctrinal differences.

Others in this quadrant take a more temperate approach in an attempt to cooperate with French Catholics who are concerned about the salvation of their friends and neighbors. These missionaries encourage their converts to attend both the missionary group and the state church. This more moderate position usually draws swift rebuke from other missionaries who insist upon doctrinal precision (Koop 1986:147).

As early as twenty years ago, Ramez Atallah, the Quebec Director of InterVarsity Christian Fellowship, pointed out that missionaries ministering under the Indigenous Church Model in post-Christian Roman Catholic lands were facing a severe ministerial dilemma (1974:881):

> In their present relationships with Roman Catholics, many Protestant missionaries and pastors are facing an acute dilemma. On the one hand, they are enjoying a new and exciting ministry among Catholics through Bible teaching, discussion, prayer and evangelistic activity. On the other hand, this involvement with Catholics is sometimes strongly questioned by the Christian worker's churches or mission boards. The latter are afraid that such activity by their missionaries may be a compromise of biblical principles.
>
> Many Christian workers, caught in this dilemma find it very hard to know what to do. Often, even when they are convinced that their activities do not involve any compromise of biblical principles, they feel forced to either cover up what they do or completely abandon their involvement with Catholics. If they do not do this, many of them face the prospect of losing financial support from their church or mission.
>
> This delicate situation is increasingly becoming the experience of many evangelical Protestants ministering in predominantly Roman Catholic countries. It requires serious, patient, and prayerful consideration by all involved.

Incarnational (Kingdom of God/Relational)

The missionaries who find themselves in this quadrant recognize that their mission is to lead men and women to conversion to Christ on the level of their worldview allegiances and commitments. They understand the need to integrate these converts into the Christian community which they see as a network of mentoring and accountability relationships which are distinguishable from ecclesiastical structures and which transcend denominational distinctives. Their ministry is done life-to-life, unobtrusively, in the intimacy of everyday relationships. They are not concerned about organizing a church or establishing a Christian institution. Their goal is to reconcile people to God without placing undue stumbling blocks in anyone's path (2 Cor. 5:11–6:10).

Furthermore, they believe that they can best proclaim the kingdom of God in post-Christendom lands by assuming the posture of "servants" who "set aside" their own ecclesiastical rights and privileges. They understand that their mission is not to establish a new, distinct, ecclesiastical body of believers or to impose their liturgical forms in these countries marked by centuries of the church's presence. Rather, they aim to place their unique theological heritage, ministerial experience, and bi-cultural perspective at the service of the followers of Jesus already present in those lands. In so doing they "become all things to all men," as it were, in order to win as many as possible (1 Cor. 9:19–23). Thus the ministry of these missionaries serves to ratify and strengthen the ties of their converts to the Christian church of their own heritage.

Concluding Thoughts

It has been my own observation and experience in France that the closer a North American evangelical ministry finds itself to point "A" in my model the more it is perceived as culturally inappropriate by the members of French society. Dr. J. Herbert Kane, the late Professor Emeritus of the School of World Mission and Evangelism at Trinity Evangelical Divinity School, pointed out that this is a major barrier to our missionary endeavors in Western Europe:

> As far as evangelism among Europeans is concerned, the evangelical missionary has a number of strikes against him, the greatest being

> their perception of him as an evangelical. They regard us as a cult, just as we regard the Mormons, the Moonies, and the Jehovah's Witnesses. Consequently they will have nothing to do with us (1986:2).

On the other hand, my own missionary experience confirms that the closer a North American evangelical ministry is to point B in the model, the more contextualized it is to the French situation. Through the years I have endeavored to minister in France from a kingdom of God paradigm stressing relational methods. This has allowed me to accompany more than two hundred French teenagers and adults as they welcomed the lordship of Christ over their lives. All of these individuals were Catholics. Less than a dozen of these people were practicing their faith when we first met, and many said that they were atheists. We accompanied some of these men and women in their spiritual pilgrimages for several months and others for more than a decade.

It has been fairly common to hear one or another of these individuals testify that they "rediscovered" their church after I helped them to ratify their baptism by acknowledging Jesus as their Lord and Savior. To my knowledge no one has left the Catholic Church because of my involvement in their life.

A good number of these people are actively accompanying their neighbors and friends in their spiritual pilgrimage; some have taken places of leadership in their parishes. It is interesting that these believers are sometimes accused of taking Jesus too seriously because they have moved from nominality to a vital relationship with Jesus Christ. They are not seen as being "cultist"; instead, they are perceived as "Catholics who are not quite like the others."

Evangelizing and discipling French people in the context of human relationships, without forming them into a visible entity which exists outside of or alongside the state church, enables them to remain in vital contact with neighbors, friends, and family members who would otherwise consider them members of a strange cult. The result is that rather than becoming a small, ingrown group of believers, the missionary, along with the French believers who have been influenced for Christ, has an ever-widening web of ministry relationships in the communities where they live.

REFERENCES

Andersen, Wilhelm. 1955. *Towards A Theology of Mission.* London: SCM.

Atallah, Ramez L. 1974. "Some Trends in the Roman Catholic Church Today." In *Let the Earth Hear His Voice: Official Reference Volume Papers and Responses/International Congress on World Evangelization.* J. D. Douglas, ed. Pp. 872–884. Minneapolis: World Wide Publications.

Beyerhaus, Peter. 1979. "The Three Selves Formula, Is It Built on Biblical Foundations?" In *Readings in Dynamic Indigeneity.* Kraft, Charles H. and Tom N. Wisley, eds. Pp. 15–29. Pasadena, CA: William Carey Library.

Blocher, Jacques. 1960. *Le Catholicisme à la lumière de l'Écriture sainte.* Paris: Librairie des Bons Semeurs.

Boon, J. Edward. 1982. "Will the Barriers Be Broken?" *The Alliance Witness* (November):5–19.

Carrier, Hervé. 1993. *Evangelizing the Culture of Modernity.* Maryknoll, NY: Orbis.

Dawson, Christopher. 1965. *The Historic Reality of Christian Culture.* New York: Harper Torchbooks.

Hodges, Melvin L. 1971. *The Indigenous Church.* Springfield, MO: Gospel Publishing House.

Hoekendijk, J. C. 1950. "The Evangelisation of Man in Modern Mass Society." *Ecumenical Review* 2(2):133–140.

Julien, Tom. 1986. *Grace Magazine, Special Europe Missions Issue* 2(1):1–8.

Kane, J. Herbert. 1986. *Trinity World Forum* 11(2):3–4.

Koop, Allen V. 1986. *American Evangelical Missionaries in France 1945–1975.* New York: University Press of America.

Packer, J. I. 1995. "Crosscurrents among Evangelicals." In *Evangelicals and Catholics Together: Toward a Common Mission.* Colson, Charles and Richard John Neuhaus, eds. Pp. 147–174. Dallas: Word.

Suenens, Leo Jozef. 1992. "Spirit of Renewal." *The Tablet* (September 19):1157.

Wessels, Antone. 1994. *Europe: Was It Ever Really Christian?* London: SCM.

Wilheim, Hans. 1986. "Chicago Consultation on Partnership in Mission in Western Europe." *World Mission Associates European Project* (December):5–24.

Part III

Means of Overcoming: Finding and Building Bridges

Chapter 8

Overcoming Resistance through Martyrdom

Karen L. White

This chapter discusses one means which may be a key in unlocking the kingdom of God for the least evangelized Muslim peoples residing in the 10/40 window which stretches from West Africa across southern Europe and the Middle East all the way to the eastern shores of Asia.[1] That means is the martyrdom of those who carry the gospel there.

People define "martyrdom," in various ways. James and Marti Hefley chose a somewhat broad definition: a martyr is "one who dies, suffers, or sacrifices everything for a principle, cause, etc." (1996:9). David Barrett, on the other hand, defines martyrdom more rigorously as "believers in Christ who lose their lives prematurely in a situation of witness as a result of human hostility" (cited in Bridges 1996). The English word "martyr" comes from the Greek word *martus*. It is related to the word *martureo*, which means to witness or to give testimony. However, a *martus*, or martyr, is one who gives testimony even at the point of ultimate sacrifice. For the purposes of this chapter,

---

1 There is no intention to denigrate the importance of other peoples in the 10/40 Window, but simply to recognize the restraints of time and space required by this particular project.

a martyr is one who is determined to be God's person in the place to which he or she is assigned and willing even to die if need be.

In spite of the fact that I spent twenty years as a missionary in the 10/40 window, during fifteen of which I lived in a guerrilla war zone, I never entertained the thought I espouse in this chapter—that severe persecution and/or martyrdom is not only a distinct possibility, especially for those who carry the gospel to the least evangelized, but that it is likely a specific means of God to bring the lost to himself. Further, it is my contention that this likelihood ought to be considered strategically by missionary sending agencies and understood (by missionaries) as integral to their call.

Martyrdom is not a new concept to the church. David Barrett estimates that fifty million believers may have died for their faith in Christ throughout the past twenty centuries (cited in Bridges 1996). David Hesselgrave points out that the missionary enterprise has always been attended by danger. In the nineteenth century the prevailing threat was disease; in the twentieth century it is violence.

> The facts that opposition may sometimes be directed against national Christians rather than the missionaries themselves, and that it may not be directed against missionaries because they are missionaries, but because they are white or American or Western, does not really change the situation very much. The result is the same (1988:202).

We do not yet have all the facts regarding the scale of martyrdom in the twentieth century. According to Wilbert R. Shenk, "preliminary estimates indicate this to be perhaps the bloodiest and most costly century in all of Christian history" (1987:62). Dr. Thomas Wang, of the Great Commission Center in Texas, stated in a recent conversation that it is probable that Chinese Christian martyrs in the twentieth century alone equal more than the martyrs of all other nationalities throughout the centuries since Christ.[2]

Those early missionaries in the modern era, who followed in the footsteps of William Carey and others, left for foreign fields knowing they would in all likelihood die within a few months or

---

2 Personal conversation, March 7, 1997, Dallas, Texas.

years as a result of disease. Many of them never saw their homelands again, having been buried in the lands to which God sent them. They followed the steps of the biblical patriarchs, prophets, people of God, and martyrs whom the Holy Spirit listed in Hebrews 11. They did not consider their sacrifice unusual. Many of them died with full understanding of the value of their sacrifice. Raymon Lull wrote before his martyrdom that Islamic strongholds would be conquered only by "love and prayers, and the pouring out of tears and blood" (cited in Bridges 1997). Betty Stam's father, upon the martyrdom of Betty and John at the hands of Chinese kidnappers in 1934, took heart in remembering the faith-statement made by the church father Tertullian when he said, "They have not died in vain. The blood of the martyrs is still the seed of the church" (cited in Hefley and Hefley 1996:57–60). Said Baker J. Cauthen regarding the martyrdom in 1953 of Bill Wallace, missionary to China, "The Communists thought they were rid of him; instead they immortalized him" (cited in Hefley and Hefley 1996:72). He was right. Many Southern Baptist missionaries and others serving today committed their lives to missionary service as a result of Wallace's sacrifice. Cauthen again commented in a eulogy for Mavis Pate,

> Her silent grave will be a permanent witness to the high calling of God. Missionaries will look at it and remember the great extent to which missionaries go in order that the love of God may be shared. Non-Christian people will look at it and be reminded of the love of God that sent the Lord Jesus into the world for our redemption, and has continued sending his messengers forth to make that redemption known (cited in Hefley and Hefley 1996:361–362).

Pilot Al Lewis, only a few days prior to his martyrdom, when his rescue plane crashed into the side of a mountain overlooking a valley where missionaries were running for their lives, had predicted, "I believe it is going to cost much to open this field, but I am ready to pay the price" (cited in Hefley and Hefley 1996:181). Upon learning of the martyrdom of their fellow workers in a landslide in the Wusak Valley in 1969, tribal evangelists of New Guinea responded, "Because our blood has been shed in the Wusak it has become our land, and we will continue to take the gospel there" (cited in Hefley and Hefley 1996:183). Lubov Kosachevich, of the former Soviet Union, was not alone in his ardor for Christ when he said, "I love God! I am willing to give even my life to serve Him" (cited in Hefley and Hefley 1996:258). Having been bathed in blood and schooled in suffering, the church in the former Soviet Union stands strong and shines brightly today in the midst of the chaotic darkness still swirling around it. Yes, many who have been martyred understood the value of their sacrifice.

There are also many people groups today who witness that "the darkness on them was dissipated only when a missionary was killed there" (Tson n.d.:465). Hear from Algeria where God made himself known in a remarkable way one evening in 1983.

> On that evening in 1983 villagers later testified, the Holy Spirit moved from house to house, revealing himself through dreams, visions and angelic visitations. Some 450 Muslims in the village eventually became believers in Christ as their Savior.
>
> Christians had nothing to do with the incident—or so they thought.
>
> But when mission workers began asking how such a miracle could have occurred, they discovered this: More than six centuries ago, Spanish missionary Raymon Lull was stoned to death by Muslims for preaching where the village now stands (Bridges 1997).

While many missionaries, and even many peoples, have understood the value of martyrdom to the kingdom of God, the concept has not been in vogue during recent years when church growth strategy has governed the work in which many of us have invested our lives. I personally formed my missionary strategy during the height of the church growth movement. During my years on the mission field I regularly made decisions about where to go, what to do, and to whom to minister, in consideration of peace and order factors. The concept that formed the foundation for such decisions was intensely practical—one ought to make every effort to stay alive because when dead one cannot carry the gospel anywhere. I did not live in fear, and I was ready to die, but I did not consider death to be a good strategic option. Martyrdom would, at best, have been one of those evils out of which God could bring some good (Rom. 8:28).

Therefore, it was a revolutionary thought for me and one that demanded serious reflection—that martyrdom might be an intentional strategy of God.

The world is full of peoples who have eagerly received the gospel. It seemed wise to many of us to concentrate our resources where the response was greatest and where the resources could be maximized. As a result, we have neglected many peoples in the 10/40 window, a vast geographical area wherein 1.7 billion unevangelized, or nearly unevangelized people live as members of at least 2,161 people groups. One hundred eighty-seven of these peoples have been identified as mega-populations which together make up ninety-four percent of the population in the 10/40 window.[3] It would still be wise to consider responsiveness and size of population in making strategic decisions regarding where to plant our resources within this region. One's life or death, as the case may be, ought to be used to do the greatest good possible. From the human standpoint, it seems that reaching the mega-populations first would be wisest because they would have the resources then to make a significant impact on the smaller people groups around them.

Be that as it may, this chapter simply calls us to recognize the fact that martyrdom will in all likelihood increase as missionaries multiply in the 10/40 window.[4] Far from being a tragedy, martyrdom may indeed be one of God's strategies for bringing this part of our world to himself.

In considering this matter of martyrdom as a strategy for reaching the least evangelized, this chapter will describe briefly the Muslim portion of the 10/40 window, noting something of the state of the church there. In the light of the situation in the Muslim 10/40 window and the mandate from God to carry the gospel to all peoples whatever the cost, the chapter will reveal some of my own theological reflection regarding martyrdom, and how its possibility fits into the call to mission. It will conclude by

---

3 John Gilbert, director of Global Research at the Southern Baptist Foreign Mission Board, telephone conversation, February 3, 1997

4 In fact, in 1995 alone, one hundred fifty foreign missionaries were murdered while at their task (Bridges 1996).

raising some questions regarding strategy for presenting the opportunity of missionary service to our contemporary young generation.

MUSLIMS IN THE 10/40 WINDOW

The General State of Affairs

There are more than one billion Muslims, most of whom live within the 10/40 window where there are thirty-eight nations in which over fifty percent of the people are Muslim. Most of these countries officially consider themselves Islamic. In these areas *Islam intends to remain dominant*. People with power in these nations tend to resolutely resist efforts of non-Muslims to evangelize (Douglas 1994:59, emphasis mine). This being so, it is perfectly clear that taking the gospel to Muslim nations is a risky business.[5]

One out of every three unreached people is a Muslim. "Muslims constitute the largest bloc of unreached people in today's world. . . . More than nine hundred thirty major ethnolinguistic groups need churches planted among them" (Douglas 1994:59). For many years only a very few have chosen to carry the gospel to the Muslim world. The work has been difficult and the results minimal. In recent years, however, Christians have begun to focus their prayers and attention on these peoples. A multi-source flood of new workers is going to the Muslim world with the result that Muslims are coming to Jesus in virtually all Muslim countries (McCurry 1994:99–104). These workers report that many who are coming to Jesus have been influenced to do so by dreams or visions of Christ.

Several examples of such phenomena were detailed last year by *National and International Religion Report*:

---

5 Most of the rest of the 10/40 Window is peopled by Hindus or atheistic Communists. Each of these religions (atheistic communism *is* like a religion), too, intends to remain dominant within its sphere of influence. For the most part, the 10/40 Window does not welcome the gospel or those who carry it there.

> Thousands of North African Muslims wrote to a Christian radio service asking for information. Many reported a similar dream: Jesus appears and tells them, "I am the way."
>
> A young Muslim angrily took a Bible tract from a Christian worker, tore it up and threatened the worker's life. The next day the same young man appeared at the worker's door, not with a weapon but with a plea: "I must have another booklet." The previous night, he recounted, he had felt two hands shake him awake and heard a voice say, "You have torn up the truth." He read the tract and became a believer in Christ.
>
> In Nigeria, Muslims savagely beat a Christian convert from their tribe. As he lay dying, they heard him asking God to forgive them. That night two Muslim mullahs who participated in the attack saw visions of Christ. Both repented and took 80 followers to a Christian church to hear the gospel (Bridges 1997).

Aside from the influence of prayer, the new openness in the Islamic world is a result of the crisis caused by secularism and the rise of Western civilization there. Muhammad's words and deeds have been absolutized as binding upon all Muslims. They have become the core not only of religion but also of governmental ideology. Muslims are consequently locked into the seventh century ethnocentric Arab behavioral pattern of Muhammad as expressed in the Qur'an. For the orthodox, then, Muhammad is the model man, not only for all Muslims, but for the whole human race. All he said and did is normative for the rest of humanity. Muslims are now

> forced either to come to terms with the supremacy of modern technological societies, at least economically and militarily, or utterly deny the accomplishments of non-Muslim countries, particularly the West, and seek to reimpose on all Muslims, and ultimately on all mankind, the absolutistic model of a seventh century Arab culture. Neither move is possible. When Muslims take the line of accommodating to Western culture, it is in opposition to the core teaching of Islam, thus weakening the grip of Islam on its followers. For those Muslims who take the other approach of ignoring the achievements of the West and reverting to an Arabic version of seventh century lifestyle as modeled by Muhammad, dilemma follows. They are forced to use the tools and skills developed by the very people they feel destined to conquer. Along with these tools and skills, comes the Western value system (worldview) that gave birth to

> them. Today we see the Muslim world in the throes of this controversy. The choice seems to be to accommodate to Western culture or to prepare to go to war with the West (and all other non-Muslim countries) to assert Islamic supremacy (Bridges 1997:102).

The very foundations of Islam are being challenged and eroded, and God is working through a growing number of laborers who are taking advantage of the burgeoning receptivity among so many Muslims today. Satan is fighting back, of course, and there is persecution and martyrdom. But Muslims are coming to Christ in increasing numbers (Bridges 1997:104; *see* also Hefley and Hefley 1996).

Islamic Fundamentalism

At a conference in 1986, meeting in Lahore, Muslims challenged Islamic nations to become free of all Christians by the year 2000 (*Missionary News Service* 1986 cited in Hesselgrave 1988:202). Nabeel Jabour helps us understand the reason many Muslims are attracted to such a goal. First, Islam is both a religion and a body politic. It has seen rapid expansion in diversity beyond national and geographical boundaries in recent years. Such growth has inflamed the patriotism of students especially those from rural areas. These students long for the return of the Islamic caliphate, the succession of orthodox Islam throughout the Muslim world. Their hope is focused on the resurgence of Islamic fundamentalism in Iran as the model for all. Second, not all economic promises made by Muslim governments have been kept because of intermittent or continued warfare. Disillusionment drives people toward fundamentalists who claim to be able to right the wrongs. Third, the fundamentalist movement appeals to those who are most deprived in society, a segment of the Muslim population which is growing rapidly in spite of the fabulous wealth of the Gulf states. Fourth, the influence of Western ideas through education, multinational corporations, and media have brought estrangement which comes in several forms: those who want to emulate the West wear western clothes. This not only sets them apart from their fellow Muslims in their own eyes but also draws the wrath of the traditionalists. Thus, they experience isolation at home and also in the community. Others harbor resentment and envy because they are not able to find jobs with the multinationals. The wealth is disproportionately distributed to a new class of millionaires, which means that increasing numbers of people find themselves living on a subsistence level. This situation leads to a feeling that life is a jungle, and survival is for the strongest and most violent (Jabbour 1994:81).

Islamic fundamentalists sometimes enforce the laws of apostasy. This doctrine allows those who leave the faith of Islam to be put to death.

> Until recently, such doctrines were routinely ignored by Islamic governments, or interpreted liberally. But particularly in the case of Christian converts and evangelical Protestants, this is no longer true (Horowitz 1995).

In a speech in 1984, the Ayatollah Khomeini expressed the viewpoint which forms the foundation of the law of apostasy:

> War is a blessing for the world and for all nations. It is God who incites men to fight and to kill. The Koran says, "Fight until all corruption and all rebellion have ceased." The wars the Prophet led against the infidels were a blessing for all humanity. Imagine that we soon will win the war. That will not be enough, for corruption and resistance to Islam will still exist. The Koran says, "War, war until victory". . . . The mullahs with corrupt hearts who say that all this is contrary to the teachings of the Koran are unworthy of Islam. Thanks to God, our young people are now, to the limits of their means, putting God's commandments into action. They know that to kill the unbelievers is one of man's greatest missions (cited in Haught 1990:203).

MARTYRDOM AND PERSECUTION

In Iran, in 1994, three of the most prominent evangelical leaders were abducted and assassinated. Bishop Haik Hovsepian-Mehr was martyred in January. In June, his successor as chairman of the Council of Churches in Iran, Rev. Tatavous Mikaelian, was killed in an execution style murder, shot three times in the back of the head. Again, in July, Rev. Mahdi Dibaj was executed (ICI Report 1996:15).

> Christian converts are effectively barred from attending services of any kind, and large numbers of converts and evangelizers have been arrested, imprisoned, tortured and forced to recant their faith. Others more fortunate have merely lost homes, jobs and businesses (Horowitz 1995).

In 1990 Rev. Hossein Soodmand, an Iranian Muslim convert to Christianity and pastor of a church in Mashad, was executed by hanging. When three Christian pastors appealed to the Ministry of Islamic Guidance of the Islamic Republic of Iran not to carry out Rev. Soodmand's death sentence, they were told, "We intend to execute all Muslim converts to Christianity and Soodmand is the first" (ICI Report 1996:20).

In 1995 it was reported by *The Wall Street Journal* that in Egypt due to fundamentalists' pressure on the government,

> Christian converts and evangelicals have been imprisoned and tortured. . . . Religious segregation unofficially exists in schools, and beatings of Christian students as "devils" now regularly occurs. Burnings of churches and lootings of Christian-owned businesses are on the rise (Horowitz 1995).

Greg Livingstone, the general director of Frontiers, a missionary agency devoted to evangelizing the Muslim world, reported the arrests in Egypt of four missionaries (three American and one New Zealander), all engaged in lawful employment in addition to being in the country as Frontiers missionaries. The arrests followed the baptism as Christians of thirty-five Muslims in Cairo. "When people start getting baptized, all hell breaks loose. . . ." Although freedom of religion is guaranteed in the Egyptian constitution, "conversion of Muslims" and "disparaging Islam" are forbidden (cited in Kennedy 1993:55).

In Sudan, conversion to Christianity is a criminal act punishable by flogging. Thousands of children have been forcibly taken from their Christian families and sold into slavery there. Algeria's Armed Islamic Group has called for the annihilation of Christians. Pakistan has a sweeping blasphemy law that prohibits speaking or acting against the prophet Muhammad, violations of which are punishable by death (Horowitz 1995).

Most of the specific reports of suffering and martyrdom in Muslim states come from Iran. This may be true for at least two reasons: one, Iran, seeking to be the standard bearer for Islamic Fundamentalism, has instituted a massive persecution of Christians, and two, the Iranian Christians International, Inc. is making every effort to document the story of Christian persecution in Iran and to disseminate the information in strategic places. They report regarding the state of affairs for Christians in Iran:

> Muslim converts to Christianity, other Evangelical Christians, pastors and church leaders continue to be arrested, imprisoned, and tortured, simply because of their religion. Some are kept under heavy surveillance, with their phones tapped and letters routinely opened, while others received written and oral death threats. Some have also escaped assassination attempts. Others have lost their jobs or have been refused gainful employment, housing and education. Since Bishop Hovsepian-Mehr's death in January 1994, government agents are concentrating their persecution more on individuals who are Muslim converts and/or those who encourage Muslims to convert to Christianity. Ethnic Christians such as Armenians and Assyrians also continue to face officially sanctioned discrimination, particularly in the areas of employment, education, housing, the court system and public accommodations (ICI Report 1996:14–15).

Even Iranian Christians living outside Iran, particularly Iranian Christian leaders, are not safe. Over sixty "dissidents" have been killed outside of Iran since 1980 (ICI Report 1996:26).

These beleaguered believers, in Iran and throughout the Muslim world, are learning firsthand, in the most graphic of ways, the meaning of the cross, even as it was learned by a little Armenian refugee from the Turkish massacre of Armenians in 1915. As many as six hundred thousand died when Muslim Turks determined to wipe out the Armenian Christians within Turkish borders. Only the strongest escaped into Russian territory where American relief camps had been set up. One of those who escaped was a young girl of eighteen who stumbled into an American camp.

"Are you in pain?" a nurse asked when she arrived.

"No," she replied, "but I have learned the meaning of the cross."

> The nurse thought she was mentally disoriented and questioned her further. Pulling down the one garment she wore, the young girl exposed a bare shoulder. There, burned deeply into her flesh, was the figure of a cross.
>
> "I was caught with others in my village. The Turks stood me up and asked, 'Muhammad or Christ?' I said, 'Christ, always Christ.' For seven days they asked me this same question and each day when I said 'Christ' part of this cross was burned into my shoulder. On the seventh day they said, 'Tomorrow if you say "Muhammad" you live. If not, you die.' Then we heard that Americans were near and some of us escaped. That is how I learned the meaning of the cross" (Hefley and Hefley 1996:343).

When Christians carry the gospel to Muslim peoples, they awaken the power of Satan that energizes them. "Satan can and does stir Muslims up to kill new believers, destroy Christian businesses and burn churches. Examples abound from the southern Philippines to West Africa" (McCurry 1994:103). Panya Baba, Pastor Director of the Evangelical Church of West Africa, says,

> if we are really serious to accomplish the work of the gospel, in the areas of the world where we know that most of the unreached peoples are found, we'll have to conclude that they will never be reached unless some people are ready and willing to go and suffer, including being willing to lose their lives (1994:39).

How Should Christians Respond to the Danger of Martyrdom?

How can one person say for another what is right when it comes to risking one's life? Certainly, I would not presume to do so. It is interesting, however, that a few people have risked making some quite pointed statements regarding this issue. For instance, Dr. Chris Marantika, the president of a Bible college in Jokjakarta, Indonesia, says that the pressure the church faces in Islamic culture has "caused her to take a very defensive position toward Muslims. This position is where the devil wants her to be so that the promise of the power to break the gates of hell will not be put into effect." He continues,

> members [are] more concerned with their safety and security than with being occupied with the challenge to accomplish the mandate for which they have been adopted to the position of the children of God's dear Son.... In some cases, the approach of retreating or even of being runaways are too much evident. Many of her leaders and members retreat to a Western missionary compound, or even to a western country where safety and security can be easily secured; and, out of sincere love, the Church in the West embraces them and, therefore, pulls out the divine instruments and power from the Muslim world (1989:106–107).

Dr. John Moldovan of Romania, in a recent conversation, revealed the frustration experienced by the Christians in Romania when, under pressure from the Communists, the Christians were standing for their convictions at enormous cost. When they asked missionaries for counsel and support, the missionaries replied that they intended to remain aloof from involvement in anything which might put them in a bad light with the government. The missionaries wanted to protect their right to remain as long as possible in the country. However, their unwillingness to take the risks to stand with their Romanian brothers and sisters in the fight for the life of the church, wounded deeply.

Panya Baba, in discussing the situation of the Arab Christians today, and their tendency to flee rather than to remain in their countries and be a redemptive influence even if it means martyrdom, says that they might be able to remain if they had more support from the Western churches. He agrees that Westerners may have to model being put in jail and persecuted in the Middle East before the national churches will try to do the same.

> It is very difficult to teach persecution, that's why I mentioned it because I know the need of it. In Nigeria, as a result of having gone through persecution, our eyes are opened. We have seen that without persecution the Church in Nigeria was lacking lots of spiritual strength and boldness. But it's a new experience, bearing much fruit, since our churches started to be bombed by Muslims (Baba 1994:39).

Believers in China, in orienting Western Christians who want to minister to them, say,

> As for our Pastors, each has served an average of seventeen years and three months in prison for his faith, much of it in solitary confinement. Don't come into this meeting to talk about or do anything that you are not willing to die for (Lawrence 1985:45).

How missionaries respond to danger is a matter of great import, one which they must consider carefully before investing their lives in the evangelization of the least evangelized peoples of the world.

THEOLOGICAL REFLECTION

Why do we need a theology of martyrdom? Perhaps one reason is that it has always been of importance to the church. In fact, "some scholars have argued that a touchstone in the formation of the New Testament canon was whether a document helped prepare the disciple community for suffering, even unto death" (Shenk 1987:63). In the twenty-first century, certainly, the missionary church will want to own a theology which prepares her to bear witness to Jesus Christ, even at the price of death. Another reason to have a theology of martyrdom is to make sense of the kinds of experiences described by the little Armenian girl who had the cross burned into her shoulder in an attempt to make her deny her Lord. Could there be a connection between martyrdom and the cross?

The obvious place to start in seeking an answer to this question is with Jesus two thousand years ago on Golgotha. Humanly speaking, the cross for Jesus was capital punishment for his refusal to recant his position as Son of God, Savior, Messiah, and Lamb of God who takes away the sin of the world. On the other hand, from God's point of view it was the culmination of a long-held plan to bring redemption to humankind. No part of what occurred was finally in the hands of the human perpetrators of it. God controlled it all, albeit through the agency of human free will. For Jesus, the cross was martyrdom. And truly, his blood became the "seed of the church." Martyrdom always has these two sides to it. One side is what humans do to God's servants. The other side is what God intends to accomplish through it. No martyrdom is an accident from God's point of view. Before those missionaries ever committed their lives to his service, God was calling them to serve and die so that their blood would mingle with that of others to become the "seed of the church" in the places where they died.

THE MARTYR AND GOD

God does not call all to literal martyrdom, but in Matthew 16:24 he does call all of us to deny ourselves, take up our crosses, and follow him. The word translated "deny" in this verse is *aparneomai*, which means to disown utterly. Almost all uses of this word in the New Testament relate to Peter's denial of the Lord. When Peter stood at the fire and denied that he knew Jesus, he was utterly disowning his relationship with Jesus in order to protect himself. He considered his relationship with Jesus to be of no value compared to saving himself. This is why his remorse was so great afterward. It is also why he was later so motivated to serve the Lord at any cost. His denial of Jesus was no light thing. Jesus is calling us to consider our lives to be of no value at all compared with following him. And following him requires us to close the deal before we know the terms of the contract. We literally place our lives in his hands. We give him full control whether we live or die.

Christians in the West have interpreted the concept of taking up our crosses to mean obedience. And we have not been wrong in this as far as it goes. We have not, generally speaking, had to face death for our loyalty to Christ. In order for the concept to have meaning to us, we must dig beneath the act which took place on the cross to find Christ's motivation for going there—obedience.[6] "Taking up my cross means obeying whatever God asks me to do." However, we have not often considered that he might ask us to die at the hands of violent people for the sake of the kingdom. "Wait just a minute, Lord! What about the kids?

---

6 I realize this was not Christ's only motivation for going to the cross. His love for humanity and his desire to redeem them also motivated his sacrifice. However, obedience is probably what most Christians see as the meaning of "take up your cross and follow me."

What about my work? What about my career plan? I'm still young! I have my life to live!" We may feel that it is one thing to commit to God that we will do whatever he commands us to do and another thing entirely if he commands us to die.

After all, we believe we are called in Romans 12:1 to offer ourselves as "living sacrifices" with emphasis on the "living." However, God's emphasis is on the "sacrifice." A living sacrifice is still a sacrifice. The word translated "offer" here is *paristemi* and carries the meaning "to put at God's disposal." A living sacrifice has no personal agenda, no long-range plan, and no hope for tomorrow on the earth. It lives one day at a time awaiting its appointment with death.

In Luke 14:33 Jesus calls us to give up everything we have as his disciples. The word translated "give up" is *apotassomai* and means "to bid farewell," "to take leave of," and "to send away." Most missionaries realize that the material things they have, while they may have great sentimental value, are expendable. They carry them in their hands, not in their hearts. But what about those personal ambitions for the future and even those God-given responsibilities? Do we carry them in our hands, too, or in our hearts? Do we really believe that God is in control, that his will is benevolent and that he can take care of all that needs caring for when what seems to be disaster strikes?

In the call to be witnesses found in Acts 1:8, the word translated "witness" is *martus*, the word from which we get our word "martyr." The early Christians understood the meaning of the term—to be a witness is to risk suffering and death. They constantly faced the danger of death and vast numbers of them were martyred. In fact, by the early fifth century, the church historian Jerome had already counted nearly two million Christian martyrs (Bridges 1996). See the testimonies of the apostles throughout Acts. Almost always their witness was delivered in a context of danger, and all but one of them died a martyr's death.

In Ephesians 6:13–20 we are encouraged to wear armor for protection in the spiritual battle to carry the gospel to all people. And so we should. But we must realize that wearing spiritual armor does not make us physically invincible. The spiritual battle breaks out into the material world. Soldiers wearing armor get wounded. Some of them die. And some of us will, too. Just as military generals make decisions for the good of the whole that require exposing some of their soldiers to death, so God, for the sake of the kingdom, exposes some of his missionaries to death. Paul faced this danger every day. To be in chains in the Roman empire meant the great likelihood of death. But what did Paul ask for in verses 19 and 20? That he would be freed? No, that he would be fearless to proclaim the gospel in spite of the likelihood of death as a result.

Martyrs and Their Colleagues

Jesus, in John 15:13, called us to lay down our lives for our friends. The word translated "lay down" is *tithemi* which denotes a condition of passivity, and could be translated "to allow to settle, or to sink down." It is the word Jesus used in Luke 9:44 when he told the disciples to listen carefully. Literally he told them to let his words sink down into their ears. It is the word he used in Acts 1:7 when he told them a matter had been set by the Father's authority. It was a "done deal," not dynamic, but static; it had been settled. It is the word Paul used in Acts 13:47 when he quoted God speaking in Isaiah 49:6, "I have made you a light for the Gentiles." It is a settled fact. That is what Jesus is saying to us in John 15:13. He says there is no greater evidence of love than this—that people set their lives into the hands of God for the sake of their colleagues. They no longer claim the right to decide what will happen to themselves. It is in God's hands for the sake of their colleagues.

Further, in Luke 14:26, Jesus calls us to hate our families for his sake. This word translated "hate" is *miseo* and means to love less. It does not connote the malevolent emotion which our English word "hate" carries. Jesus calls us to love our families less than we love him and to put his concerns above theirs. This must be balanced with the commands of Scripture to take care of our families. However, it is easy for Christians today with the strong contemporary emphasis on the Christian family to put family concerns above God's concerns. In Luke 16:13 we learn the reason a believer must love his family less than Jesus—

because it is impossible to serve two masters equally. We will certainly love one less than the other. Jesus must have first place even when it means sacrificing other precious relationships. As concerns martyrdom, God has promised to be father to the fatherless and spouse to the widow. He has also commanded his church to take care of the orphans and widows. Can we take God at his word and trust his heart? Eddie Carswell and Babbie Mason have said it well in their song, "Trust His Heart."

> [God] is too wise to be mistaken.
> God is too good to be unkind.
> So when you don't understand,
> When you don't see His plan,
> When you can't trace His hand,
> Trust His heart.

When Jesus called his disciples to follow him, not one of them was unemployed. They were not standing around looking for something to do. Each was busy about his livelihood. When he called them, they immediately left their life work and followed him. There was sacrifice involved here. It required the abandonment of their occupation and the family income it represented, and also it called for separation from loved ones. These twelve men left their families behind and went with Jesus wherever he went. No doubt they saw their families from time to time. But they left them in the hands of God. And to what purpose? So they could go to the "next towns" where there were people with little or no opportunity to hear the gospel (Mk. 1:38). Jesus had the "next towns" on his heart. He pursued his course to reach them even though doing so eventually cost him his life. He called his disciples, and eventually us (1 Pet. 2:21), to follow in his steps. Are we willing to say with the Christians of the first century, "for your sake we face death all day long; we are considered as sheep to be slaughtered [living sacrifices]. [But] in all these things we are more than conquerors through him who loved us" (Rom. 8:36–37)?

THE MARTYR AND HIMSELF/HERSELF

A promise is given by Jesus in Matthew 10:39 that whoever loses his life for his [Jesus'] sake will find it. The word translated "lose" here is *apollumi* which literally means to destroy fully. Figuratively, as it is here, it means "to destroy, die, lose, mar, or perish." Almost always it is translated "kill," as with Matthew 2:13 or 10:28 for instance, or "lose" in terms of a final loss, as in Matthew 5:29–30 or with some euphemism for death. In a different phrasing of the same promise in John 12:25, Jesus says that the man who hates [loves less] his life will keep it. The promise is that when we consider ourselves dead to our own plans and dreams, love ourselves less than we love our Lord, we will experience life as it is meant to be lived—free of anxiety and inner pressure, full of heavenly purpose, and alive with the emotional freedom to be his person in our place for his glory whatever the cost. What peace!

PRESENTING THE OPPORTUNITY TO THE CHURCH

I recently read an advertisement posted by one mission agency:

> Wanted: Missionaries to Muslims. Bitter cold, scorching heat, long hours. Sickness almost certain. Possible imprisonment. Safe return not guaranteed. Honor and recognition from peers doubtful. Eternal rewards. Interested parties apply . . . (*IJFM* 1994).

This is an honest appeal. The dangers are projected up front along with the rewards. Those who wrote this ad are looking for those whom God has called and who are ready to take risks because they have entrusted themselves to God.

When missionary sending agencies present the opportunity to serve the Lord in difficult assignments, they must consider the pool of potential missionaries and try to couch their appeal in words and graphics which will catch their interest and stir up their reflection.

Volumes have been written describing Generation X, that pool of the population from which most of the career missionary appointees come these days. Generation X characteristics can be briefly summarized as follows: they most urgently long for meaningful relationships in life. They search for a way to live guilt-free lives. They do not want to wait for anything; rather, they want immediate gratification. They also do not want to pay the price for what they get; they are looking for the ultimate windfall. Finally, they are thirsting for prosperity, but most of them are destined to live a less affluent lifestyle than that afforded by their parents.[7]

Certainly the presence of the Holy Spirit living in the lives of born-again members of Generation X will make a vast difference in the characteristics of their lives. Nevertheless, it is likely that the basic generational description will be apparent in the decisions that they make regarding how they live their lives.

Two facets of this description should be of particular concern to missionary sending agencies: the longing for meaningful relationships and the search for freedom from guilt. A majority of Generation Xers, even Christian ones, have grown up in broken homes where relationships have been distant and/or painful and where fear has forced them to erect walls of emotional protection around themselves. Many of them have experienced abuse of one variety or another, and they are deeply wounded. They long for meaningful relationships, but find it difficult, if not impossible, to take down the protective barriers so that their longings can be satisfied.

This has incredible impact on missions. Carrying the gospel to someone else is an intensely personal matter. It has to do more with successful interpersonal relationships than it does with the ability to preach, teach, lead, or write effectively. This would be even more important in missions to Muslim peoples where the open evangelization of people is prohibited. Raymon Lull and Samuel Zwemer said it long ago, each in his own way, and it has never been more true: Muslims will be reached

---

7 I am indebted to Dr. O. S. Hawkins, pastor of the First Baptist Church of Dallas, for the concepts reported here.

through love—love that stimulates prayer, burden, and sacrifice.

People with wounded hearts find it deeply difficult to love others. They are constantly concerned, even though it may be at a subliminal level, with self-preservation and with self-protection. The focus is on self rather than on the people around them. This is not a problem which can be solved by knowing the right doctrine or memorizing Scripture verses. Those who have surrendered their lives to Christ know that God is love and that he has called them to love others for the sake of the kingdom. They want to do that, but their own wounds have often been sealed over with hard scabs of repression so that the infection continues presently but cannot be seen by them. They struggle to be what they believe God wants them to be, but they can never let go and be vulnerable. They live in a constant state of frustration if they truly seek to be God's people in their circumstances.

Such people are also burdened with guilt. Most of the guilt they feel is false guilt which is the result of blaming themselves for the pain of rejection. They believe that if they had just been better children that their lives would not have been disrupted as they have been. They struggle with the need to be perfect and to somehow earn the benevolence of God and other people. But they never feel they have achieved the necessary perfection, and so the struggle goes on and on and on, with guilt piling up upon guilt. Most who struggle with these inner pains cannot readily discern where their pain comes from. They only know they are driven.

People who struggle this way, whose inadvertent focus is inward, rather than outward, would have a painfully difficult time bearing the difficult stresses of ministering where they are not welcome. They are already carrying a full load of emotional stress because of unresolved childhood pain. Many may not have the emotional strength to bear up under the additional load. Some have had to leave the field because they could not manage the stress. Others have remained until their families disintegrated. Others have finally suffered nervous breakdowns. It is conceivable that others might welcome martyrdom as a means of release and thus live carelessly.

How much weight needs to be given to these problems which Generation Xers wrestle with in their personal lives? Certainly God is able to overcome a multitude of personal problems in the lives of his ambassadors. None of us would dare claim otherwise, for we are ourselves prime examples of it. Nevertheless, it would probably be foolish to ignore them altogether. God will never leave himself without witness, so we must not feel hopeless. On the other hand, it may be time for the church to look clearly at the needs of the youthful generation and discover ways for it to truly be the church to them, to find ways to administer the *shalom* of God to them so that they might be healed. It is a discussion for another venue, perhaps, to wrestle with these questions.

CONCLUSION

Almost thirty years ago, Joseph Kenny wrote,

> Any hope of converting more than occasional Muslims is unrealistic. A Muslim's adherence to his religion implies a deeply rooted social identity, prized alike by the individual and the community. While the Muslim community tolerates occasional individuals who are willing to forego the social benefits of being a Muslim by joining another religion, it certainly would actively resist any mass conversion movement. Perhaps more numerous conversions will eventually be possible, but only if generations of social evolution change the traditional situation (Kenny 1970:35).

Yet, today Muslims are coming to Christ by the hundreds in many Muslim countries. Reaching the Muslim world is "a do-able task, given the innate power of the gospel, the power of the Spirit at work in the hearts of men and women, and the willing and able hands and hearts of the Lord's laborers" (Weerstra 1996:161).

The cost, however, is very great. Missionary martyrdoms may not have increased greatly, but, as David Barrett says,

> the fact that national Christians have been hunted and hounded and even killed in ever-larger numbers in recent years (and that number is projected to increase in the future) is equally significant for missions (cited in Hesselgrave 1988:203).

He estimates that an average of one hundred sixty thousand Christians are killed for their faith every year (cited in Bridges 1996). These martyrdoms will continue in spite of the fact that as many as one hundred seventy-five million Christians will worship and serve the Lord as crypto-Christians by the year 2000 (Hesselgrave 1988:204).

The call remains the same since our Lord Jesus Christ presented it to his church almost two thousand years ago: "You will be my witnesses [*martures*] in Jerusalem, and in all Judea and Samaria, and to the ends parts of the earth." Some will be called upon to be martyrs in fact, others in spirit. But martyrs, nevertheless. Let us pray and work that the laborers might be called out and sent healthy into the fields, that they might have the stamina to reap the harvest the Lord is preparing in Muslim lands and to pay the ultimate price should they be called upon to do so.

Long ago E. H. Hamilton penned words of great power in response to the death of Jack Vinson, the first Southern Presbyterian martyr in China:

Afraid? Of What?
To feel the spirit's glad release!
To pass from pain to perfect peace,
The strife and strain of life to cease!
    Afraid—of that?
    Afraid? Of what?
Afraid to see the Savior's face
To hear His welcome, and to trace
The glory gleam from wounds of grace?
    Afraid—of that?
    Afraid? Of What?
A flash, a crash, a pierced heart;
Darkness, light, O Heaven's art!
A wound of His a counterpart!
    Afraid—of that?
    Afraid? Of What?
To do by death what life could not—
Baptize with blood a stony plot,
Till souls shall blossom from the spot?
    Afraid—of that? (cited in Hefley and Hefley 1996:57).

REFERENCES

Baba, Panya. 1994. "The Seriousness of the Mission Vision." *International Journal of Frontier Missions* 11:39.

Bridges, Erich. 1996. "Silent Night of the Martyrs: Time to Break the Silence." *Northwest Baptist Witness* (December 18).

______. 1997. "Pray for Muslims during Ramadan." *Baptist Standard* (January 22).

Douglas, Robert C. 1994. "Editorial: Time for the Muslims." *International Journal of Frontier Missions* 11:59.

Haught, James A. 1990. *Holy Horrors: An Illustrated History of Religious Murder and Madness*. Buffalo, NY: Prometheus.

Hefley, James and Marti Hefley. 1996. *By Their Blood: Christian Martyrs of the Twentieth Century*. 2nd edition. Grand Rapids: Baker.

Hesselgrave, David J. 1988. *Today's Choices for Tomorrow's Mission: An Evangelical Perspective on Trends and Issues in Missions*. Grand Rapids: Zondervan.

Horowitz, Michael. 1995. "New Intolerance Between Crescent and Cross." *The Wall Street Journal* A8 (July 5).

ICI Report. 1996. *The Continued Escalation of Persecution of Evangelical Christians in the Islamic Republic of Iran*. Colorado Springs: Iranian Christians International.

IJFM. 1994. Advertisement. *International Journal of Frontier Missions* 11:back cover.

Jabbour, Nabeel T. 1994. "Islamic Fundamentalism: Implications for Missions." *International Journal of Frontier Missions* 11:81.

Kennedy, John W. 1993. "Frontiers on the Frontline." *Christianity Today* 37:55.

Kenny, Joseph. 1970. "Reassessment of Apostolate among Muslims." *International Review of Mission* 233.

Lawrence, Carl. 1985. *The Church in China: How It Survives and Prospers under Communism*. Minneapolis: Bethany House.

Marantika, Chris. 1989. "The Church in the Islamic Context." In *Christian Suffering in Asia: The Blood of the Martyrs*

Is the Seed of the Church. B. R. Ro, ed. Pp. 106–107. Taichung, Taiwan, R.O.C.: Asia Theological Association.

McCurry, Don. 1994. "What's Happening among Muslims Today?" *International Journal of Frontier Missions* 11:99–104.

Missionary News Service. 1986. 33(February).

Shenk, Wilbert R. 1987. "The Future of Mission." *International Review of Mission* 76.

Tson, Iosif. *Suffering Martyrdom and Rewards in Heaven*. Unpublished manuscript.

Weerstra, Hans M. 1996. "Editorial: The Challenge of the Muslim Frontiers." *International Journal of Frontier Missions* 13.

Chapter 9

Overcoming Resistance Through Prayer

John D. Robb

Introduction

Prayer Through the Window is a global prayer effort focused on the nations of the "10/40 window." In 1993, more than two hundred seventy teams went out to pray on-site in these countries. It was my privilege to lead one of these teams to the country of Bhutan. Since that time, with the help of World Vision, I have worked with national Christian leaders to set up similar prayer initiatives in several other countries. These interdenominational prayer efforts have focused prayer on mission breakthrough in unreached peoples and/or sociopolitical transformation. Thus, I come at this subject from two angles: a concern for the removal of spiritual hindrances which keep unreached people groups from responding to the gospel (which is my AD2000 hat, if you will) as well as a concern for the overthrow of the evil which brings injustice, suffering and exploitation of the poor (which is my World Vision hat). Increasingly World Vision personnel in various countries are asking for prayer support because they are finding themselves wrestling with spiritual darkness in the communities we serve. For example, just a few weeks ago, in meetings with our staff in Indonesia, the major topic was how to deal effectively with the demonic forces that we are encountering.

Since the late 1960s, as a student involved in university evangelism, and during my field missionary experience which followed, I became convinced that prayer was our major resource in dealing with spiritual resistance. I continue to believe this but also realize acutely that I am still in the process of learning and hope that you will take my comments in that light. Perhaps the most solid conclusion I have reached is that we need to be humbly dependent upon God and to admit that we do not understand, so that as trusting, curious children he can lead us by the hand. King Jehoshaphat, when faced by overpowering resistance in the form of an invasion against his people by a combined force of three hostile nations, prayed, "We do not know what to do, but our eyes are upon you" (2 Ch. 20:12). This, it seems to me, is the safest posture for us to take as well.

Resistance to the church and its missionary endeavor, of course, springs from both human and demonic origins. Theologian Walter Wink's writings demonstrate that the Bible tends to use the same language for human and spiritual authorities or powers as in Ephesians 6 (1984). But since the apostle Paul says very explicitly that we wrestle not against flesh and blood (Eph. 6:12), I want to focus on the spiritual resistance which animates human beings and their institutions to oppose the kingdom of God.

We Must Discern the Real Source of Resistance and Use Spiritual Weapons to Combat It

Jesus said "The kingdom of heaven suffer[s] violence, and the violent take it by force" (Mt. 11:12, NKJV). A number of biblical scholars think that the meaning of this text is that the kingdom has been under attack from violent foes (Albright and Mann 1971, *Interpreter's Bible* 1951:382–83). Human beings and their institutions like King Herod and his soldiers captured and killed John the Baptist. Religious leaders in league with the Roman authorities opposed Jesus and had him executed. But behind these human forces, Jesus saw the one whom he often called "the prince of this world." And in Mark 3:27, speaking of Satan, he said that this "strongman" needs to be "bound" if his goods—presumably those human beings and their institutions held captive—are to be liberated from his control.

How did this strongman become strong enough in our world to put up such a violent resistance to the kingdom of God? The Genesis story teaches that the first people were given dominion of the earth to rule as God's vice-regents over all creation (Gen. 1:28). But through deception and disobedience, the serpent usurped our dominion, and become the veritable ruler of this world. In my opinion, prayer is the way we who have been redeemed from his slavery apply the victory of Calvary to take back that dominion in the specific situations and places for which we intercede. This, I believe, is the theological reason why prayer can be used of God to overcome resistance from the evil one. It is not that we are powerful in and of ourselves, but that our prayer invites the almighty Lord into the equation, and thus invited, he, as Lord of hosts, will put the enemy to flight.

Scripture attests over and over again that prayer is the mightiest weapon that we have been given for overcoming spiritual resistance. When Moses faced Pharaoh and the gods of Egypt, it was a power encounter that he won through a relationship of prayerful dependence on the Lord. On forty-six occasions in Exodus chapters 3 to 14 the Lord spoke to Moses. Only eleven times did Moses speak back to the Lord. In other words, he listened to God's instructions and acted upon them. Later on he revealed his understanding of what we might now call "spiritual warfare." At the crossing of the Red Sea he urged the Israelites to "Stand firm and you will see the deliverance the Lord will bring you today.... The Lord will fight for you; you need only to be still" (Ex. 14:13–14). In the struggle against the Amalekites, Moses took the high ground of intercession, standing on the mountain top with his arms raised before the Lord. As he kept his arms outstretched, the Israelites prevailed over the Amalekites in the valley below (Ex. 17:8–13). At the end of his life, he summarized his learning concerning spiritual warfare. He assured Israel that God would be their "shield," "helper," and "glorious sword" and said, "he will drive out your enemy before you" (Dt. 33:26–29).

Moses passed down what he had learned to Joshua, who, time and again, prayed for and received guidance from God as to the exact strategy for overcoming Israel's enemies during his conquest of Canaan. It is also important to note that the armies with which Israel fought went forth to war in dependence upon and under the control of false gods. For example, Moloch of the Ammonites and Chemosh of the Moabites were worshipped through human sacrifice and should definitely be called demons (Bromiley 1986 1:640, 3:401). Thus, there was an element of spiritual warfare even though these battles were fought on the physical plane.

Daniel the prophet mourned and prayed for three weeks before the angel of the Lord broke through the cosmic resistance of the princes of Persia and Greece (Dan. 10:2, 12–13). This story demonstrates both spiritual resistance and the power of prayer to prevail over it. The angel told Daniel, "Since the first day that you set your mind to gain understanding and to humble yourself before your God, your words were heard, and I have come in response to them" (10:12). Walter Wink, commenting on this passage, writes: "Recognizing the role of the Powers in blocking prayer can revolutionize the way we pray. We will be more energized and aggressive" (1992:317).

Jesus' own ministry, characterized by intense conflict with the demonic, was always undergirded by much prayer. This was his modus operandi whether he was enduring the temptation in the wilderness, confronting evil spirits in possessed people, or sweating blood at Gethsemane before his triumph over Satan on the cross. The apostles James and Peter both urge us to "resist" the devil so that he will flee from us. We are to do this in a context of submitting ourselves to God and humbling ourselves before him which is the posture of prayer (Jas. 4:7, 1 Pet. 5:9).

The apostle Paul repeatedly uses warfare terminology to describe his mission and that of God's people. There was no more violent image in Paul's day than an armor-clad Roman soldier. This is the image he uses in Ephesians 6 to describe our battle with the powers. He tells us that we do not wage war as the world does in a fleshly or purely human manner. Rather, the weapons we fight with have "divine power to demolish strongholds" (2 Cor. 10:4). Strongholds are points at which the "strongman" has a grip over a people group or human institution. They may be false political ideologies, such as communism, which mislead people or false religious beliefs, like the Hindu concept of caste, which lock people into an oppressive lifestyle. Ethnic stereotyping is an awful stronghold. For example, before the Rwandan genocide Hutu extremists constantly referred to the Tutsi as "cockroaches," dehumanizing them to the point where it was acceptable to eliminate them.

Paul says, "The god of this age has blinded the minds of unbelievers, so that they cannot see the light of the gospel of the glory of Christ, who is the image of God" (2 Cor. 4:4). People everywhere are perishing and being destroyed through the deception of this false god. They are also being turned against each other in senseless national and ethnic conflicts in which thousands, even millions, die, and no one wins except Satan, the destroyer. But Paul reminds us that the weapons which God has given us are mighty because Jesus has given us his power for the pulling down of demonic strongholds. After the seventy-two returned with joy and said, "Lord, even the demons submit to us in your name," he said, "I saw Satan fall like lightning from heaven." Then he said "I have given you authority [the legal right or power] to trample on snakes and scorpions and to overcome all the power of the enemy; nothing will harm you" (Lk. 10:19).

When you tread on snakes and scorpions, you do not do so lightly or with bare feet. You crush them so that they will not keep biting or harming other people with their deadly venom or sting. I remember the fury with which I killed a rattlesnake which appeared under the feed trough upon which I had just been sitting in our friend's stable. I cut him up into a dozen pieces to make sure he was really dead! In that situation, I became angrily violent because of the danger to myself and others. Speaking of spiritual warfare, Pastor Jack Hayford affirms, "Prayer is an act of violence" (cited in Roth 1995:105). When will we in the missions community and in the church at large get angrily violent enough to take up the spiritual weapons we have been given to really deal with the enemy? We often just treat the symptoms and let the evil one stay around to keep causing havoc.

THE DEGREE OF RESISTANCE TO THE GOSPEL CORRESPONDS TO THE PRESENCE OF EVIL SPIRITS

George Otis's research demonstrates that people groups renew covenants made by their forefathers with the powers of darkness through recurring religious festivals and rituals (1991:89–93). Even though Satan has gotten significant control over the world as we have seen, he seems to need the ongoing compliance of human beings to maintain or intensify his grip. Deborah Glick, a missionary working in Taiwan, describes "occasions when the presence, influence or empowering of evil spirits . . . is particularly obvious." She writes:

> During the time of a festival in honor of a god's birthday, the atmosphere may seem to be particularly heavy or oppressive, especially in the vicinity of the participating temple(s) as incense is burned, music played, and spirits are called down to be present or to make their presence known. In other instances *tang-ki* [mediums] may become spirit possessed or under the influence of spirits performing superhuman feats. [Her conclusion is:] in all of these cases missionaries and Christian workers ... may expect God to demonstrate his power by nullifying satanic power. Thus spirits may fail to manifest themselves at festivals, *tang-ki* may be unable to perform their feats, spells may no longer produce the desired effects and so forth. Missionaries and other Christian workers must be prepared to pray unabashedly either privately or publicly toward this end (1989:85).

Joy Boese, a missionary friend from Thailand, described the increasing spiritual oppression she felt which was accompanied by inexplicable apathy on the part of the people with regard to the gospel. "Spirit pillars" had just been erected in her town. She writes,

> From our local people I've learned that many cities have a "protective and ruling/controlling spirit" residing in a recognized "pillar." The provincial governor decides to erect a pillar and invites a spirit to come and inhabit that pillar to protect his city or province.

She mentions the rising interest in city pillars all over Thailand and, along with this, the occurrence of widespread drought and tremendously increased vices—gambling, prostitution, and drugs.[1]

Vernon Sterk writes about his missionary experience in a particular Mexican village:

> Since the gospel was first communicated in this village, there has been a great increase in the number of spirits and deities. This has been reflected in both the increased number of "saint" images in the local church-shrine and in the amazing multiplication of house "talking saints." The resistance to the gospel has corresponded with the increase in these spirits (1989:11).

Earlier this year a Japanese pastor told me that the majority of new converts to Christ would fall away from the faith unless he and his staff prayed with them personally, severing any preconversion connections with specific shrines and temples.[2] Anthropologist David Lewis adds:

> In Japan, which has been regarded as a "difficult" country for Christian missionary work, there is a need to pay attention to the country's "spiritual geography," the foci of demonic power at certain locations and the manner in which there may be interlinkages between them. The "resistance" to the gospel is not merely cultural but also spiritual. This is also a contributing reason why the Japanese appear to be more receptive to the gospel outside Japan than when they are in their own country (1993:82).

His conclusion is:

> Christians in Japan and those elsewhere who pray for Japan need to "avoid wasting valuable spiritual ammunition on inconsequential or phantom targets." There is a need for increased prayer against the spiritual forces of darkness in each area.

---

1 Joy Boese, in a letter, March/April, 1987.

2 Pastor Jun Takimoto, in a conversation, March, 1997.

He therefore calls for extending praise marches and prayer walks throughout the country (1993:82).

THE PRAYERS OF GOD'S PEOPLE CAN OVERCOME DEMONIC RESISTANCE, BRINGING SPIRITUAL BREAKTHROUGH AMONG THE UNREACHED AND SOCIAL TRANSFORMATION

I have talked with Christian workers all over the world who maintain that the prayer of God's people weakens the occult powers. An Assemblies of God pastor in northern Ghana, attending one of my Unreached Peoples Seminars, relayed how a witch doctor had been stubbornly opposing the work of his church, inciting the people against the Christians. However, when the believers united in prayer for that village, the witch doctor lost all his powers, and the villagers began to turn to the Lord.[3]

A doctor and his wife, who have devoted themselves to evangelism and church planting in the vast Indian state of Madhya Pradesh, describe what a difference prayer has made in overcoming resistance in Hindu villages. Before beginning the work of evangelism, they and their team members first pause at the outskirts of the target village to exert the authority of Jesus in prayer, binding any forces of the enemy that would seek to hinder the proclamation of the gospel. They often find a new receptivity and willingness to embrace the gospel and have seen increasing numbers of Hindus turn to Christ.[4]

If it is true that the prayers of believers make such a difference, how should we then pray?

It is important that we pray unitedly if resistance is to be overcome. Jesus promised us in Matthew 18 that if two of us agreed as touching *anything* it would be done by our father in heaven. The difficulty is in getting Christians to agree. It has been said, where there are two Christians there are three opinions! In the book of Acts major expansions of the church and spiritual break-

---

3 During an Unreached Peoples Seminar, Tamale, Ghana, March, 1993.

4 Victor Choudhrie, in a conversation, Varanasi, India, September, 1994.

throughs followed the believers praying in "one accord." According to the writings of J. Edwin Orr and David Bryant, united prayer has preceded every great revival in the history of the church (Bryant 1987:121). During our international prayer initiatives, we have found that reconciliation is a critical first step if believers are to pray in unity. In Bosnia, one month before the war ended, local Christians from Serb, Croat, and Muslim backgrounds first repented to one another, identifying with the sins of their peoples. It was then that they were able to pray effectively for peace and the healing of their land.

Unity in prayer is also essential for spiritual breakthrough in a resistant, unreached people. Missionary efforts for fifty years failed to make any dent upon the Bateke people of the Congo. It was only when Christian workers prayed unitedly and authoritatively against the spirit of the river which had enslaved this people with fear that sudden breakthrough came. Within weeks they saw dramatic response to the gospel with three thousand coming to the Lord followed rapidly by another five thousand![5]

In the summer of 1992, a group of occultists aggressively opposed the mass evangelism efforts some Russian friends and I were carrying out in the city of Saratov. They tore down the advertising posters and sought to create a diversion by holding a competing meeting on extrasensory perception. During our morning worship service two hundred believers united their prayers against the spirits of darkness who were controlling these human enemies. That evening, in spite of all the earlier opposition, between six thousand and seven thousand people made public commitments to Jesus Christ, which was an impact that was far beyond all we could have asked or thought!

We must pray specifically. We need to gather information and insights from documentary study, conferring with local Christian leaders and even interviewing members of the people group we are concerned to reach. All of this helps us know how to pray accurately. What is the nature of the grip that the forces of

---

5 Rev. Kividi Kikama, in an interview during 1994.

darkness have on this people group or city? This will involve a look at culture, history, religion, economics, and politics.

We need to pray holistically. Every dimension of a people's existence is important and all these dimensions—political, economic, social, cultural, and spiritual—are interconnected. In 1995, in the city of Cali, Colombia, the believers focused their prayers on the entrenched structural evil of their society. The infamous Cali drug cartel had used obscene amounts of money to buy over both government officials and police and had killed everyone who stood in their way, making Cali the most violent city in the world. A series of all night prayer vigils attended by tens of thousands of local believers did what nothing else could do. Shortly thereafter all the cartel leaders were either dead or behind bars, and an anti-corruption investigation began, resulting in the dismissal of hundreds of corrupt police officers and the imprisonment of cartel-linked politicians.[6]

In India, when Pastor Arthur Paul and his wife moved into a Hindu slum area of Bangalore, they were first greeted with a hail of stones. They persisted in much prayer for the community and then with the support of World Vision began to reach out to the people, caring for little girls who would have been sold into prostitution and praying for the terminally ill. Deeds of love and mercy plus miracles of healing and deliverance demonstrated the reality of Jesus. There and elsewhere in the state of Karnataka they have so far baptized about five thousand, of which the great majority have come from a Hindu background. According to Pastor Paul, more than anything else it was prayer that brought the breakthrough.[7] In the same way we need to pray holistically for the needs of individuals and the entire community.

We need to praise God and proclaim his word. It was at the decisive moment when Judah's singers of praise began to sing and "give thanks to the Lord, for his love endures forever" that the Lord set ambushes against their enemies (2 Chr. 20:21–23).

---

6 Rev. Hector Torres, in an interview, September 16, 1997.

7 Rev. Arthur Paul, in an interview in Bangalore, India, September, 1996.

The invading armies were thrown into confusion and put to flight. The apostle Paul indicates that it is through the church that the manifold wisdom of God is proclaimed to the rulers and authorities in the heavenly realms (Eph. 3:10). Praise and the proclamation of the word of God are powerful tools to do this. In our prayer initiatives we have found that worship and praise to God, as well as proclaiming passages of his word, are essential parts of changing the spiritual atmosphere where there is difficulty or resistance. During a prayer seminar in Bangkok in April 1995, a member of our team led in proclaiming Moses' words to Pharaoh, "Let my people go." We proclaimed this word in the face of the division which was keeping God's people in that city from coming together to pray in unity. Several months later, more than five hundred Christians from across the denominational spectrum, including those who had been at odds, gathered to pray together for the first time. One of the prayer leaders attributed it to the April seminar in which the participants had made this proclamation.

We Must Hold to the Central Focus of the Kingdom of God—Bringing People to Christ

As Tom White puts it,

> Power encounter like any other aspect of ministry is not to become a preoccupation. There is a danger of a holy crusade to rid the world of evil strongholds. If the vision of the heart of God aching for the lost is blurred by a commando operation to storm the gates of hell, we miss the point of the Great Commission (1989:13).

The whole point of this kind of praying is to bring liberation to those groups of people whose minds are still blinded by the god of this world and who are hindered from understanding and responding to the gospel (2 Cor. 4:4). Therefore, like Jesus, we need to keep focused on individual and social redemption and transformation.

We Also Need to Face the Fact That Sometimes Resistance Will Not Be Overcome or That We Will Have Mixed Results

Pharaoh still hardened his heart against the prayers of Moses. The Sanhedrin, for the most part, rejected Jesus and crucified him. The apostle Paul was stoned, whipped, and ultimately beheaded. We Americans sometimes bring a success mentality to prayer along with a materialistic, technological way of thinking which assumes we can just pull a lever and get a particular result. In Colombia, even while marvelous breakthroughs have been occurring in answer to united prayer, over two hundred pastors have lost their lives during the same two year period due to attacks by guerrillas and paramilitary forces.[8] Backlash from an utterly fierce and ruthless foe is to be expected. In Matthew 24, Jesus warned us about persecutions that his people will experience and that sometimes we may not be delivered.

There is still a profound air of mystery surrounding prayer and how God uses our praying to transform our world. Walter Wink wisely affirms:

> Prayer is not magic; it does not always "work"; it is not something we do, but a response to what God is already doing within us and the world. Our prayers are the necessary opening that allows God to act without violating our freedom. Prayer is the ultimate act of partnership with God (1992:312).

References

Albright, W. F. and C. S. Mann. *The Anchor Bible: Matthew*. Garden City, NY: Doubleday.

Bromiley, Geoffrey, ed. 1986. *The International Standard Bible Encyclopedia*. Vol. 1. and Vol. 3. Grand Rapids: Eerdmans.

Bryant, David. 1987. "Prayer Movements Signal New Light for the Nations." *Evangelical Missions Quarterly* (April).

---

8 Torres interview.

Glick, Deborah. 1989. "Toward an Application of a Power Theology in Inner City Taipei, Taiwan." M.A. thesis, Columbia Biblical Seminary and Graduate School of Missions.

Interpreter's Bible. 1951. New York: Abingdon-Cokesbury.

Lewis, David C. 1993. *The Unseen Face of Japan*. Tunbridge Wells, U.K.: Monarch.

Otis, George, Jr. 1991. *Last of the Giants*. Tarrytown, NY: Chosen Books.

Roth, Randall. 1995. *Prayer Powerpoints*. Wheaton.: Victor.

Steck, Vernon. 1989. "Territorial Spirits and Evangelization in Hostile Environments." Unpublished paper, Fuller Theological Seminary School of World Mission.

White, Tom. 1989. "A Model for Discerning, Penetrating and Overcoming Ruling Principalities and Powers." Unpublished paper presented at Lausanne Congress on World Evangelization (July).

Wink, Water. 1984. *Naming the Powers*. Philadelphia: Fortress.

______. 1992. *Engaging the Powers:Discernment and Resistance in a World of Domination*. Minneapolis: Fortress.

Chapter 10

OVERCOMING RESISTANCE THROUGH THE PARANORMAL

Sobhi Malek

INTRODUCTION

During most of the twentieth century, the Western world has drifted dangerously toward materialism. Western civilization has clearly aligned itself with secular humanism. It seems to me that in the West the average person is skeptical of the supernatural and does not believe in miracles. It is easy to trace this attitude to the eighteenth century Enlightenment that refused to believe in divine intervention and exalted reason over revelation and materialism over spirituality. An example of such thinking is David Hume's argument that since a miracle is a violation of the laws of nature, and since such laws are firmly established and cannot be violated, miracles do not exist (1748:s.10, p.1).

Now, at the end of the twentieth century, we are encountering a disheartening shift, particularly in America, where New Age thought and practices have people delving into spiritism and dealings with the underworld which produce supernatural phenomena. Europe and other parts of the world are following closely behind!

These are two dangerous extremes that have one thing in common: they exalt humans to take the place of God. Here we will support the biblical assertion of the existence of paranormal phenomena, which I will describe under the category of miracles.

Definition and Explanation of Miracles

Ahmad (not his real name) was a Muslim college student. He accepted Christ, and six months later he was baptized and manifested the indwelling of the Holy Spirit. He liked to skin dive. One day after he was converted, he was skin diving in the Mediterranean Sea. Down under the water where he was diving, he caught his foot in the crevice of some rocks. He tried and tried to get free, but nothing worked. Finally, he said he actually began to feel the life leaving his body. Then he said in desperation, "Jesus" he said. Just his name, but he said it as a prayer. And he still does not know how it happened, but he found himself at the surface of the water. This was apparently a miracle.

What is a miracle? Simply stated, a miracle is a supernatural intervention of God in human affairs or nature's course to magnify God's name and comfort humans. The result of this typically cannot be explained scientifically.

I believe that the Bible teaches us that all Christians living for their Lord can be empowered and entrusted to perform miracles. But miracles can also be performed by magicians, sorcerers, spiritists, Muslim Sufis and holy men, and practitioners of some oriental religions. Yet signs and wonders that come from God take place by the power of the Holy Spirit, in the name of Jesus Christ, who is the Son of the living God, and on the foundation of the cross of Calvary. This more narrow definition of a miracle is what will guide my discussion.

Miracles should point beyond themselves to God, who created the natural order of the universe and life and is able to disrupt that order, suspend it, interfere with it, go beyond it, or control it. You may use whichever expression you prefer! Thus miracles should not be ends in themselves but should always bring glory to God.

As the disciples preached the message of eternal salvation, God "worked with them and confirmed his word by the signs that accompanied it" (Mk. 16:20). "The apostles performed many miraculous signs and wonders among the people" (Ac. 5:12, NIV).

Paul states the same idea when he says: "My message and my preaching were not with wise and persuasive words, but with a demonstration of the Spirit's power" (1 Cor. 2:4, NIV). The Greek word *apodeixis*, translated here "demonstration," literally means "proof" and "something that is forceful enough to bring conviction."

"The things that mark an apostle—signs, wonders and miracles—were done among you with great perseverance" (2 Cor. 12:12).

Most interpreters agree that signs, wonders, and miracles are synonyms. They do not describe three categories of miraculous acts, but rather three different aspects from which mighty deeds are seen:

- They are signs in their ability to authenticate the message and point to its validity.
- They are wonders in the sense that they evoke awe and astonishment.
- They are miracles in their display of divine supernatural power and extraordinary marvelous acts.

Miracles Can Help Overcome Resistance

People are seeking relief for their emotional stress, solutions for their relational, financial, and economic pressures, and cures for their physical sufferings. Normally, they look for answers and help wherever they can find them.

As ministers of the gospel, we have Christ's power available to us to help others. Miracles can be achieved through prayer in the name of Jesus to bring to immediate needs answers that have been considered impossible to receive in the natural realm. In other words, we are talking about prayer that produces a miracle. Miracles also take place through the manifestations of the gifts of the Holy Spirit.

Such demonstrations of God's mighty acts and his power to meet people's deep daily needs are important catalysts to quell antagonism and hostile feelings toward the gospel. These demonstrations often help people to take a step of faith toward Christ. In the Bible, the supernatural often gave the people of God an open door to speak on God's behalf and declare his glory (1 Ki. 18:36–39; Ac. 28:3–10). It also motivated people to listen to the message (Ac. 8:6–7).

In many cases in the New Testament, miracles took place to break people's resistance to Christ's message and to lead them to repentance and faith. Toward the end of his story about Christ, John says: "Jesus did many other miraculous signs in the presence of his disciples. . . . But these are written that you may believe" (Jn. 20:30–31).

When supernatural demonstrations take place in the name of Jesus, evidence of the superiority of Christ over heathen lords and belief systems is demonstrated.

I believe that miracles today can have the same results as in the time of Jesus and the apostles. Through miracles, people see the glory of God at work as they hear the good news of Jesus. The Holy Spirit will minister to their needs, cast out evil spirits, deliver a demonized person, heal sick bodies, alleviate pain and suffering, supply a job, send rain, give someone a wife or a husband, dispel fears of the unknown and the future, and grant security and assurance. Such happenings can help lessen people's resistance to the message.

When resistance is overcome, hearts can be more open to hear the message. When people hear with open hearts and minds, they are more disposed to accept the claims of Christ and his offer of free grace. Then the living Christ can be recognized as Lord over all. The gospel record, however, indicates that despite the signs some become hardened in their disbelief.

Saul's resistance to the message of Jesus was completely demolished through the complex miracle on the road to Damascus (Ac. 9:1–18; 22:5–16; 26:12–18):

1. A bright light from heaven flashed around Saul in broad daylight.
2. Saul must have believed the high priest's story that Jesus' disciples had stolen his dead body and had hidden it somewhere in a secret tomb. What a surprise to Saul that

Jesus himself who was alive, well, and mighty, appeared to him and spoke with him!
3. Saul's companions saw and heard some of the things that happened.
4. Saul lost his sight for three days and regained it only after Ananias prayed for him.

Result? Saul could not resist anymore. His defenses and attack system were overpowered by the miraculous.

Why Miracles Can Help Overcome Resistance

Miracles can help overcome resistance because they can be:

A Witness to God's love

People have needs. Sometimes those needs are impossible to meet apart from supernatural intervention. When that happens, people often realize that God cares for them. He loves them and is concerned about them. He is a God who is interested in his creation.

The Bible tells us that because of his compassion and love, Jesus performed miracles (Mk. 8:2–10; Lk. 7:11–17), healed the sick (Mt. 20:33, 34; Mk. 1:41), and cast out demons (Mk. 5:18, 19).

> During those days another large crowd gathered. Since they had nothing to eat, Jesus called his disciples to him and said, "I have compassion for these people; they have already been with me three days and have nothing to eat. If I send them home hungry, they will collapse on the way, because some of them have come a long distance"....
>
> When he had taken the seven loaves and given thanks, he broke them and gave them to his disciples to set before the people, and they did so. They had a few small fish as well; he gave thanks for them also and told the disciples to distribute them. The people ate and were satisfied. Afterward the disciples picked up seven basketfuls of broken pieces that were left over. About four thousand men were present (Mk. 8:1–3, 6–9).

> Jesus had compassion on them and touched their eyes. Immediately they received their sight and followed him (Mt. 20:34).
>
> As Jesus was getting into the boat, the man who had been demon-possessed begged to go with him. Jesus did not let him, but said, "Go home to your family and tell them how much the Lord has done for you, and how he has had mercy on you" (Mk. 5:18, 19).

Miracles can help overcome resistance also because they can be:

A Confirmation of the Claims of Christ

In one of the heated debates the Jews had with Jesus, he told them that his works were a clear confirmation of who he claimed to be. He said:

> Why then do you accuse me of blasphemy because I said, "I am God's Son"? Do not believe me unless I do what my Father does. But if I do it, even though you do not believe me, believe the miracles, that you may learn and understand that the Father is in me, and I in the Father (Jn. 10:36b–38).

In this passage, Jesus cites his works as a witness to his divinity. He tells the Jews that they should accept him as God's son because of the works he does. Those works showed that he was exercising divine, supernatural power. His ability to command the winds and the waves, to heal the sick, and to raise the dead all proved that his claims were divinely supported and accredited .

> Believe me when I say that I am in the Father and the Father is in me; or at least believe [me] on the evidence of the miracles them selves (Jn. 14:11).

Further, no one else could do those works. They were his distinctive acts.

Nicodemus made a comment in line with this. He said to Jesus: "Rabbi, we know you are a teacher who has come from God. For no one could perform the miraculous signs you are doing if God were not with him" (Jn. 3:2). When Jesus fed the multitude, the people who saw the power of God working through him concluded: "Surely this is the Prophet who is to come into the world" (Jn. 6:14). Manifestations of divine power confirm Christ's claims and point people to him.

We should never forget that often there are spiritual forces behind humanistic and religious systems, and we need to encounter them with the supernatural power of our God.

The Bible says that many people came to meet Jesus because they heard about the miracle of raising Lazarus from the dead.

> Now the crowd that was with him when he called Lazarus from the tomb and raised him from the dead continued to spread the word. Many people, because they had heard that he had given this miraculous sign, went out to meet him (Jn. 12:17–18).

Around 1912, a Muslim Iranian, Mer'at-es-Sultan, was the police commissioner of the province of Azerbaijan. At that time, Azerbaijan belonged to Iran and was a northeastern province of that country.

The Russians invaded the area, occupied it and started looking for the police commissioner. Sultan fled toward Turkey, but his efforts were frustrated because of severe weather conditions. Snow, cold, and the pursuing enemy forced him to take refuge in the home of an Armenian priest who compassionately hosted him. For forty days, the man provided him with the shelter, protection, and care he badly needed.

When it was time for the fugitive to continue his flight, the priest told him that during all forty days of his stay he had been praying for him "in the presence of Jesus Christ" for his safety so that he would return unharmed to his family. "But are you ready," asked the priest, "to promise Christ that when you arrive safely at your home you will not forget him but will yield yourself to your Savior?" Sultan said he was and went on his way. The priest testified confidently to Jesus' ability and willingness to help out the Muslim officer.

Later on, Sultan was captured by the Russian forces and put in a cold, dark prison awaiting execution. During his months in prison, he prayed in every conceivable Islamic way. He invoked all the prophets and imams by name to help him out. But there was no help; he was to be executed.

Finally, the morning of his appointed death came. At nine o'clock he was seized with fear and panic—there was no hope.

Suddenly, the words of the priest came back to him. Immediately he turned his heart to Christ. "Jesus Christ," he said, "if you are alive today and are the Savior of sinful men, deliver me, a sinner, from this plight that I may believe on you."

The door to the cell opened and the prisoner was taken to the gallows. When he saw the gallows, he was gripped with absolute despair and distress. Yet suddenly a group of mounted soldiers appeared and handed the officer in charge of the execution a letter from the Russian government, telling him to let Sultan go free.

Sultan fell on his knees and worshipped Christ. He acknowledged Christ's power and pledged to follow him the rest of his life. At the close of his prayer, this police commissioner of the province of Azerbaijan said: "So long as I live, I shall continue to live in the hope of the love of Christ . . . [who] is the Savior of sinners."

When he returned home, Sultan found out that his wife had received Christ as her Lord and Savior because someone had witnessed to her. Moreover, a friend informed him that he had been praying for him to receive Christ! (Allen 1952:176–184).

Miracles can help overcome resistance also because they can be:

A Proof of the Truth Proclaimed

Miracles also can help overcome resistance because they serve as a proof of the truth we preach. God said to Moses and the Israelites that he would show his miracles to Pharaoh so that the children of Israel might know that he is the Lord.

> Then the LORD said to Moses, "Go to Pharaoh, for I have hardened his heart and the hearts of his officials so that I may perform these miraculous signs of mine among them that you may tell your children and grandchildren how I dealt harshly with the Egyptians and how I performed my signs among them, and that you may know that I am the LORD" (Ex. 10:1–2).

Miracles are an important means of proving what we say. I am always amazed when I read the story of Joseph's brothers when they went back to Canaan to tell their father that Joseph was still alive. I expected Jacob to be so happy and ready to go to

Egypt to see his long-lost son. Yet the Bible has this to say: "They told him, 'Joseph is still alive! In fact, he is ruler of all Egypt.' Jacob was stunned; he did not believe them" (Gen. 45:26).

He was stunned! The King James Version says, "Jacob's heart fainted."

> But when they told him everything Joseph had said to them, and when he saw the carts Joseph had sent to carry him back, the spirit of their father Jacob revived (v. 27).

Their own words caused his heart to faint, but Joseph's words and the carts which he sent to carry them to Egypt sent life into Jacob's being. The carts were tangible signs of Joseph being alive and well and in a position of authority and power.

Peter and John were arrested and jailed for preaching Christ to the throngs that gathered in the wake of the miraculous healing of the paralytic (Ac. 4:1–3). After deliberating on their case, their judges decided to release them but at the same time commanded them not to preach Christ (v. 18). The two apostles went back to the other believers, and all of them prayed: "Sovereign Lord . . . stretch out your hand to heal and perform miraculous signs and wonders through the name of your holy servant Jesus" (vv. 24, 30). As a proof of the truth they were proclaiming, they asked for manifestations of the power of God.

Fadila is a Muslim young lady who came to our house with some questions about the Christian faith. My wife and I shared with her about God's love demonstrated in Christ. After I learned that she had attended a Christian meeting a few times, I asked her what most impressed her about the meeting. I was not surprised when she answered, "The music and people speaking in languages they did not learn!" Today, Fadila is a keen believer serving Christ.

Miracles can help overcome resistance also because they can be:

A Weapon for Spiritual Warfare

In building the church of Jesus Christ, we are engaged in spiritual warfare. When we attack the kingdom of darkness to deliver precious souls from the grip of Satan, the enemy does not stand by and watch his demise without reacting! He attacks and counterattacks.

Dialogue, intellectual debate, life-style evangelism, social assistance, hospitals and medical work, agricultural development, food aid, schools and education, literacy programs and the like are often helpful endeavors, and they can have their place and time in proclaiming Christ to the nations and in the dynamics of God's kingdom. But working in the realm of the supernatural adds a dimension of the gospel that can be decisive in the spiritual warfare against Satan.

Jesus said:

> When a strong man, fully armed, guards his own house, his possessions are safe. But when someone stronger attacks and overpowers him, he takes away the armor in which the man trusted and divides up the spoils (Lk. 11:21–22. *See* also Mt. 12:29).

Miracles can help us to challenge the power of the enemy, overwhelm him, and gain victory over him.

Miracles can help overcome resistance also because they can be:

A Manifestation of the Kingdom Coming in Power

Supernatural power is an important manifestation of the kingdom of God.

> The Kingdom, the final rule of God, manifested itself in healings and cures which liberated individuals at every level of their being, including not least the physical and mental. Wherever Satan exercised his sway, the proclamation and power of the Kingdom was concerned to bring about release and liberation (Dunn and Twelftree 1980:220).

As God's kingdom advances today, the Lord continues to work out his purpose, utilizing the miraculous to break people's opposition to the gospel in order to free them from Satan's fetters. Their deliverance from demonic spirits in the name of Jesus is clear evidence that his kingdom has come among us.

George Eldon Ladd points out that

> God is now acting among men to deliver them from bondage to Satan. . . . The exorcism of demons is proof that the kingdom of God

> has come among men and is at work among them. The casting out of demons is itself a work of the kingdom of God (cited in De Wet 1982:26).

In 1925 Watchman Nee, the famous Chinese writer and preacher, went with six other young men to preach the gospel in a village called Mei-hwa. The villagers, mainly fishermen and farmers, had never heard of Christ.

When the party of seven evangelists arrived, the village was celebrating the annual festival of the god Ta-Wang, the great king. People were eating, drinking, gambling, engaging in ancestor worship, and giving their offerings to the local gods. There was neither room nor time to hear or heed the preachers' message. The villagers said that they needed only to depend on Ta-Wang. Divination showed that his festival should be held on the eleventh day of that month. For two hundred eighty-six consecutive years he had always provided sunshine on his day.

Upon hearing this, one of the Christian preachers challenged them: "I promise you," he said, "Our God who is the true God, will make it rain on the eleventh." The villagers accepted the challenge. "If there is rain on the eleventh," they said, "then Jesus is indeed God and we'll be ready to hear him." Watchman Nee and his friends felt that they put themselves on the spot. The preachers went into special prayer.

Then the eleventh came. The sun was shining bright. Watchman Nee prayed for rain. As the seven evangelists and their host sat at breakfast, they were all very quiet. There was not a cloud in the sky! They bowed to thank God for the meal and also to remind him that they needed the rain.

Before they said "Amen," they heard drops of rain on the tiles! While they were eating their breakfast, they gave thanks to the Lord and asked for heavier rain. The rain came down in bucketfuls. Some young people of the village shouted: "There is God; there is no more Ta-Wang! The rain has kept him in!"

But the worshippers of Ta-Wang brought the idol out on a chair hoping that he would stop the rain. After walking only a few yards, they stumbled and fell. And down went the god, fracturing his jaw and his left arm. After he was repaired, they took him out again. The streets were flooded, and they and he fell again. So they decided that the eleventh was the wrong day. The procession was to take place at 6 p.m. on the fourteenth. When the sky cleared later in the afternoon of the eleventh, people came to hear the preaching of the gospel. Thirty villagers accepted Christ as their Lord and Savior.

The evangelists prayed that rain would pour down at 6 p.m. on the fourteenth and that there would be good weather until then. The sky was clear on the twelfth and the thirteenth. The fourteenth started as another perfect day. But exactly at 6 p.m. there were torrential rains and floods!

Christ manifested his glory in his mighty power over nature. The servants of Christ had challenged Ta-Wang, and he had lost his centuries-old reputation. Satan's power represented in the idol was broken (Kinnear 1984:92–96).

Further, miracles can help overcome resistance also because they can be:

A Live Encounter with Christ

True religion starts with what God does. People then respond to his divine provision by experiencing and expressing faith, repentance, worship and joy; by being baptized and by receiving communion; and by other manifestations in their daily lives.

Why are some of us afraid to emphasize experience?

The basic reason is that for two centuries some theologians have been telling us not to depend on experience. But why should biblically founded and validated experience be a negative notion? It should not be. As a matter of fact, it should play a significant role in our spiritual growth.

John White asserts that:

> In the real world experiences often validate truth. Biblical writers affirm the truths they present by describing their experiences. Isaiah tells the awesome story of his subjectively experienced call to be a prophet, as do Jeremiah and Ezekiel. Jesus himself tells Nicodemus "... we speak what we know, and we testify to what we have seen ..." Peter assured us that we do not follow cunningly devised fables, but the result of firsthand observation. Paul makes the same kind of reference to the gospel revealed to him in Arabia as the prophets. Ordinary people call experience to validate truth also. The Samaritan

> prostitute, on the basis of her experience of him, cries, "Is not this the Christ?" And throughout the history of the Church, God repeatedly gives people the experience of being taken by the scruff of the neck as he shakes them and says, "Wake up! Let's get back to basics!" (cited in Williams 1989:ix).

Reading 1 John 1:1–14, we encounter several verbs that are related to experiencing Christ: "we have heard," "seen," "our hands have touched," "life appeared," "we have seen it," and so forth.

It seems also that for some people, the manifestation of God's power in miraculous signs intensifies their hatred for Christ! Jesus referred to that when he said to his disciples:

> If I had not done among them what no one else did, they would not be guilty of sin. But now they have seen these miracles, and yet they have hated both me and my Father (Jn. 15:24).

CONCLUSION

Demonstrated by miracles, the victorious gospel can be proclaimed. When poor, imprisoned, and enslaved people hear, they will sense freedom. When they accept the message, those groping in the darkness will see the light. The overcoming church will go on victoriously, and the kingdom of God will prevail over the kingdom of Satan.

An Asian worker in a Muslim country was saved and filled with the power of the Holy Spirit. His host country absolutely bans preaching the gospel. Soon after his conversion, this new Christian started to share the gospel with others. The Lord gave him power to heal the sick in the name of Jesus. About that time, a little girl from the host country's royal family was diagnosed with leukemia. The doctors gave her family no hope for her living.

A princess who had heard of the Christian foreign worker contacted him to go and pray for the sick girl. He did. The little girl was healed, and the princess who made the contact accepted Christ and began to share her faith quietly and wisely with other members of the royal house. As a result, today there is a small but growing group of believers in that family (as told to the author by an expatriate living in that country).

In Malaysia, a Chinese Buddhist teenage girl gave her heart to Christ. Shortly afterward, she received a call to serve the Lord in the ministry. To prepare herself, she wanted to attend Bible school, but she knew her family would be against it. When she asked her pastor what she should do, he told her to spend time in prayer first and then tell her parents she wanted to attend Bible school. She followed his advice, and as she had feared, her mother became very angry and refused to allow her to go. The young girl, now sad and afraid, told her pastor what happened. He once more advised her to pray and then talk with her mother again. When she followed his advice, her mother locked her in a room for one month to force her to renounce her faith in Christ.

At the end of the month, the mother asked a Buddhist priest, who was also a medium and was possessed by a spirit, to come to her house to help her change her daughter's mind. When he arrived, he asked her to open the door of the room where her daughter had been locked in for one month. The priest/medium then approached the girl and looked her straight in the eyes in an attempt to influence her. Suddenly he stopped, turned around, gathered up all the things he had brought with him, and prepared to leave. Before going, he told the mother that he could do nothing because the spirit in her daughter was stronger than the spirit in him. As a result, the mother and the girl's entire family became Christians (as told by the young woman's pastor in Malaysia).

It is when believers courageously preach the gospel of salvation and avail themselves of the supernatural power available to them in the person of the Holy Spirit working through manifestations and gifts that they can overcome satanic opposition.

> Where is our Christ, who is alive and lives in power? In the preaching of our churches, he has become a beautiful ideal. He has been turned into a myth, embodying a theological concept. The witness to his objective reality has largely been lost. . . . [Many] churches have never even heard of the power of prayer in his name. The church has become an organization of well-meaning idealists, working for Christ

> but far from his presence and power (Wuellner cited in Willard 1991:22).

In closing, I would like to report another miracle in the life of Ahmad, the young man I mentioned at the beginning. After Ahmad graduated from college, he was appointed to a very good position with the government. A few months later he was called in for military service. Since there was no guarantee that he would be re-hired after serving in the military, he had to confront the real possibility of losing his good job. But he had to go.

On his first day at the military camp, they shaved his head and gave him military fatigues. During a break, he sat under a tree and was discouraged and despondent. He said that he tried to pray, but words would not come. Yet his soul was crying out to God for help. All of a sudden, he heard a voice from behind him saying: "Where is Jesus whom you have been following? Ha! Jesus is not the mighty God. Muhammad is the prophet of God. Can Jesus help you now? Renounce your faith in him and call on Muhammad." A power encounter was definitely at hand. He said that the voice was almost audible. He immediately rebuked the voice and said: "Satan, get away from me. You're a liar." Then he continued, "Jesus, I believe in you. You are the son of God. You are my Lord, my Savior, my everything. I love you Jesus. Help me." Only a few hours later the young man was discharged from the military and was able to return to his job. No explanation was given for his release (from Ahmad's personal testimony given in a Christian meeting two days after his discharge). Such signs in the name of Jesus communicate Christ's victory and confirm the validity of the gospel to the millions who need to hear.

References

Allen, C. H. 1952. "Why a Muslim Official Changed His Faith." *The Muslim World* pp. 176–184.

De Wet, Christiaan. 1982 "Biblical Basis of Signs and Wonders." In *Signs and Wonders Today*. Christian Life

Magazine and C. Peter Wagner, eds. Wheaton: *Christian Life Magazine*.

Dunn, D. G. and Graham H. Twelftree. 1980. "Demon Possession and Exorcism in the New Testament." *Churchman* 94(3):220.

Hume, David. 1748/1926. *Concerning Human Understanding*. Chicago: The Open Court Publishing.

Kinnear, Angus. 1984. *The Story of Watchman Nee—Against the Tide*. Wheaton: Tyndale.

Williams, Don. 1989. *Signs, Wonders, and the Kingdom of God*. Ann Arbor: Servant.

Willard, Dallas. 1991. *The Spirit of the Disciplines: Understanding How God Changes Lives*. New York: HarperCollins.

Chapter 11

Overcoming Resistance through Tentmaking

Gary Ginter

By way of introduction, resistance is fundamentally a spiritual issue. It will only be broken through spiritual weapons:

- by faith,
- by prayer, and
- by the Spirit-filled life

The Spirit-filled life consists of an active blend of faith and prayer which is really just Christian action. Any discussion of how to overcome resistance must start by recognizing that only God's Holy Spirit overcomes resistance. It is true that he has chosen to use people and techniques to do so, but those techniques are lifeless if they are not characterized by being acts of faith, prayers in motion, if you will. If, at the end of the day, our hope lies in our cleverness, rather than in our cooperation within God's plan, then we will see only the results that our cleverness can achieve. We will not see happen what God desired but in which we failed to cooperate. Only genuine Christian action will overcome resistance, and even then only in God's time and because of his enablement.

When Christians speak of *tentmaking*, they all too often are thinking of either an access strategy or a financial strategy. To view tentmaking that way is to confuse two possible effects of tentmaking as a process with the essence of what a tentmaker is.

Today, I want to reflect on one small but important distinguishing feature in what determines who are or are not tentmakers and how effective they may be in overcoming barriers to resistance. That key determinant is time: the tentmaker and time. How persons use their time has a major impact on how effective they are as tentmakers.

Medical personnel are the most common (and perhaps the most consistently effective) examples of tentmaking. Doctors and nurses have been such successful tentmakers that most mission boards do not even think of them in those terms anymore—they are just missionaries, like everybody else. Precisely correct! But they are the best examples of healthy tentmaking that we have. And they wrestle with the problem of how to spend their precious time: healing physical needs or spiritual needs. They can never meet all the crying needs of those with whom they work. So, what do they do?

My father once asked A. C. Osterholm, a medical missionary in Africa, how he ever managed to get enough time to share the message of Christ with those he served. The kindly surgeon replied that he never had enough time; he had to make time available to talk to patients about the gospel. He did so knowing that when he did some of the sick would not receive medical attention. It is a hard choice for these medical tentmakers to choose to spend time ministering in ways besides those of their medical calling. However, this problem of the tentmaker and time is not limited to medical workers. Though they may face the problem more obviously, they face it no more truly than many other types of tentmakers or professionals. To help us think through this issue, perhaps an intellectual map or framework of how time and ministry relate in all of our lives might prove helpful. You are all professionals. You all need to be about kingdom work wherever God places you. I have faced that challenge as a manager in commodity option trading firms. It has helped me to think of life as being composed of three different types of ministry time: vocational, intentional, and serendipitous ministry time.

VOCATIONAL MINISTRY TIME

Vocational ministry is serving God (hence "ministry") via one's job. A pastor's vocational ministry time is time spent preaching, teaching, and shepherding God's people. An evangelist's vocational ministry time is time spent winning people to Christ; a businessperson's vocational ministry time includes building organizations which provide jobs and valued goods and services; and a medical doctor's is in practicing medicine. You get the idea. The point is that vocational ministry time is the time spent serving God by serving others through your job. For all Christians, whether in professional ministry or "secular" work, more time is spent serving God through your vocation than through any other category of time usage.

The most effective tentmaking springs from the melding of the Great Commission and the theology of work as vocation. Good tentmakers know in their bones that when they are performing their specialized skill which allowed them to reach their particular CANUPs (= Creative Access Nation's Unreached Peoples) that they are doing part of those good works which God foreordained for them to do. It is not "wasted" time; it is not just "a necessary evil"; and it is not just a "cover" to allow them access to those people.

Effective tentmakers know that God is pleased to see them do their work well. His will for the tentmaker includes serving people through a vocation. That is why he gave them the natural abilities and spiritual gifts they have. The tentmaker's giftedness is a strong hint by God about which specific types of vocational ministry he wants that person to pursue. One's vocational ministry can be lived via any one of thousands of different professions. There are potentially as many different types of vocational ministries as there are jobs in a modern society.

The variety of gifts and abilities of God's people find their proper expression in the vocations of his people. This is the theology of work perspective which justifies calling one's job a "vocational ministry." The world would call it one's vocation, but to the Christian, and especially for the tentmaker, all of life is ministry: in both vocation and avocation alike, the tentmaker serves God. Therefore, it follows that the single largest block of ministry time for any tentmaker (as for any Christian) is his or her vocational ministry time. This is how most of his or her ministering hours will be spent. This is why effective tentmakers see their vocation in terms of service rendered to God. This is a missiological application of the theology of work to cross-cultural communication of the gospel among unreached peoples in nations closed to traditional missionary visas. This is vocational ministry to CANUPs; this is tentmaking.

This is how most of one's time as a tentmaker will be spent. Yet, in each of these specialized tasks, as Christians, tentmakers know that God has called them not only to this specific vocational ministry, but also more generally to help fulfill the Great Commission as part of the body of Christ. This is where intentional ministry time plays a central role in evangelism and discipleship.

Intentional Ministry Time

People need focused, goal-oriented communication designed to confront them with the claims of Jesus Christ. Such time may happen spontaneously, but it is more likely to happen if it is planned. Hence, the modifier *intentional* is used to distinguish these planned segments of ministry time which supplement one's vocational ministry time. Included in this category of time use might be the Bible study with a seeker which you hold over lunch hour from noon to 1:00 each Wednesday, or the evening discipleship meeting you host every Thursday night. These activities are not part of your job description. Nobody pays you to do these things. You do them with a ministry goal in mind. They are intentional in their evangelistic or discipleship orientation. They are voluntary. In sum, the key distinguishing feature of intentional ministry time is its planned nature. Christians living overseas who have not included this type of intentional ministry time in their time budgets are not likely to be effective tentmakers.

From Christian Professional to Kingdom Professional: The Difference Intent Makes

There are most likely millions of Christians living, working and studying in E-2 (a similar culture for evangelism) and E-3 (a different culture for evangelism) cultural contents. Many are Korean, Filipino, Nigerian, Dutch, Kenyan, Indian, North American, Brazilian, South African, Mexican—from every part of God's world to every major city in his world, and thereby to be among most of the cultures of the peoples of his world.

God has used modernity and its handmaiden, technique, to break down some of the traditional walls of resistance such as:

- Geographic isolation
- Language barriers (more people speak English than any other language)
- Cultural hegemony

Of course, this is not meant to minimize the corrosive effect of modernity on the life of his Church. Modernity, and especially its fixation on technique as embodied in science and technology, has been a subtle but devastating tool in Satan's hands. He has used its secular leverage to pry our hearts away from a moment-by-moment reliance on the Holy Spirit. Instead, we all too quickly allow the world's standards to press us into its mold:

— "you must be credentialed!"
— "there are techniques that are effective—use them."
— "here is how our mission does things, son!"
— "you need to use proven fund raising techniques!"

But the deleterious effects of modernity on mission is neither my assigned topic, nor my forte. I will leave such weighty matters to the late Lesslie Newbigin and David Bosch and other such intellectual giants from whom God has granted us the privilege of learning.

Let us return to the difference intent makes in the life of a tentmaker. Of the millions of Christians living in E-2 or E-3 cultures, very few are having much of an impact in terms of kingdom priorities. They just happen to be Christians living in a different culture. These Christians are, for the most part, no more (and no less) effective in terms of kingdom impact in those strategic locations than they were in their home cultures. They are not really tentmakers—they are just Christians living their day-by-day lives in potentially strategic places. But that potentiality needs a catalyst to make a difference in kingdom terms, and that catalyst is intent.

What distinguished effective tentmakers from those who were just Christian professionals? It was their intentionality. There are no accidental tentmakers! If you allow God's heart to move you into a strategic E-2 or E-3 context, you need to be focused and intentional about living as a winsome witness among those people. Ruth Siemens describes this sort of intentionality when she writes about fishing evangelism. Don Hamilton measures the visible outworking of such intent in his surveys on the characteristics of effective tentmakers. So, if you want to be a tentmaker, you need to be intentional about it. You need to seek prayerfully God's leading as to the people toward whom he would lead you. You need to maintain a mature balance between self-initiated activism and constant readiness to respond to the Spirit's unexpected moves in your life. You also need to reject Satan's counterfeit of openness, which is a debilitating passivity born of a fear of doing the wrong thing, of looking stupid, or even of being arrogant and presumptuous on God's grace. Tentmakers, just like all other Christians, must learn the Spirit-led blend of initiative and proactive opportunism that so believes that our God is in control that we choose to see his leading in the circumstances of our life. Because we believe that he is involved with our lives, we are willing to seize any opportunity life sends us, subject to the normal checks on rampant individualism that ought to be part and parcel of how we discern God's will for our lives. Here, I am referring to the counsel of one's spouse, one's accountability group, and the affirmation of one's church.

Kingdom professionals define success in terms of kingdom values. They do not define success as would the non-Christian professionals beside whom they work. Kingdom professionals seek to serve God and people by faithfully fulfilling the roles given to them by their professions. In doing so, they exercise their giftedness and apply their accumulated experience and marketplace skills in effectively meeting the real felt needs of the people they serve.

When kingdom professionals catch God's heart for the unreached peoples, they then turn their accumulated experience, resources and intensity toward the intentionally chosen task of impacting those people for God. When they do this and successfully involve themselves with that E-2 or E-3 culture, they are tentmakers. It is effective intentionality that distinguishes tentmakers from Christian professionals living oversees. Of course, in real life, such distinctions are not so black and white. In reality, there is a continuum between being a Christian professional and being a tentmaker, but at some point along that progression, the difference in degree becomes so large that it is more correctly seen as a difference in kind. And it is intent that moves one along that continuum from Christian professional toward kingdom professional and perhaps to tentmaker. The latter is a strategic choice made by a kingdom professional to reach out to an unreached people group. The strategy is but the visible outworking of the heart's intent. Tentmaking is a matter of choice, not geography. It is an issue of the will, not of one's job description.

To review so far, we are looking at the issue of time as it affects one's ability to minister effectively in seeking to overcome spiritual barriers of resistance. We have considered how a Christian view of work sees all of life as a ministry. We posited three types of ministry time:

- First, vocational ministry time,
- Second, intentional ministry time, and
- Third, serendipitous ministry time.

SERENDIPITOUS MINISTRY TIME

What is serendipitous ministry time? It is ministry which is:

- unplanned
- spontaneous
- often inconvenient
- often awkward

- usually wrapped in an uninvited interruption

Life just happens. You cannot plan it all; you should not try! Overseas, among CANUPs, this is even more true. So, "go with the flow" knowing that our loving heavenly Father will insert into our plans those unplanned, spontaneous ministry opportunities which constitute serendipitous ministry time. It is the serendipity of the sovereign Spirit of God that seats you on your flight next to a person ready to talk about spiritual things. It is his serendipity in our lives that transmutes all such "chance encounters" into signs of his gracious willingness to use us in accomplishing his will. These ministry opportunities are not under our control. All we can do is respond to the ones God gives us. If we respond, he gives us more. If we do not, he gives us fewer such opportunities for serendipitous ministry.

Not all of life is ministry. Life is more than ministry. It is also worship. For the purposes of clarity in communication, let us use the term *ministry* to refer to those blocks of time in which we are seeking to serve others in Jesus' name: one's vocation; one's intentional ministry time; and one's serendipitous ministry opportunities. There are, of course, many other helpful ways to dissect a day's ministry time: family ministry time, corporate ministry time, ministry to one's own needs for silence and reflection, and so forth. The goal here is not to suggest anything more than a helpful way to think about the problem of the tentmaker and time and to give you as professionals a useful framework with which to think about these issues. By focusing on these three categories of time usage, it is hoped that kingdom professionals can easily evaluate the time trade-offs they are making as tentmakers.

The Tentmaker and Time

Effective tentmakers accept the call of God to a vocation as ministry. They also accept the call of God to accomplish the Great Commission and use intentional ministry time toward that end. Of course, they have no more control over the amount of serendipitous ministry time available to them than does a professional Christian such as a traditional missionary, an evangelist, or a pastor-teacher. Therefore, it is in the use of vocational and intentional ministry time that professional Christians differ from Christian professionals, that is, from tentmakers. Remember, among many CANUPs, professional Christians are unable to practice their vocations at all, thus requiring help from Christian professionals. In such situations, it is either tentmaking as the means of communicating the gospel, or it is nothing at all. But tentmakers are not just God's second string team! They are especially important in reaching some CANUPs because professional Christian workers are not as effective, for whatever reason, in reaching those people. Tentmakers are equally called to the battle as are the professional missionaries. The difference is one of fit, of function, and of consequent appropriateness rather than of quality. But the time trade-offs required by the ministry context must be seen as being fully in God's will if kingdom professionals who are serving as tentmakers are to avoid unnecessary stress. For if one feels second class, if one's work is seen as a necessary means to a more important end rather than as being part of God's will for one's life, then the very magnitude of time that is consumed vocationally becomes a source of discouragement. This is not how God has called kingdom professionals to live. This is neither honoring to God nor likely to prove winsomely attractive to the watching CANUPs. It is missiologically and vocationally deadly. May I be so bold as to suggest that it may even be sin?

THE TENTMAKER TIME TRADE-OFF

If a person could discover a legal job that would allow him or her all of the benefits of access and all of the finances that person needs for only one hour's work per month, how much time should that he or she spend in vocational ministry rather than in intentional ministry? This trade-off between these two types of ministry time constitutes a major strategic variable in tentmaking. This is the tentmaker teeter-totter. How you balance it, heavy to vocational ministry or heavy to intentional ministry, is a decision that strongly influences your approach to being among a particular CANUP.

I would like to suggest that the effective tentmaker should engage in vocational ministry no less than half-time. This leaves half-time available for intentional ministry. It is my opinion that if you spend less than half of your time as a kingdom professional serving people through your vocation, that you will soon begin to look, act, talk, and "smell" like something other than a professional in your field. You become what you practice and what you do. Therefore, if you are more something else than you are a kingdom professional, then, in time, you will come to be seen as being that something else by the people you are among. That may be a problem in terms of its impact on your long-term ability to be among those folk. It may also be a failure to adequately model for them how a Christian melds life and ministry into one integrated whole. In any case, it may leave you unbalanced if you fail to fulfill God's call on your life to serve people through a certain vocation, for you, too, must balance the tentmaker time-trade-off teeter-totter in your own life.

You have to be sensitive to God's leading in every circumstance, for no single formula can capture the beauty of God's variety in his people, in his world. If you are called overseas, go; but go as who you are. The way God made you was no mistake! Discover his pattern within you; believe it to be a sign of grace rather than dumb luck or environmental conditioning; and by that same grace, go in faith. And God will undergird your faith-steps by his going before you and preparing the way, just as he promised.

REFERENCES

Hesselgrave, David. 1991. *Communicating Christ Cross-Culturally*. 2nd edition. Grand Rapids: Zondervan.

PART IV

PREPARING FOR THE FUTURE: PLANNING BRIDGES

Chapter 12

Equipping Missionaries for the Resistant

Timothy C. Tennent

Introduction

The purpose of this article is to explore how we who are involved in the training and preparation of a new generation of missionaries can best prepare them to reach resistant peoples with the gospel of Jesus Christ. The first part of this article makes a general observation about the phrase "resistant peoples." The latter part of the article examines several strategic points which provoke us to reflect on some new ways in which we might be able to do a better job of training missionaries to reach resistant peoples. In both sections this chapter is designed to be practical in its orientation.

What Is meant by "Resistant Peoples"?

When we raise the question concerning how we can best train people to reach "resistant peoples," we are met at the very threshold of such a question with an important challenge—namely, what do we mean by the phrase "resistant peoples"? The term "resistant peoples," while widely used in our classrooms, in our literature, and in the local church is, in fact, an insufficient phrase for those of us involved in strategic planning. It is an insufficient phrase because, frankly, it is too vague and too broad to say anything meaningful at the strategic planning level.

For example, one can quickly note that there are at least four categories of resistant peoples which make up the unreached world with an accompanying host of variations and combinations on each of the themes.

First, there are those groups which are *culturally resistant*. Recall, for example, how Dr. Hesselgrave has reminded us of Nietzche's and Ruth Benedict's analysis of certain societies which may be termed "Apollonarian" societies as opposed to "Dionysian" (Hesselgrave 1991:591). It is a simple rubric underlying an important point. Namely, some societies resist change simply because all change, indeed, any change, is perceived to be bad. The truth claims of the gospel cannot easily undermine a pre-existing cultural bias not to accept any new beliefs or practices. We can re-state the gospel in a dozen different ways, it still does not matter, because it represents change.

Second, there are those groups which may be called *theologically resistant*. These groups range from the Mormons to Muslims and have been predisposed to reject certain Christian doctrines out of hand because of their own theological self-understanding which has been shaped by an explicit rejection of certain particulars of Christian theology, whether real or perceived, genuine or caricatured. "Allah has no partners," claims the Muslim and to affirm the Sonship and deity of Jesus Christ represents a fundamental theological impossibility.[1] We must be prepared to discuss detailed theological questions and issues regarding the deity and Sonship of Jesus Christ.

Third, there are those groups which are *nationalistically or ethnically resistant*. Such a group's very identity—not theological but ethnic identity—involves a rejection of another group, including their beliefs. The Tiv in the middle belt of Nigeria, for example, resisted Islam, not because of its theological content, the insufficiency of its truth claims, or the weakness of its worldview, but because the Hausa were Muslim.

---

1 *See*, e.g., such passages in the Qur'an as 2:116, 117; 10:68; 17:111; 51:51.

Precisely because the Hausa were committed to Islam would mean that the Tiv would be predisposed to resist Islam. Likewise, there are groups which identify Christianity with Westernization or with colonialism or some other alien factor which causes the group out of ethnic or nationalistic pride to reject Christianity. Many of the nineteenth century Hindu revival groups such as the Arya Samaj and Brahmo Samaj rallied around a revitalized Hinduism because it was a way of reasserting traditional "Indianness" in a context dominated by British colonialism. My Ph.D. dissertation focused on the Bengali theologian Brahmabandhav Upadhyay. Before he came to Christ, he was convinced that being a Christian meant having to wear pants, eat meat and drink alcohol. Once he came to Christ, he spent the rest of his life seeking to demonstrate that being a Christian was not tantamount to renouncing his Indian heritage and culture.

Finally, there are resistant groups which are *politically resistant*. There are many groups which are behind political walls which do not permit traditional missionary work, and since this is often accompanied with a national situation where there is not a viable witnessing church, we assume that they are resistant. In fact, many have never had the opportunity to even hear or respond to the gospel, and therefore our assessment that they are resistant may be premature. How does one compare the twenty-three million Koreans who have not heard the gospel because of the political realities in North Korea with the Malayalam speaking Mappillas off the coast of Southwest India who have repeatedly rejected the gospel and remain fiercely Islamic?[2] There is a significant strategic difference in our approach to such groups.

Therefore, we must do a much better job of articulating what we mean by "resistant peoples" because the world encompasses a wide variety of reasons for resistance or perceived resistance: cultural, theological, national, and political, among others, as well as combinations of these, and each requires different kinds

---

2 Joshua Project 2000 Unreached Peoples List, pp. 4, 8.

of strategies if we are to be effective in the task of training which God has given to us.

With this observation in mind, let us now turn to some strategic reflections. At Toccoa Falls College we are currently seeking to equip around one hundred forty mission majors, many of whom are committed to reaching resistant peoples in several of the above categories. I would like to highlight six principles which are helping to guide our training process.

First, without Sacrificing the Time Spent Grounding Our Students in the Biblical Message, We Must, Nevertheless, Become More Receptor Oriented in Our Training

That is, we must help our students to not only understand the gospel message but understand it in light of the beliefs, worldviews, perceptions, and challenges of those on the receiving end. This means an increased emphasis on anthropology, world religions, cross-cultural communication, and cross-cultural theologizing. Put quite plainly, it is not unusual for people-groups in the 10/40 window to ask a whole range of new questions which our Western theologizing has not prepared us to answer. I have had the privilege for several years of teaching during the main academic year here in the United States and then teaching in India during each summer. Teaching many of the same courses on two different continents has been a very constructive way to observe how theology is formulated on two different continents. What has struck me is that my Indian students persistently ask their own set of questions. I have been singularly impressed with the need to do a better job in formulating theology cross-culturally.[3]

Our program at Toccoa Falls College is rooted in an anthropology core of four courses in sequence as well as courses which acquaint students in the beliefs of the target people

---

[3] For two of the most helpful books in this area, *see* Sanneh 1989 and 1993. *See also* Nida and Reyburn 1981 and Gilliland 1989, which provide excellent demonstration of the need for a contextualized theology. Much of the work of such theologies is still quite young.

groups.[4] We offer courses in belief systems, world religions and even individual courses in Islam and Hinduism and Buddhism which not only give us sufficient time to explore the beliefs of the receptor groups but also to examine specific strategies currently being used to reach these unreached people groups. We have become far more intentional in preparing our students to understand the beliefs, worldviews, thinking processes, cultures, and so forth, of the target group. This emphasis has helped us in the task of contextualization as well as in the task of de-contextualization (i.e., learning to separate the Christian gospel from elements in our own culture which we have unwittingly united with the kerygma).

Second, We as Missiologists Need to Increase Our Discussions about Bolder Forms of Contextualization

Whether we are talking about Jesus mosques in Bangladesh or Christian Sannyasins in India or Soka Gakkai-styled lay discussion and discipleship groups in Japan, new ideas are being promoted today in ways which we have not seen on this scale. The last few issues of *Mission Frontiers* have been highlighting this issue. I was pleased to read the report in the *Commission* magazine of the Southern Baptists in August and later reprinted in *Mission Frontiers* about the Jesus mosques and the work in Benin which is, of course, only one part of a larger movement within some mission circles to experiment with bolder forms of contextualization. One of the comments made in the *Missions Frontiers* article by those opposed to Jesus mosques was the following statement: "Muslim forms cannot be divorced from their meanings" (*MFB* 1997:19 citing Chastain). That has to be one of the most theologically loaded phrases I have read in some time. If that statement is true, then it reverberates outward affecting all of our missiological strategy. If it is not, then we have to discuss seriously how Islamic or Hindu or Buddhist forms might be redirected toward Christian ends. We

4 We offer the following anthropology core: cultural anthropology, applied anthropology, ethnography, and religious belief systems.

desperately need far more interaction about the pros and cons of using and/or redirecting and/or replacing non-Christian religious forms with Christian ones.

Third, We Must Train Our Students to Be Trainers and Equip Them to Be Equippers

Three of the four types of resistance outlined earlier all demand an increased emphasis on our promoting "in culture" changes rather than using external agents of change from outside the culture such as is sometimes promoted overtly or inadvertently in traditional Western missionary outreach. Consider for example, an Apollonian culture which is against change for change's sake or a culture proud of its own ethnic heritage and suspicious of a Westerner or a culture with political restrictions which make long-term residency of Western missionaries illegal. In all three of these cases, the answer is found in an increased emphasis on the non-Western missionary—someone who is either a member of the target culture or a near culture member.

Certainly one of the most dramatic changes in the twentieth century has been the emergence of Third World missions. For example, since the early 1970s, India ceased issuing new visas for Western missionaries, and the missionary force began its rapid decline from thousands down to just a few hundred. For every Western missionary which left India, God has raised up at least two national Indian workers who are crossing cultural boundaries with the gospel. It would be foolish for a Western organization today to target India without networking with indigenous believers. It would be foolish for a Western organization to target Muslims in Nigeria, for example, without taking into account the growth of new Christians among the people-groups in Middle-belt Nigeria.

Networking with national believers also helps to prevent the notion that we have been set apart as the guardians of global orthodoxy. Are we really in a position, for example, to decide which African Independent Churches (AICs) are "in" and which ones are "out" based on *our* understanding of *their* orthodoxy. Western formulations of theology may not always be applicable in their contexts, and often we are simply unable to "hear" their orthodoxy because it is not being expressed in the familiar strains of our own theological expressions.

I have been involved for the last ten years in a church planting ministry in Northern India which trains Indians from Southern India to plant churches in Northern India.[5] Southern Indians are culturally distant from Northern Indians but are still far more effective and culturally similar than a missionary from the West. I applaud several new ministries such as the International Institute of Christian Studies which have committed themselves and their resources into sending missionaries not to do missions per se, but to train and equip national believers to carry out more effectively their God-given task of reaching the unreached people groups in their country for Christ. We need to acquaint our students with these kinds of ministries both in the classroom as well as on the field during their field internships. Networking with Third World missions is not the first step in relinquishing our role in global evangelism. On the contrary, every church on every continent should be both a sending and a receiving church. We have gifts which the global church needs. Likewise, we need the insights and experiences of our brothers and sisters around the world to help in our own appreciation of the full grandeur of the church of Jesus Christ.

Fourth, We Must Continue to Be Vigilant in Recognizing the Vital Link between Missiology and Theology

Solid biblical theology should lie at the heart of our missiological task. I see theological challenges both from without and from within which deserve our attention.

First, as noted earlier, we face unique theological challenges from without. We must help our students to understand the difference, for example, between the theological challenges which

---

5 The Indian church planting organization is Bharat Susamachar Samiti and is primarily known for its theological training institute in Dehra Dun, U.P. called the Luther W. New, Jr. Theological College or NTC.

face us in an Islamic context versus the theological challenges which face us in a Hindu context. We must give our students the theological preparation to face new questions which often are not raised or are not raised in the same way in our typical biblical and theological courses. In our courses on Islam and Hinduism respectively, a great deal of time is spent dealing with the theological issues and challenges which arise out of these unique contexts.

Second, we face theological challenges from within. We must increase our vigilance in defending historic doctrines such as the uniqueness of Christ, the importance of personal response, and the centrality of the Great Commission in the church's mission among our own. It takes spiritual conviction to give your life to reaching resistant peoples. Granted, many of our students want to go and "do" missions for a summer "here" or have a cross-cultural experience "there," but we need people prepared to commit their lives to full-time mission work. The problem is that the very basis for missions which provides the motivation for students is being eroded even within evangelicalism. The most blatant example is the problem of inclusivism which continues to seep into the consciousness of the post-modern evangelical community. I want to say clearly that from my understanding of Scripture, any theology, whether it comes from Catholic or Protestant circles, which says that Christ's death is central, but a response to the name of Jesus is not central, undermines the very foundation of the Great Commission and is in direct violation of Acts 4:12 and Romans 10:13–15. To say that Jesus' death is ontologically necessary but not epistemologically necessary is nothing but a thinly veiled theological construct which repeats the old problem of separating the Jesus of history from the Christ of faith. Faith must be explicitly in the historical, objective work of God in Jesus Christ, not merely a subjective experience of "faith" which is not necessarily or cognitively related to Jesus Christ. Our evangelical students coming to us in the last several years are already pre-disposed towards inclusivism. We can no longer assume that our students share our theological convictions. This has led us to be more intentional in the theological preparation of our students who are considering a career in cross-cultural work.

Fifth, We Must Continue to Encourage the Training of Christian Tentmakers

If ninety percent of the unreached people groups are in the 10/40 window and the vast majority of the political countries within the 10/40 window prohibit traditional missionary access, then it is only logical that a much higher percentage of our resources should be utilized to equip and to provide the missionary structures so that our students can enter into restricted access countries as professionals and not as traditional missionaries. Our program at Toccoa Falls has two main tracks with several different majors under each track. We have a missiology track which trains and equips our students for traditional missionary access, especially church planting, which is essential to any bona fide missionary program. But we also have a second track titled "Cross-Cultural Studies." The very name of the degree diffuses possible problems for our students entering sensitive countries. Within the track we have two majors: medical professionals for those training to be doctors or nurses and TESOL, Teaching English to Speakers of Other Languages. Approximately one third of our majors in the School of World Missions at Toccoa Falls College are preparing to be English language professionals. In addition to our normal anthropological and missiological training and the required hours in Bible and Theology, they will take Introduction to TESOL, Methods and Materials of TESOL, TESOL Practicum, and Communicating Values Through TESOL. The result is that a number of our graduates are being trained to teach English and are landing jobs in China, Japan, Mongolia, and Kazakhstan, all countries within the 10/40 window. Tentmakers have the advantages of being able to get to the field quicker, to get into the 10/40 window with long-term visas, and to require far less resources from the sending church since they are all either fully or partially self-supporting.

Sixth, We Need to Integrate the Strategic Role of Prayer and Personal Devotion into Our Overall Professional Training

We no longer have the luxury of assuming that our students have solid personal lives with deep relationships with Christ who only need the professional skills and tools to get the job done. Our students need to be taught and given models of prayer and personal devotion to Christ. Spiritual formation is as important as professional formation. The recent "Praying Through the Window III" which culminated in the "Praying Through the Window" daily during the month of October has been one of the best initiatives in recent years to help our students in this area. Spiritual strongholds such as those found in the 10/40 window do not collapse because we have applied the right technique but, in part, because our efforts have been bathed in prayer and in dependence upon the Lord Jesus Christ to go before us. We begin classes by praying for an unreached group, and we set aside regular prayer times when we as the faculty can get before God with our students and pray for unreached people groups. This will not only give our teaching more credibility, but it will model the most important part of our task as missionaries.

In conclusion, in addition to challenging us to re-think what is meant by the expression "resistant peoples," I have attempted to point out some practical ways which might help us in our common calling to equip a new generation of missionaries to complete the Great Commission. May the new rally cry of "*all peoples—nothing less*" be increasingly true as we seek to finish the task given us by our Lord Jesus Christ.

References

Gilliland, Dean S., ed. 1989. *The Word Among Us: Contextualizing Theology for Mission Today*. Waco, TX: Word.

Hesselgrave, David. 1991. *Communicating Christ Cross-Culturally*. 2nd edition. Grand Rapids: Zondervan.

MFB. 1997. *Mission Frontiers Bulletin* (July–October). Reprinted from *Commission*. 1997. Magazine of the International Mission Board, Southern Baptist Convention (August).

Nida, Eugene and William Reyburn. 1981. *Meaning Across Cultures: A Study on Bible Translating*. Maryknoll: Orbis.

Sanneh, Lamin. 1989. *Translating the Message, the Missionary Impact on Culture*. Maryknoll: Orbis.

______. 1993. *Encountering the West: Christianity and the Global Cultural Process*. Maryknoll: Orbis.

Chapter 13

GLOBAL PLANNING FOR THE RESISTANT

Luis Bush

INTRODUCTION

The blessings seen and lessons learned over the first seven years of this decade through the AD2000 Movement vision have been vivid and many, most recently being seen from the launch of Joshua Project 2000 in December 1995. This now sets the stage for a second phase of reaching all peoples everywhere, which is proposed in this chapter under the name Joshua Harvest: All Peoples All Persons.

With the ultimate goal of a church for every people by the year 2000 and beyond, I believe there are practical principles that have been learned through trial and error with regard to reaching resistant peoples.

Ten key words representing ten general principles are presented in outline form in the first section of this chapter. A specific proposal to integrate these principles into a working strategy for reaching resistant peoples comprises the second section and major portion of this chapter.

Lessons Learned from the First Seven Years of the AD2000 Movement

Identification

The task has been broken down as follows:

- The 10/40 window (between the tenth and fortieth degree latitude in Africa and Asia, identified as containing the most unreached peoples).
- Twelve affinity blocks of peoples identified.
- One hundred forty clusters of peoples identified.
- Joshua Project 2000 selected 1739 peoples of over ten thousand members for special attention.
- All peoples, including smaller ethno-cultural groups, are an ultimate concern (to be treated in the second section of this chapter).

Investigation

Research on the resistant peoples has been done on site and through global networks. The Bethany World Prayer Center in Colorado Springs contains the 1739 profiles of the Joshua Project 2000 Unreached Peoples.

Information Sharing

The Global Guide of Unreached Peoples involves the information sharing of twenty-five thousand pieces of information from fifty mission organizations in eighty countries which is now available for mission agencies and churches to adopt unreached people groups.

Illumination/Intuition

Key Christian leaders held consultations to share information, interact, and pray to see what the Holy Spirit is saying to the churches.

Increased Awareness

Increased awareness was facilitated through 1) communication materials, 2) computer conferences, and 3) "face to face" consultations such as GCOWE '95, GCOWE '97, HIMCOE '96, SE Asia

Joshua Project 2000, Latin America 2000, and other regional/national consultations.

Intercession

Prayer was focused on resistant peoples and places through:

- Praying Through the Window I/'93, Praying Through the Window II/'95, and Praying Through the Window III/'97, in which Christians worldwide prayed for the peoples in the 10/40 window.
- Ten churches and ten cell groups which prayed for each of the 1,739 selected peoples.
- "Praying with Power" conferences held throughout the world.

Involvement

Church and mission leaders around the globe became involved through specific task assignments.

Integration

Coalescing efforts included:

- Country-wide networks (e.g., African National Initiatives consultation at GCOWE '97, two hundred sixty peoples adopted and affirmed in country by country follow up consultations).
- Strategic networks (e.g., GCOWE '97, mission executives committed to seeking ministries among over three hundred peoples).
- Theological networks (e.g., GCOWE '97, presidents and academic deans declared commitment to integrate curriculum distinctives toward a church for every people).
- Resource networks organized to support specific programs.
- People-specific networks.
- Task force networks.
- Continent-wide networks.
- Organizational networks.
- Regional (within a country) networks.
- Mission agency partnerships.

Implementation

All kinds of initiatives encouraged local, national, regional, continental, and global resources and tools to assist in implementing the vision.

Impartation of Vision

The Holy Spirit transformed the perspective of those at gatherings such as GCOWE '95 and GCOWE '97 and regional events.

JOSHUA HARVEST: ALL PEOPLES ALL PERSONS: A PROPOSAL

Introduction

The Viability and Components of the Joshua Harvest

The *All Peoples All Persons Proposal* is now being assessed by Christian leaders around the world. Inputs are being solicited. Upon receiving adequate understanding, broad ownership, and commitment to the vision, an official launch would take place, currently envisioned at Celebrate Messiah 2000.

For example, the input from Patrick Johnstone, author of *Operation World*, is as follows:

> I am delighted with the initiative and fully endorse the need for such. We had to simplify and focus for these three to five years. We should bequeath to the church of the twenty-first century the full challenge. I believe we now have the attention, interest and concern of many Christians, and we now also have a commonly agreed upon set of terms and categorizations to make the complicated analysis more practicable.
>
> As for the launch, I would suggest this be the focus of Celebrate Messiah 2000 in the Holy Lands (Dec. 27, 2000–Jan. 3, 2001). I am deliberately aiming for the next *Operation World* to be published later in 2000, because I want it to be forward-looking into the challenges of the still unfinished task. If the Joshua Harvest vision is launched, *Operation World* can give written focus and undergirding even if AD2000 as a structure will have handed over the torch. I think that this

> Joshua Harvest vision could do this for Celebrate Messiah 2000. I am certainly desirous of doing all I can to make this a successful launch.

Because of God's blessings on existing initiatives worldwide, Joshua Project 2000, and Praying Through the Window efforts, there has been evident mobilization, cooperation, and penetration among the peoples identified as the largest and most spiritually needy. Common goals, a common information base, and common values have contributed to this global cooperative effort. Now, many leaders within the Movement have considered the idea and importance of expanding the scope to all peoples worldwide.

We believe that to continue toward the fulfillment of the AD2000 and Beyond Movement vision of "a church for every people and the gospel for every person," we need to expand the criteria of the Joshua Project from those ethno-linguistic groups over ten thousand to include *all* peoples regardless of population. While the broader All Peoples effort will encompass all known ethno-linguistic and ethno-cultural peoples, AD2000 seeks to continue the primary focus of making disciples of Christ among the most spiritually needy and unreached peoples of the world. Where data is available, the less than two percent evangelical and less than five percent Christian adherents' criteria would be applied to all peoples to determine this primary focus.

The purpose of this document is to expose much of the detailed thoughts and supporting aspects of this recent vision for your careful review, prayer, and response.

THE PROPOSAL

Vision of Joshua Harvest: All Peoples All Persons

To catalyze a movement for Christ among all peoples and to present the gospel to all persons worldwide.

Purpose of Joshua Harvest: All Peoples All Persons

The purpose of Joshua Harvest: All Peoples All Persons is to network Christians worldwide who are committed to establishing a life-giving congregation of believers among all peoples and making the gospel available to all persons by means of a common purpose, common values, and a common information system.

Rationale: Why This New Thrust within the On-Going Vision at This Time?

1. God is a sending God, reflected in the compassion of the Father, the commission of the Son, and the compulsion of the Holy Spirit.
2. God is at work today. In Africa, follow-up meetings to GCOWE '97 in every country are focusing on church planting among every people beginning with Joshua Project 2000 peoples. In Nigeria, leaders met in October 1997, and all but seventeen of the one hundred seventy unreached peoples of Nigeria were adopted. In South Asia, an India ethno-cultural peoples list was prepared and presented for adoption in July 1997. In Brazil, in January 1997, a commitment of leaders to establish churches among each of the one hundred seventy unreached peoples in Brazil was made. Regarding all persons, Mission America has a specific challenge of presenting the gospel to each person in the United States as do many other countries through their own national initiatives.
3. It is technologically possible. Development of a unique and complete interactive information system to accommodate pursuit of the vision of All Peoples All Persons is already underway. This will enable the transfer of all the information residing at the AD2000 and Beyond International Office to the larger Christian community as needed.

Nature of Joshua Harvest: All Peoples All Persons (What Is It?)

Common Information

The coordination of a global effort to collect accurate data regarding all peoples is required so those global, continental, national, and local initiatives can work off the same page.

A Common Information System

The development of an information support system is underway through an alliance of Christian entities committed to the stewardship and maintenance of interrelating information sets related to the harvest field, harvest force, or harvest yield.

A Common Database

The communication of non-secured, interrelated, user-friendly information through the preparation of a common information database, to be distributed by CD-ROM and hard copy, is being prepared.

A Common Purpose/Goal

To cultivate a common purpose/goal that expresses the mandate of Jesus Christ and the common conviction of his people throughout the world today.

Enhancement of Existing Efforts

To encourage all existing efforts that are working toward the goal of "a church for every people and the gospel for every person" to continue toward fulfillment.

Catalyzation of New Efforts

To catalyze new global, regional, national and local initiatives where they do not exist for the spiritually and materially neediest peoples.

A Cooperative Venture

To further cultivate cooperative, coalescing, practical affinity networks and partnerships to advance the goal of All Peoples All Persons.

FACTORS BEARING UPON THE PURPOSE

1. Intensification of prayer efforts on behalf of all peoples and all persons in all places is underway.
2. Perception exists of "Joshua Harvest: All Peoples All Persons" as a natural enhancer of existing movements and networks.
3. Harvest Database Information System is in full development and view.
4. Local churches are taking ownership of specific target peoples.
5. Mission agencies worldwide are engaged in the vision.
6. Funding sources are identified, created, and supportive.
7. Cooperation and networking currently exist among those who share this similar vision.

NEAR-TERM GOALS

In the light of these factors and full process, several key near term goals are as follows:

1. Pursue understanding, goodwill, and cooperation among existing movements and structures to work together towards this common vision.
2. Intercede to the end that new leadership is raised up to carry forward this vision into the new millennium.
3. Focus appropriate energies on a key event(s) to launch the vision and catalyze the worldwide efforts.
4. Establish adequate accountability and reporting mechanisms for follow-through towards completion.

A Strategy Model

An excellent model that illustrates a working strategy for Joshua Harvest: All Peoples All Persons can be observed in North India today.

North India is strategically important in completing the unfinished task of world evangelization. The church in India has a rich and very long history, and may date back to the apostle Thomas. In fact, India is where the era of modern missionary effort began over two hundred years ago with the arrival of William Carey, called by many the father of modern missions. But historically, most of the growth of the Indian church has been concentrated in the southern and northeastern parts of the country. Pastors and missionaries both within and without India have long noticed the special needs and strategic importance of the northern part of the country—an area often called "the North India-Hindi Belt."

This area stretches across north and central India and covers nine states: Bihar, Rajasthan, Madhya Pradesh, Uttar Pradesh, Delhi, Jammu Kashmir, Punjab, Himachel Pradesh, and Haryana.

North India is important because: 1) It is a major population center. The Ganges River belt contains one of the most heavily populated regions of the world. If Uttar Pradesh were a country, it would be the seventh most populous country in the world; if Bihar were a country, it would be the thirteenth. Forty percent of the total Indian population live there, some four hundred million people. 2) Within North India are located massive numbers of people who have historically resisted the gospel and are gripped by Hinduism and Islam.

It is in this context of resistant peoples that a working model for reaching resistant people has emerged. Many Christians and organizations have come together as the North India Harvest Network, a loosely-organized forum established for mutual encouragement and strength in evangelism and church planting efforts. Totally managed by volunteers, it has sponsored seminars in sixty of the two hundred districts of North India to build networks and mobilize workers for the harvest they truly believe is coming. Their goal is reaching "every people group in every city in every language in every geographic district."

Their mission is expressed in the phrase "PLUG, PREM and be NICE," a series of acronyms that describe their focus and methodology for reaching their goals.

PLUG refers to the different targets their networks are trying to reach: every *people*—in every *languages*—in every *urban* center—in every *geographical* division (district, block, and PIN code).

At the heart of the strategy are five hundred target groups or units in North India based on this PLUG approach.

200 *people* groups
50 *languages*
50 *urban* areas
200 *geographical* districts

Much like a net, each target group serves as a thread drawn from a different direction to ensure that every person has a chance to hear the gospel, regardless of the language they speak, their cultural grouping, or the city or the geographical district in which they reside. These target groups have become the focus of the network's prayer and mobilization efforts.

Through their seminars, the NIHN seeks to identify, prepare, and train local leaders who will coordinate the resources and personnel to reach each of these target groups in their area.

PREM and be NICE describe how that work will be done: *prayer* must be offered; *research* into the harvest field must be performed and then utilized; *equipping* and training those who go out to labor must occur; *mobilization* must be ongoing.

It is recognized and understood by all concerned that this can only occur by *networking*, especially in pioneer situations, by taking *initiative* when nothing is happening or a gap is realized, by being a *catalyst* (an agent that provokes or speeds significant change or action), and by *encouraging* all the existing ministries and efforts that advance the cause of Jesus Christ.

In so many ways, India is learning to work together to reach its own resistant peoples. The networks of concerned individuals and churches are stretching across the entire country. However, in the process the North India Harvest Network is providing a working model strategy on reaching resistant peoples.

CONCLUSION:

"Joshua Harvest: All Peoples All Persons" seeks to advance the goal of establishing a church planting movement among all peoples and to present the gospel to all persons worldwide.

APPENDIX

Values

1. *Faith expectation* in the Captain of the Host to advance his kingdom purposes and enable his people to fulfill their God-given faith goals.
2. *Full participation* of Christians from all peoples and all cultures and all places.
3. *Freeing up* of God's people to be the kind of people that God has called them to be and to do the kind of things in God's will that they have dreamed of doing, especially women, business executives, youth, children, and others.
4. *Focus* on the spiritually and materially poorest persons and peoples. Providing a holistic, integrated response by drawing upon the combined resources of the whole body of Christ in its various agencies to meet their needs.
5. *Fierce* spiritual warfare through a growing prayer army linked in heart, mind, soul, spirit, and purpose around the world.
6. *Formation* and extension of all kinds of networks to catalyze different groups for advancing Christ's kingdom purposes, optimum to the place and point of need.
7. *Fostering* of countrywide initiatives to fulfill the Great Commission and the Great Commandment in their countries.
8. *Finish* the task that the Lord has commanded and committed to his followers.

9. *Flexible* organizational style that provides freedom for the work of the Holy Spirit.

	Too Often Yesterday's Style	*Joshua Harvest Style*
Individual power	Positional	Personal
Structure	Hierarchical	Network of team
Focus of loyalty	Institution	People
Style	Structured	Flexible
Source of energy	Stability	Change and innovation
Leadership	Dogmatic, authoritative	Inspirational, facilitator
Leader	Order giver	Coach, teacher
Quality	Affordable best	Excellence
Expectations	Security	Personal growth
Status	Title and rank	Making a difference
Resources	Cash, time	Information, people, networks
Motivation	Complete a task	Build people

Developing a Common Information System

Name: Harvest Database

The People Information Network (PIN), under the coordination of Ron Rowland, has been led to develop an interrelating information system to support the vision of all peoples and all persons. A strategic alliance has been established to incorporate organizations and ministries in the development, interface, and maintenance of this database.

Summary Functions

1. Encompasses all peoples—by language, culture, religion, and physical location.
2. Encompasses all persons—it identifies who a person is both individually and collectively by languages spoken, country and state/province of residence, religion, and physical location to the level of neighborhood within a community/district within a city.

3. Built upon the perception of how people see themselves.
4. Based upon the information sets called info-sets that unite and/or divide people.
5. Based on relationships. This is a relationship and relational information system.
6. Built upon effectiveness. Only one change will change the information in the entire system.
7. Built upon the concept of harvest with three major phases in view—the harvest field, the harvest force, and the harvest yield.

Contents

Harvest Field

There are five principal descriptors which cause a people to be seen as the same or different.

1. Cultural descriptor identifies the people by the group to which the people feel they belong.
2. Linguistic descriptor identifies the people by the language they speak.
3. Religious descriptor identifies the people by the traditionally accepted religion that they practice.
4. Political descriptor identifies the people by the country of citizenship.
5. Spatial descriptor identifies the people by the geographic space they occupy as their primary location of residence.

Harvest Force

1. Mission organizations, recognizing four (or more) levels/tables.
   a. First level mission organizations, any organization, regardless of size.
   b. Second geographic level for large mission organizations, as needed.
   c. Third geographic level for larger mission organizations, as needed.
   d. Specific ministry level for mission organizations, regardless of levels.

2. Mission ministries, recognizing three potential levels.
   a. Group of ministries, being the broadest definition of category.
   b. The type of ministry in which the person is engaged.
   c. The specific ministry in which the person is engaged.
3. Mission networking, recognizing three levels/tables.
   a. Network between organizations or individuals for a specific purpose.
   b. Sub-network between organizations or individuals for a specific purpose.
   c. Networking among peoples—already twenty-two thousand pieces of information are available of four hundred fifty organizations in eighty collecting organizations
4. Individual persons, recognizing one level. Persons who operate independently of organizations or individuals within organizations whose special roles should be separately recorded. There are twenty-five thousand individuals from almost two hundred countries in the AD2000 database of persons who have shown some interest in the vision.
5. Individual skills, recognizing four levels/types.
   a. Leadership skills.
   b. Administration skills.
   c. Ministry skills.
   d. Supporting skills.
6. Individual relationships, recognizing one level/table. Ministry relationships for a specific purpose.
7. Mission products, recognizing four types of mission product.
   a. Products related to ministry through God's Word.
   b. Products related to ministry directly to people.
   c. Products related to ministry publications.
   d. Products related to visual and audio-visual communications.

Harvest Yield

"Churches in Habitat" is a snapshot of the church using spatial identification and statistics. The "one hundred believers" measure used by AD2000 is analogous to the first baby photo—showing that the baby is born. "Churches in Action" is analogous to a photo album containing a series of snapshots in temporal sequence. The "Agency Work" and "Church Planting Status" scales are by analogy a series of "parents" and "child" snapshots.

Church Planting Status

0 = Nothing happening, no known believers
1 = No known churches, individual believers
2 = One known church of at least one hundred believers
3 = A group of churches, no missiological breakthrough
4 = Missiological breakthrough, ready for DAWN-type program
5 = A discipled church, churches widely spread through the people

Mission Agencies Work Status

0 = Nothing happening, no agency or group targeting
1 = At least one mission agency, called and committed evangelizers
2 = At least one agency with evangelizers on site
3 = Multiple agencies committed and involved in outreach
4 = A functioning partnership of committed agencies
5 = People with missions sending vision

"Churches in Christ," by contrast, is analogous to living with the child and understanding his or her character, etc. This is not "objective" information, but our "subjective" information can be described—and it really tells us much more about the child. So, we end up with a threefold view of the church:

a. Table one: Information about "Churches in Habitat"; locations, statistics, "one hundred believers," et al.
b. Table Two: Information about "Churches in Action," including Agency Work and Church Status.

c. Table Three: Information about "Churches in Christ"—the spiritual life of the church.

Design, Development and Maintenance

A strategic harvest alliance will share responsibility for the database. Currently the Peoples Information Network (PIN) and the Global Research Office of the International Mission Board integrate this alliance and welcome others to join.

How Do I Get Personally Involved in Joshua Harvest: All Peoples All Persons?

Jesus Christ is not only the Master but also the Master Multiplier. When you stop to consider that almost two thousand years ago he began with but twelve followers and today there are estimated to be more than two billion who claim to be his followers, it is abundantly clear that the process of discipleship he followed in his brief three year ministry works. In his ministry of discipleship you can observe at least six basic steps of development of a committed disciple with a vision to reach the world.

These same six steps are the steps that are envisioned as the process of involvement for Joshua Harvest: All Peoples All Persons. They are:

1. identification
2. selection
3. recruitment
4. communication or association
5. mutual discipleship
6. challenge—ALL PEOPLES ALL PERSONS

Where might you and/or your organization fit in this picture and process?

INDEX